Zen Rising

366 SAGE STORIES TO ENKINDLE YOUR DAYS

COLLECTED BY *Tamarack Song*

Illustrated by Jan Zaremba

Snow Wolf Publishing

Snow Wolf Publishing
7124 Military Road
Three Lakes, Wisconsin 54562
www.snowwolfpublishing.org

Snow Wolf Publishing is a division of Teaching Drum Outdoor School

Song, Tamarack, 1948 –
Zen Rising: 366 Sage Stories to Enkindle Your Days

ISBN 978-0-9894737-2-9

Illustrations © 2017 Jan Zaremba

Book design by Carole Sauers/Penny Lane Studio

To send correspondence to the author of this book, mail a first class letter to the author c/o Snow Wolf Publishing, 7124 Military Road, Three Lakes, Wisconsin 54562, and we will forward the communication, or email the author at info@snowwolfpublishing.org. Visit the author's websites at www.tamaracksong.org, www.teachingdrum.org, and www.brotherwolffoundation.org.

Contents

THE ART OF CRACKING NUTS

If I were allowed only two words to describe the Way of Zen, they would be *conscious living*. Our modern lives tend to be quite un-Zen-like: we tolerate a humdrum existence on the promise of a peak moment at some point in the future. It might be a concert, a movie, or connecting with an old friend. If nothing else, there is always the weekend or a distant vacation to dream about. Yet these events are over all too soon; and again, time drags on.

The stories in this book have helped put me and others back in touch with another way of living, where every event and every conversation becomes a peak experience. For me, it's like being a child again, always engaged and finding fun—and mischief—wherever I find myself. I lost much of that in school, and in the process of becoming a responsible adult. It wasn't until I started living life the way it is presented in the following stories that I was again able to be fully engaged in the moment and revel in its gifts.

My transformation didn't happen overnight, and it often manifested in ways that took time to recognize. Yet in retrospect, I see how step-by-step I reclaimed my life from the doldrums of mere existence. With these stories' guidance, I have been able to convert seemingly insignificant events into conscious ones. In doing so, I have gifted myself an awakened life.

I would like to share one of these everyday events with you, as it has become my metaphor for how something mundane can be transformed into a rich and sacred ritual.

Our food co-op stocked shelled nuts in bulk, which I felt good about purchasing. They were organic, and I could cut down on packaging waste by using my own recycled bags. Yet I developed no real relationship with those nuts—I just brought them home, mixed them in my granola, and ate them. It was a far cry from my experiences growing up with the black walnuts and wild hickory nuts that my family would gather and clean together. Dad knew how to dry and husk them, and Mom was deft with the shell-cracking hammer and nut picker. We kids chipped in; yet if it weren't for our parents, we'd be waiting a long time between nut breads and nut-topped pies.

While absentmindedly chewing my granola, I would sometimes drift back to my family's sense of presence and engagement with the food we ate. I realized how much I missed that feeling, and I wondered how I could bring it back into my life.

Let me help you visualize how I accomplished this: Imagine that I invite you to breakfast with my family. You arrive, and we lay a tablecloth over the living room rug. In the center we place a flat rock the size of a saucer, surrounded by several stones around the size of a lemon. Beside them, we set a basket of fruit and two bowls of nuts. In one bowl are wild-for-aged black walnuts and hickory nuts, and in the other is a mix of almonds, hazelnuts, English walnuts, Brazil nuts, and pecans that we purchased in 50-pound sacks. As though the center arrangement were our altar, we sit in a circle around it, hold hands, and express our gratitude for the gifts that will be brought to us by every moment of the coming day.

Each of us then chooses a few nuts, and we begin cracking. To get you started, one of us gives you a few tips on how to execute a deft crack without smashing your fingers.

Soon you see that each of us has evolved a cracking style that matches our personality. Lety, my mate, cracks a couple dozen at a time, as fast as she can set them on the anvil stone. She then sits back to sort shell from meat. When finished—and with a self-satisfied smile—she mixes her handsome handful of nutmeats into her bowl of already diced fruit, to make the freshest fruit salad there is. On the other hand, I— ever impetuous—crack one nut at a time and eat it immediately.

At the same time, I am exacting: I will not crack a nut just any old way. I wrap a finger around each side, to keep shell fragments from flying asunder. Next, I give the nut just enough of a tap to crack the shell without crushing the meat. Each variety of nut has its preferred way of being cracked. While I gently tap a Brazil nut on its upturned narrow ridge, I give black walnuts a good rap. But not too hard, or I'll end up picking shrapnel-like shell bits out of my mashed nutmeat.

Each nut requests special attention. While heavier nuts mean a thicker shell and a proportionately harder tap, odd shapes ask to be held at just the right angle, or they could fly out of hand. We make a game of it, aiming to crack each nut on the first hit, without striking it so hard as to damage the nutmeat. For dexterity training, I crack a nut by holding it and the stone in the same hand; then I shell and eat the nut with the same hand as well.

My family finds that active engagement in the meal, along with sharing the cracking rock, encourages animated conversation. I am especially nurtured by the ritual aspects of the meal. When someone cracks a nut with twin meats, one of them is shared with another person. For serving, we pass our bowls around the circle clockwise (which we call sunwise), with Elders first, followed by women and nurslings, then men and older children. Servers dish themselves out last, along with setting aside food for anyone missing. Those who want seconds will first check to see that everyone else—slow eaters in particular—have had their fill.

Even cleaning up is participatory. One person will put the nut bowls back atop the refrigerator, while another burns the nutshells in the woodstove, and a third brushes off the cracking stones and returns them to their place beside the woodstove. Someone else takes the tablecloth outside to shake it out.

I sometimes wonder if Bonobos, a chimpanzee species indigenous to the Congo, have feelings similar to ours when a troop of them returns to use the nut-cracking stones it has set beside a particular tree. Stones are scarce in the Congo, so Bonobos remember their stone cache locations and return to them time after time, even over generations. Like us, they gather around their stones to crack nuts together, then return the stones to their proper place.

Sometimes while cracking nuts with my circle, I imagine that we have been invited to breakfast with a Bonobo family. While we pass the cracking stones back and forth, it occurs to me that Bonobos might live more consciously than we do. They must be present and engaged in their daily activities, as any disconnection could spell hunger—or worse.

At the same time, I fancy that their conscious presence brings them pleasure and fulfillment in the sharing of a simple meal of nuts and fruit, just as it does for us. I like to think of their mealtime ritual, just like ours, as a metaphor for mindfulness—for being fully present and engaged in every gilded day. May the stories in the following pages bring you a stone to crack open every moment to the succulence it holds.

THE STORY BEHIND THE STORIES

To understand why Zen literature and oral tradition are blessed with such a large number of rich teaching stories, we must look at 6th-to-8th century imperial China—the fabled time of the first Zen sages. At that time, there was a growing aversion to pageantry and adherence to any specific philosophy, ritual, or exercise. Juxtaposed with that antipathy were the diverse philosophical influences from around the empire and beyond. Imagine a Chinese monk wearing a Buddhist robe, a Confucian hat, and Taoist sandals while going to visit a Siberian shaman, and we have a picture of the fertile mix from which Zen arose.

Yet today, most of us know Zen for what it has largely reverted to since its origin: a school of Buddhism with specific practices based on meditation and sutras.

Rather than a spiritual practice or a way of life, classic Zen is simply a state of being, with the stress on *simply*. Zen claims nothing: there is no philosophy and there are no practices or exercises. Its approach is to strip away the habits, pretenses, and illusions that relegate us to mere existence, which then frees us to have vibrant, unfettered lives. Think of Zen as a continual explosion of the now—an unending journey into the frontier of fear and unknowing. There is comfort, but not complacency; there is pleasure, but not satiation.

Story Origins

Around fifty years ago, I began collecting Zen stories. I presently have over 1000, not including variations of the same story. I learned some stories directly from the sages who pass down the oral tradition, yet most came from my research of the classical literature (see *Selected Sources*).

Some stories are attributed to the Confucian and Taoist traditions, while others come from Chinese and Indian folklore. Many are said to have been told by Buddha, and a number can be traced back to Rumi (a 13th century Middle-Eastern mystic), yet the stories could be much older. The origins of most stories are lost to the folds of time. Most likely they were selected over the centuries from the greater body of stories that existed at the time.

I have found versions of supposedly Zen stories in Slavic, Persian, and Arabic storytelling traditions. It still amazes me to read the same story in sources as diverse as a classic Zen text, *One Thousand and One Nights*, and a Swahili folktale collection. As a story travels, the Sage becomes a Zen Master in the Far East, a Swami in South Asia, and a Mulla in Islamic lands. He plays the character of Afandi in Central Asia, Nasreddin in Western Asia, Joha on the Arabian Peninsula, and Giufa in Italy. The cross pollination is due to migration, conquest, trade (particularly on the Silk Road), and wandering storytellers.

A number of stories originated as *mondos*, which are reflective dialogues between Sages and Seekers, while others took form from consciousness-raising riddles, or *koans*. Others have been used as parables and fables. Yet whatever their origin, label, or distinction, all are now part of the vast body of traditional Zen literature.

In my research, I've found that many stories considered to be of contemporary origin are actually modernized versions of ancient stories. Some stories have survived only as fragments, while others have been divided or combined. Still others appear to have been stripped down to bare outlines, probably for ease of memory. Different translations of the same story can differ significantly from one another: one might be lush and another sparse; one could be literal and a second will reflect the bias of the translator.

My Presentation

I chose the stories in this book to represent the full spectrum of the Zen tradition, which not so coincidentally covers the spectrum of our life experience. Most of them are personal favorites that I have used in my teachings, counseling work, and writings. Some of the stories have been transcribed from talks I have given, while others are fresh versions that I edited specifically for this collection.

When I had multiple versions of the same story, I usually chose the earliest form. The later the version, the more it tended to have aristocratic or pontifical overlays. Some stories accumulated sermonizing or political baggage on their journeys through time, and I relieved them of those burdens before including them. When stories existed only in outline or anecdotal form, I constructed dialogue and context—a common practice for storytellers.

Virtually all Zen stories come to us out of the context of their cultures of origin. When storytellers adopt stories, they need to take this cultural impregnation into account and refashion the stories in ways that make sense to their audiences. This has been the tradition with Zen stories as well. As they migrated across Eurasia and northern Africa, terms, cultural concepts, and characters were substituted for those familiar to their audiences. I have done the same when necessary. For the characters, I use the generic terms *Elder, Sage, Wizard, Scholar, Seeker, Nun, and Monk.* I simply refer to a Seeker's aspiration as The Way or Awakening. This decision is in keeping with the earliest forms of the stories, along with following the Zen tradition of stripping down to the essence.

To draw the reader out of the ordinary, I tell the stories in the traditional formal air. To maintain that feeling, I use very few contractions, such as *don't, hasn't,* and *I'm.* I employ capitalization to distinguish symbolic words, as well as to draw attention to words and phrases with depth of meaning.

The Artwork

Jan Zaremba, Master of Japanese Brush Painting, created the story illustrations. His symbols that end each story are mostly variations of this character: ⟨♡, which is Japanese-Chinese-Korean for *heart-mind.*

After spending several years as a monastic monk, Jan studied ancient Buddhist cave paintings in India, then went on to paint in Afghanistan, Kurdistan, and the Himalayas. In 1979, he began his study of Oriental Painting with Zen Master Dr. Hisashi Ohta, who was designated a Living National Treasure of Japan.

Several years later, Dr. Ohta presented all of his Japanese students to Jan. He then became Sumi-e instructor at the Japanese Cultural Center in Los Angeles for eighteen years. In 1994, he was invited by Chinese painters to join the prestigious Chinese Calligraphers and Painters Association. He exhibits his work regularly in the United States and Europe.

Jan's style is inspired by the classic East Asian ink-and-wash painting tradition. In the West it is commonly known by its Japanese name *sumi-e* (墨絵), and in China it is called *shui-mo hua* (水墨画). As with the brush-strokes of Nantembo, the most revered Japanese Zen monk of recent times, Jan's are a superb example of the exquisite balance of boldness and subtlety for which sumi-e is noted.

Jan uses traditional sumi-e ink, which is made by blending finely-ground bamboo or pine soot with glue extracted from fish bones. The ink comes in stick form, which the artist pulverizes and mixes as he needs it. This allows him to vary the shade and texture of the ink, which provides its expressive range. It is typically the only ink used, and it comes primarily in black.

"To fully appreciate sumi-e," says Jan, "it helps to know a little bit about the technique. What you see are paintings on sensitive, absorbent rice paper, made with a delicate brush loaded with pure ink. Brush, ink, and paper of such responsiveness are unknown in Western art. These materials respond to the slightest variation in pressure and speed; hesitation, corrections, or revisions are fatal."

The Eastern world, Jan says, is one to which man belongs, but which he does not dominate. This is reflected in the approach of the artist, who "is performing an uninhibited dance with the brush. The personality of the painter, his mood, and even the speed of execution are discernible from a single brush-stroke.

"I paint because what appears to us as the world wants to be known. And I am convinced that even in its exquisite horror, it is profoundly beautiful."

HOW TO USE THIS BOOK

Without the help of story, we grow too close to our own life experiences to view them objectively and with perspective. The intent of Zen stories is to liberate us from the familiar, so that we might discover the treasures awaiting us in our Awakening.

Story is metaphor, so be careful of taking anything literally. A story's characters are aspects of ourselves, created to help us see through new eyes and relate to themes common to the human experience. We discover that we are not alone, and that we are not so different from others.

Here you will find the raw stories, without interpretation. They are bigger than any insight I could lend them, and we each need to wear the stories as they fit us. In addition, the stories seldom remain as we initially perceived them. They have a habit of speaking differently at different times—especially as we change.

Use these stories for daily meditation, or as inspirations to start your day. Don't feel bound to the order in which the stories occur; let them call you, and let intuition be your Guide. Take advantage of the subject index at the back of the book, as it will take you directly to the story that addresses your need. Or you may want to peruse the index, to see what speaks to you.

Above all, remember that words exist to encourage the wordless—to help us realize Zen, the essence. ᴖᴥ

The Stories

January
1

A TALE OF TWO VILLAGES

A Nun and a Seeker, traveling together, approached an affluent village. The villagers perceived them to be beggars and closed the gate, all the while hurling stones, sticks, and verbal abuse at them. The two travelers quickly continued on their way.

The next town they came to was a poor fishing village. When they approached, nearly everyone came out to extend a welcome, which was their longstanding tradition. The tired and hungry travelers were given the best that the villagers had to offer, and it was graciously received.

The Nun and the Seeker told stories of their travels to the villagers and gave insights from the Teachings they had received. There was so much to share both ways that the days turned into weeks, then months.

One morning, the Nun and the Seeker realized that a year had passed. They announced that it was time for them to continue on their way. With loving tears, they all wished each other well.

Ten years went by, and one day while the two were resting by the roadside, the Seeker asked, "Do you remember that village where they locked us out and stoned us? Have you heard how they are doing?"

"Their families have grown, their fields are lush, and their Cows grow fat."

"That makes no sense!" the Seeker exclaimed. "What about the fishing village? They were kind people who welcomed us openly, and we so enjoyed our stay with them."

"I hear that a hard fate befell them: an earthquake destroyed the village, and many perished. Those who survived scattered in all directions and settled where they landed."

The Seeker, sitting in reflective silence for a long time, finally asked, "Where is the justice in that? How can it be that the open-hearted people of the fishing village got repaid as they did?"

"The way of things is often beyond our grasp," replied the Nun. "The refugees of the fishing village each carried the bright flame of kindness and generosity in their heart—a fire that is needed everywhere—and they kindled their tradition in every community in which they settled." ⤳

January

2

THIS OR THAT

"The Fish are back!" shouted a boy as he ran up from the River to the town. Every spring the townspeople waited for the Fish to come up from the Sea and pass by the town on their way up to spawn in the River's headwaters.

Upon hearing the news, everyone got together to decide whether it was the beginning or the end of the spawn. If it were the beginning, they would wait a few days until the peak, when they could catch the greatest number of Fish with the least effort. If it were the end of the spawn, they would have to travel upstream to intercept the Fish.

However, the people could not decide which it was. They reconvened the next day after they had gathered more information, and again on the next day, yet there were always conflicting reports.

The following day, the children came up from playing along the River and reported that there were no more Fish. Once more, the townspeople met to decide what to do.

"We did our part," they concluded. "Why are the Fish not cooperating?" They decided that the spawning run was no longer reliable, so they turned to raising Goats. ➺

January
3

REVERSE LOGIC

A woman was leading a Goat down the lane with a rope. Tugging and biting at the rope, the Goat obviously had something in mind other than walking down the lane with the woman.

Coming from the other direction was a group of Nuns. When they approached the woman and Goat, the eldest Nun said, "Kind Goat tender, we are Wisdomseekers. We ask if you will be part of a Teaching we wish to gain."

"I would be honored," she replied.

"Let us begin by determining who here is leading whom," said the oldest Nun.

Everyone agreed that the woman was clearly the lead. "She is in control," one of them said, "as she is forcing her will upon the Goat."

The oldest Nun then drew her knife and cut the rope. The Goat took off across the fields, with the woman running frantically after him. "Who now appears to have the rope around her neck, being dragged along against her will?" asked the Nun. "Such is the way the mind works. Always look at the shadow side of what it tells you." ➤

January
4

THE VALUE OF OPINION

In the village lives an Elder of whom nearly everyone speaks well. Yet she makes it a point to associate with those who nearly everyone demeans. When she invites guests for a meal, those who the other guests gossip about and work to demonize are nearly always in attendance.

A Seeker who studies with the Elder asked her why she would tarnish her reputation and cause her honored guests such discomfort by having them sit beside the objects of their criticism.

"Have you noticed how some people are quick to react to what a person will say or write? If that person says or writes something else, they will react in another way. Rather than responding to the person's words, they are actually formulating opinions to judge the person's character."

"Aren't our opinions all we have to go on?" the Seeker responded.

"Opinions are like the weather: is it cold or is it hot? Is it wet or is it dry? And we react accordingly. When we base our assessment of the season's weather on whether or not sunshine or sleet are hitting our faces at that particular moment, how accurate—or realistic—are we?"

"Are you saying that opinion is not knowledge?"

"Someone who sees me as virtuous is as ignorant as someone who sees me as evil."

A confused look washed over the Seeker's face.

"Let me clarify," said the Elder "Opinion is the bane of Truth. While opinions shift like a change of clothes, Truth remains solid and hidden, like the flesh and bones underneath the garb." ᴖ

加州第一風顛生

January
5

WHO CARES?

A Hermit lived in a most inhospitable place. It was cold and damp the year round, the Trees were scraggly, and the ground was barren and rocky. Yet she found beauty there, which was why she chose it for her abode.

The occasional Pilgrim would venture there to learn how to find value within a ragged exterior. One such person said when she arrived, "The journey was treacherous, and it took me three days of climbing over slippery rocks to get here."

"What does that matter?" asked the Hermit.

"I have come to sit at your feet and be guided in your ways."

"Who cares about that?"

"What is this nonsense you are giving me about not caring? Are you not the famed Hermit-Nun who chose this despicable place for beauty?"

"So what?"

January

6

THE CLAY PITCHER

Too sick to leave his bed, a man's thirst grew stronger and stronger. There was no one around to care for him, so all he could do was look longingly at the water pitcher standing on the other side of the room. Finally he had to close his eyes and rest.

The pitcher was so filled with compassion for the man that with all her might, she managed to roll almost within his reach.

After a while, the man opened his eyes and stared in wonderment at the pitcher right beside him. Mustering what meager scrap of strength he had, he stretched out to grasp it. He raised it to his parched lips.

The pitcher was empty.

With his last spark of energy, he threw the pitcher against the wall and it smashed into a thousand useless pieces of clay.

January
7

WHEN

Impatience is a symptom of youth—nearly every young Seeker would like to experience Awakening sooner rather than later. Even the Quest for Knowledge is driven by yearning. One such restive Seeker asked a Sage, "When will I start gaining some of the Knowledge I need to know?"

The Sage replied, "When does the sun show in the Sky?"

"When it is clear, of course."

"When does the sun first make his appearance?"

"When it comes his time to rise."

"And when is a drought over?"

"When the rains come."

"Do you see how useless it is to talk of this?" asked the Sage. "It's like tossing words to a Lizard when she already knows what Lizards know. Besides, a lizard has no use for something as useless as words."

"I see now that my impatience creates words," replied the Seeker. "Kind Sage, you have helped me to be the clear Sky and the parched Earth." With that, she bowed. ❧

January
8

WISE AND NOT

"Why," asked a Seeker, "will a person sometimes appear wise and at other times seem unenlightened?"

"Oftentimes," replied the Sage, "a Seeker will come to me with a question—a very informed question, I might add—and after she receives an answer, she will beg her leave."

"How does that show Wisdom and lack of Wisdom?"

"One part of the person may be ready to Awaken and another part may not, which is why someone can look dull and uninformed, then later appear to be wise beyond her years."

"That confuses me," responded the Seeker. "It would seem that if I were to gain Wisdom in one area of my life, it would spill over into other areas as well."

"Have you ever had a fruit that was ripe on one side, yet green on the other? This is the way with some people. They can be compassionate and understanding with one person, yet intolerant and oppressive with another. At one moment, they might be open to exploring the deeper meaning of things, yet at the next, they appear completely closed. It is part of the Way to Awakening."

"I still do not see it, for it seems disjointed and out of Balance."

"Does the fruit not start ripening on one side, with the ripeness then spreading through the whole fruit?" the Sage asked.

"Is it not also possible that a fruit will ripen on one side and the rest of the fruit will never mature?"

"That is fear speaking. One of its curses is that it lets us venture beyond our boundaries only a little here and a little there. It will let us timidly ask a question, then it will have us retreat back behind the false bravado of our judgments and criticisms and righteousness."

"How does that relate to Wisdom or its lack?" asked the Seeker.

"It is as though we have stolen a tidbit of Wisdom and scurried back behind our self-protective wall to savor it. What we don't realize is that the wall keeps us trapped in the same state as when we built it." —

January
9

READING SIGN

Twelve Seekers traveled to a distant land to study with a snowy-haired Wise One whose reputation had spread far beyond the confines of his region. After two months of travel on foot, they finally arrived at the doorstep of the Sage, weary yet energized by the completion of their journey.

After the traditional greeting protocols, one of the Seekers addressed the Sage: "Wise One, we have come from a distant land to study at your feet. We thirst to know the nuances of The Way, and we ask that you consider guiding us to that end. Nothing you request of us will be denied."

"I am touched by your passion for The Way," the Sage responded. "Will you all stand before me?"

After a short while, which seemed uncomfortably long to the Seekers, the White-Haired One pointed to two of them and said, "You may stay and pursue The Way with me."

The other Seekers were left speechless and frozen in their places. Finally one of them got up the wherewithal to ask, "Honored One, how is it that you can choose from among us without knowing us?"

"Have any of you kept animals?"

Most of them nodded.

"When you look for breeding stock to improve your animals, how do you select them?"

The unchosen Seekers bowed and took their leave. ➤

January
10

THE VALUE OF WISDOM

Two women were talking one day. Said the first to the second, "I have become the possessor of quite the Wisdom. I surprise even myself sometimes with my depth and perspective."

"That sounds like bragging," replied the second woman. "How can you be so sure that you are wise? In order for me to believe that, you will have to show me."

"Surely," said the first woman. "I will impart some of my Wisdom to you, and you will then know: a Tree's branches hang low when they are full of fruit, in order to make its picking easier for us."

"I never knew that!" cried the second woman. "What a tremendous piece of insight. Surely you are not bragging about being a Wisdom Carrier— you are merely stating a fact."

January
11

THE TEACHING OF NO-TEACHING

Many of us believe in the system of becoming a Master by studying a discipline or receiving a title from someone who holds a higher title. Yet anyone who claims or uses such a title disproves it by the mere act of doing so. The following story will illustrate this point.

A Sage of renown realized that his living days were numbered. At his bedside sat a Seeker, who for many years accompanied the Sage and had an undying devotion to the Awakening Journey.

"I have a book for you," said the Sage to the Seeker. "It has been passed down from Sage to Sage for generations more than I know. It contains the Wisdom Teachings of The Way; and each Sage who has held it, including me, has added to it. Take it, for you are the next rightful Carrier of the Wisdom."

"I am honored that you have chosen me," replied the Seeker, "yet I must tell you that I have no need for the book. I have traveled with you on this Journey thus far without a book, so why would I need one now? What I carry is already within me, and what I speak and hear is not in words."

"This you and I know," replied the Sage, "yet the book is a symbol, and in this way it has value. Take it."

At that, the Sage handed the book to the Seeker, who immediately tossed it into the glowing fireplace in front of them.

"What have you done?" exclaimed the Sage.

"What have you said?" replied the Seeker. ～

January

12

MUSIC TO NAP BY

The Meadow was sprinkled with fragrant spring flowers and the lazy after-noon sun warmed the soft grasses, creating an inviting carpet on which to lie. Two Monks who were passing by decided to stop for a rest.

"Tell me," said the older Monk, "what you have learned thus far from your studies."

Feeling both honored and encouraged by the request, the younger Monk talked on about the mysteries that were unfolding before him.

After a while, he looked over at his companion and saw that he was fast asleep. Gently nudging him, the younger Monk said, "You must have drifted off, and I am sure you want to hear all of what I have discovered."

"Oh, that is so! Please go on so that I can drift back to sleep." ༄

January
13

THE WAY OF GIVING

Nearby lived a Sage who would regularly give things away to other people. "I am not eating right now," he would say to one. "Here is some food." To another, he would say, "Here is a tool, do you have a use for it?"

"But they do not appreciate what you give to them," commented a Seeker. "They think you are just getting rid of something that you don't need."

"I would rather they not appreciate it," replied the Sage. "For if they did, that would be giving me praise."

"I think you deserve some praise for your kindness."

"That would defeat the purpose of the gift."

"How so?" asked the Seeker.

"I wish them to benefit from the gift, rather than it benefitting me. What most people cherish in a gift actually distracts them from what could truly help them. In gifting as I do, I want to show people that it is important to embrace the Teaching, rather than getting caught up in how the Teaching came to them." ━

January
14

LEAD OR FOLLOW?

"We are out of water," commented a Seeker.

Another Seeker got up to grab the pail and take it to the well, and a third Seeker followed to help. When the two returned, the Sage asked, "Which of you has gained, and which of you has lost?"

A lively discussion followed. Some thought the first one to get up was the one who gained, while others figured it was the follower.

After the discussion wound down, the Sage commented, "It appears that my question was not heard, as it is not about gain or loss."

"But those were your words," said a voice in the group.

"And what are words but vain attempts at expressing Truth? You heard well, but did you listen? A Parrot can repeat my words as well as you did, yet does that mean he understands them?"

"What good is it, then, to listen to words?"

"Words are good when they are ignored," replied the Sage.

"That goes way beyond my grasp," stated another Seeker.

"Only because words are sacred to us—we do not ruffle the sacred. Let's look at it this way: when the Sky invites, ignore it; when the Breeze speaks, ignore it."

"But when they call me, I want to listen."

"You want to escape, which is refusing to listen."

Several Seekers understood, and they bowed in gratitude.

January
15

THE FORSAKEN GIFT

He was a fabled wrestler and Guardian of his people, and he had grown old. Yet aspiring young Guardians would come to learn by sparring with him, and he never tired of the game.

One day a young man came who had anything but the look of wanting to learn in his eyes. "I will defeat you," he hissed to the Elder Guardian. "No one has been able to best me, and I doubt that a wrinkled old fart like you will be the first."

The trainees who had gathered round whispered to each other, "That gorilla will kill our venerable Teacher. We must talk him into refusing the challenge."

The Aged One heard their talk, yet he stepped forward with an air of serenity and said to the visitor, "I consider it an honor to accept your challenge."

The two grapplers assessed each other, then positioned themselves to take full advantage of the one who made the first move. The young stud growled and spit in the Elder's face. He cursed the Elder's mother and kicked dirt at him, which stuck to the spit. Yet the Elder remained as centered as when he first greeted the challenger.

This went on for half of the morning, until the challenger finally realized he had a formidable opponent. Or more accurately, he had no opponent. Yet as much as the rival needed to win, he would not attack. He knew it would make him vulnerable to even an old man, as all the Elder would have to do is turn the energy of the attack back upon itself.

There was one insult the challenger knew would work. It was now all or nothing, as he could not go home and face jeers after being defeated by an old man. The young buck took off his sash, stood naked in front of the serene Guardian, and peed on his feet. Tensed and ready for a lightning response, the young man took a quick step back.

Feeling the heat of combat course through his body, he studied the Elder's form, looking for any sign of tightness or twitching that would indicate a reaction. The Elder's face showed nothing but tranquility.
The pompous one gingerly backed away, and when he felt it safe to turn around, he briskly disappeared down the road.

"How could you stomach such abuse for so long?" asked a voice in the crowd.

"Why didn't you teach him a lesson?" asked another, and many similar questions came flying rapidly at the Balanced One.

After everyone relaxed and quieted, he finally spoke: "When someone offers a gift and it is not accepted, whose gift then is it?" 〜

January
16

HUNGER FOR TRUTH

"Honored Elder, there is nothing more important to me," began a desperate Seeker, "than the Quest for Truth. It is all I think about, and I want to devote my entire energy to it."

"Desire will not bring you Truth," replied the Elder, "nor will devoting all of yourself to it."

"But must I not give in order to receive?"

"It is true. However, what is asked of you is acceptance rather than giving."

"What do you mean?" asked the Seeker.

"Can you accept doing things you have no interest in or desire to do? How about things that make no sense to you and may even contradict your beliefs or better judgment? Could you refrain from doing things that your needs and desires draw you to?"

"How will that bring me closer to Truth?"

"Because it is not what we give or don't give," said the Elder, "but what we want or don't want, that diverts us from seeking Truth." ⇝

January
17

THE STAFF

One Sage went to market with a stout staff. When she reached the center of the square, she began to swing the staff wildly and shout incoherently. Soon a large group of people gathered around her, wondering what had possessed their venerable Wise One.

She suddenly grew silent, and the benevolent look on her face relaxed the crowd. Then without warning, she ran madly from one stand to the next, slashing her staff through canopies, upsetting fruit carts, and tossing all manner of wares asunder.

Several people sprang to action, quickly restraining her. Then they took her before the village constable.

"Why would a person like you behave in such an unbecoming manner?" he asked.

"There are many in our village," replied the Elder, "who are valued for the way they act. A person could have the worst of intentions, yet if he behaved properly, he would be well regarded. Yet if someone merely *does* something that is considered improper—even though his heart may be pure—he is chastised by his community."

"I understand the valuable gift you have brought us," responded the constable. "How can we make it benefit us?"

"When we use traditions, regulations, and expectations to control people, we tell them that their outward actions are more important than what is inside, and we reward them thusly. Let us instead encourage the Inward Journey. Then what we manifest outwardly will be a reflection of that." ～

January
18

THE NATURE OF YEARNING

"Revered Elder," the Seeker began, "there are things I desire—things that please me—and sometimes I feel ashamed for my yearnings. I do not know why, and I would like to understand."

"It is because pleasure and desire are not as they appear," replied the Elder. "It can be said that the true nature of things is never as it appears."

"I can imagine that. Yet how does it help with my feelings of guilt and shame over what I crave?"

"You are truly a Seeker, as you will not settle for an answer that only taunts you to ask another question. When we are pleased, we have fulfilled a yearning. Yet through its fulfillment, the yearning only grows stronger. The stronger the yearning, the harder it becomes to maintain centeredness while fulfilling that yearning. This is when virtue turns to vice and benevolence to malevolence."

"Then what can a person with desires do? Must I shun the world and go live the life of an Ascetic?"

"That, of course, is an option. There are some who take it, and their logic is sound, for whenever we fulfill a desire, we take from someone else."

"Then please help me! Or I will have no choice but to become a recluse."

"Let me illustrate with this question the trap you have just sprung on yourself: what would you rather be, courageous or cowardly?"

"I suspect that is a trick question, and that excites me. I will take the bait because I am a hungry Seeker. I would rather be courageous."

"Now what if I told you that there was no difference between courage and fear?"

"I would have to call you a liar," responded the Seeker. "Yet if I do, I know that I would only have swallowed the bait."

"Wise you are for your tender years. Imagine the brave man who attacks a Bear head-on, then the coward who waits until a Bear is asleep to stalk up and kick her. Who here is showing the most bravery?"

"I bow to the Wisdom you give voice to." ᜊ

January
19

MORE IS LESS

It was autumn, and the cold and rain came sooner than expected. A wandering Monk who was making his way down a lonely country road got caught in a storm. He was cold and his clothes were soaked through. Looking out her window, a farm woman saw him passing by and went out to invite him in. He gladly accepted.

After he warmed himself by the fireplace and had a hearty meal, the woman did not ask—but outright told—him that he was going to stay overnight. In addition, he was not to continue his journey until the rain abated. "My husband likes to gamble," she continued, "and win or lose, he drinks. When he goes to town, I never know when he will be back. The children and I sometimes go hungry because of it. If he comes home tonight, it will be late and he will be very drunk, so pay him no mind."

"I understand," replied the Monk. "Will you be so kind as to bring me a large bottle of wine for the night?"

The woman was surprised at such a request. Still, he was a Monk, and her guest besides, so she obliged.

Late in the night, the husband came stumbling in. The Monk was roused by the racket. "Who are you?" bellowed the man.

After the Monk explained his presence, he asked if the man would sit down and share a bottle of wine with him. The man relaxed immediately, and after a few swallows, he passed out on the floor.

The next morning when the man awoke, he remembered nothing. He had to be told what happened the night before. The realization of his behavior in front of the Monk triggered his immediate Awakening. He felt the need to renew his life by traveling with the Monk, and he asked his wife for her consent. Feeling both his need and sincerity, she gave him her blessing. ➤

January
20

BECOMING SHAME

A Philosopher and a Sage got together to explore a variety of esoteric topics. "Humans are the red-cheeked animals," stated the Philosopher out of the blue.

"Why would that be?" asked the Sage.

"It is because our cheeks often taste shame—so much, in fact, that they want to stay red."

"I see," replied the Sage. "From what you say, it sounds as though you think shame is the mark of our kind."

"Oh yes, and you see it everywhere! We are ashamed for doing this, ashamed for not doing that, ashamed for giving too much, ashamed for giving too little. We are sometimes even ashamed for being Human."

"Do you think that is why the virtuous man strives to not make others feel shame?" asked the Sage.

"He would rather take on the shame himself than have another endure it," stated the Philosopher with a tinge of scorn.

"Is that not a noble trait?"

"Not only does the virtuous man's sympathy happily deprive another of her shame, but it keeps him from knowing his own shame."

January
21

HOW TO SPEAK

A young woman from a tiny hamlet moved into town, where the night life swept her in. She enjoyed dressing lavishly and going to parties, so she slept late into the morning and was not very productive. Her aged father grew more and more concerned for her welfare. One day, he made the journey into town to see her.

"It has been a long trip for you, Father," she said to him. "I am so glad that you have come. Will you stay with me for a couple of days and rest up? We will have time to talk, and I will show you the beautiful sights around town." Throughout the visit, the father said nothing of his concern. The two just shared the joy of being together after so long.

On the morning of the father's departure, he said to his daughter, "My fingers are getting stiff with age, and I am having trouble with these buttons on my overcoat. Will you help me?" In that instant, the daughter came to the realization that she was also a father—to herself and to her mother back home. From then on, life brought her a new kind of joy. ━

January
22

ADVICE UNMASKED

"What am I to make of a person who comes to give me advice?" asked a Seeker of her Sage.

"That person has come to train you to hear the voice of the heart," replied the Sage.

"How can that be?" asked the Seeker.

"No matter how sound his advice," replied the Sage, "it is merely a distraction from his true intent. If you were able to truly listen, you would soon see that he is trying to convince you of something that is unrelated to his advice. He may either want something from you or want you to take something. He might be trying to gain comfort from you or give you comfort. Or he may want nothing more than to elevate himself in your eyes."

"How am I to know this?"

"Not by what he says, but by how he says it and how he acts, will you be able to hear his heart's voice. With every sentence of his supposed advice, he is reaching deeper into you, so that he can manipulate you to achieve his ends."

"That sounds creepy, like I should flee to protect myself."

"On the contrary. Now that you are aware, you can sidestep his intent and attune to the voice of his heart—he is totally unaware of the fact that this is what he is speaking. He may be presenting the most rational and studied of arguments, and he may come across as purely altruistic and genuinely helpful. He may have even convinced himself of such."

"I never imagined this to be the case. How, then, can I appropriately respond to him?"

"Even though his advice may be worthless," said the Sage, "you can genuinely thank him for it, as he has given you invaluable training in listening to the language of the heart." ᨊ

January
23

WHAT I KNOW BEST

"I have this problem," began the Seeker. "I can tell what people are thinking, and I can see when they are making mistakes and engaging in hurtful behaviors. I want to tell them what's wrong with them and help them mend their ways."

"How is it that you know so much about these people?" asked the Elder.

"I don't know. It's like I can see inside their heads."

"Are you sure it's inside their heads?"

"I don't know what you mean," responded the Seeker.

"You are very wise to know so much about other people. Tell me this: If you want to see dirt on your face, what do you do?"

"I look in a mirror."

"And what do you see in the mirror?"

"I see myself."

"Yet is the mirror not outside yourself?"

"Well, yes."

"Can you see anybody but yourself in that mirror?"

"Honorable Elder, what have you just done? All of a sudden, it is as though I have fallen in love with myself! Here all this time I have been frustrated with others, and all I have been seeing is my own dirty face."

"This is what I meant when I said that you are very wise. You know yourself so well and are able to express it so eloquently that you will now be able to embrace your beautiful face and care for it." ◞

January
24

THE HIDDEN TRUTH

Two men found an abandoned puppy in a back alley. She had silky fur the color of jasmine and eyes that sparkled intelligently. Both of the men wanted her, and they soon got into an argument over who would get to take her home.

As words turn to pushes and shoves, a stranger came along and wedged himself between them. "What is this all about?" he demanded. "You are not drunk, you are not starving. Surely there must be some reason that you are treating each other this way."

Both of them jumped on the opportunity to plead their case for the pup, each hoping that the stranger would help him get his way.

The stranger picked up the puppy, drew his sword, and said, "You each want it your way, so the only way for that to happen is to slice this puppy down the middle and give each of you half."

He raised his sword, and both of the men at the same time shouted, "Wait!"

After a cooling-down moment, one of them said, "Neither of us is worthy of this puppy. We are not looking at what is best for her, but rather at what is best for us. We just made the puppy a pawn in our own neediness game. Kind sir, will you take her? We will view this experience as a sign that it is time to commence our Awakening Journey."

The other man nodded in agreement, as did the stranger.

Walking by the market on the way home with the chubby little animal, the stranger wondered what vegetables he could pick up for the evening pup barbecue.

TRAPPED

"I have come to you, Learned One, because I feel trapped," said a Seeker. "I have gotten myself into a predicament, and I don't see any options. My world is so small now, and I know from my Journey thus far that my mind creates that world. Yet my mind will not let me be free of it. What am I to do?"

"First, we must recognize that *free* and *trapped* are relative terms," responded the Guide. "One person's bondage is another's opportunity, and vice versa."

"Are you saying that I could see entrapment as being free?"

"Seeing is not being," replied the Sage. "Many a person is gifted with awareness, only it means nothing unless it is actualized."

"How, then, do I actualize awareness?"

"You don't have to do it. The only thing that stands between awareness and actualization is fear. Your world and your choices within it will expand to the degree that you can enlist your fear as your Guide."

"But what is it that I fear, so that I may find where it resides and go befriend it?" asked the Seeker.

"Close your eyes and let your fear rise, then tell me where it came from."

The Seeker did as suggested, then stated, "From my tiny world."

"Where does your tiny world come from?"

"I see it now…it comes from my mind. Sagacious One, I bow deeply to you. I will now go into another world."

January
26

MATCH-MAKING

An aspiring Scholar liked to argue. More and more she responded with crude and demeaning statements to the Sage who was guiding her. When she resorted to such tactics, the Sage would not respond to her.

"Why do you not call her on her behaviors?" asked another Seeker. "Why not show her what she is exposing of herself?"

"She does not seek that," responded the Sage. "What she wants is someone who will engage her in debate. If I do not, she will assume that I am unable to do so, and she will eventually leave to find what she is after."

"I see. It is a way to encourage irritating people to leave."

"It may appear that way, yet I am actually helping her to get what she desires. I have no qualm with her, for I honor her Truth. However, even that makes her want to argue."

"Are your efforts then not self-defeating?"

"Again, it may appear so. She will go from here with all the more passion to find someone to debate. Though I cannot share with her what I have, I will still have served her by helping her along to someone who can meet her present needs." ⤳

 *January* 27

OIL AND WATER

A woman, who enjoyed studying different approaches to Awakening, asked a Sage to help her see the merits and limitations of the various ways.

"What happens," asked the Sage, "if you put a wick in oil and light the wick?"

"It will burn."

"Now, what if you put a wick in water and light it?"

"It would go out."

"If you were to put oil and water together and shake them up, then insert a wick and light it, what would happen?"

"I think it would sputter and probably go out."

"Perhaps, then," concluded the Sage, "there is no need for a lengthy exploration with words, as a clear and simple approach gives you what you seek."

January
28

THE VALUE OF ARGUING

There is the story of the Sage who did things that a certain Scholar considered to be very un-Sage-like. The Scholar, only having knowledge of the external manifestations of what it is to be a Sage, would criticize the Sage for not living up to her expectations.

"It is the way of a Sage," a bystander once told the Scholar, "to be involved in real life, and to do and say things that seem contrary to the typical way of Sages. It is in these ways that he keeps centered in the greater reality and protects himself from becoming dogmatic and opinionated."

"I feel shame for my shallow perspective," replied the Scholar. "I have gained great awareness from your words. Yet there is something I do not understand: how does the Sage share Knowledge and inspire Wisdom if he does not formulate opinions and argue them?"

"In the same way that the Sage does things that defy the popular definition of the Sage. One who spends time with a Sage is often affected in ways that are at first undetectable."

"How does he do that?" asked the Scholar.

"The Sage can touch people deeply because he does not argue. Presence and listening create a trusting, respectful environment, along with inspiring far deeper inquiry than argument ever could."

"But that is not the way of the Scholar. We are trained to challenge and probe."

"Why challenge when all we have to do is listen?" asked the bystander. "When we probe, are we not just feeding our self-interest?"

"You speak as though you were a Sage yourself. You share insights that I would expect only from a Sage."

"But I am one," the bystander replied, "and so are you. When we come to realize this, we can talk about something as seemingly banal as the weather and come to great realizations about topics that are seemingly unrelated. Even more, there is much we can discover in the shadow of words. In the Deeper Truth of things, words only get in the way."

January
29

THE AWAKENED PERSON

"We yearn for our Awakening," stated a Searcher for Meaning to her comrades. "However, do we know what it is to be Awakened, so that we might recognize it if we were ever to achieve it?"

"We have met many Awakened people on our Journeys," stated another. "Let us see how many of their qualities we can recall."

"She has understandings that can be applied to real life."

"He struggles with neither poverty nor wealth, as he does nothing that either would serve."

"For the same reason, she is not tormented by failure or inflated by success."

"She offers no resistance, so she experiences little fear or pain."

"He breathes deep and sure."

"Living in this breath, her sleep is not haunted by dreams, and she wakes up refreshed."

"Content with what is, she does not have to first taste her food to accept it."

"The words of imbalanced people hurl like vomit, where his fall like warm rain."

"She has no lust or cravings, as she knows her needs and wants and satisfies them in the moment."

"He has no fear of life, so he does not fear death."

"I have noticed that an Awakened One enjoys giving, yet he holds no attachment to what he gives. He also enjoys receiving, yet he soon forgets what he received or gives it away."

"Those who disagree with her still love her."

"He is content within himself, radiating a vast emptiness."

"She doesn't try to get others to feel as she does."

continued on page 44

continued from page 43

"The flow of her heart doesn't let her hang on to love or hate."

"He knows the harmony in what others see as opposites."

"She might appear aloof; however, it is only because she is not needy."

"He could appear deficient in areas, yet he needs nothing and takes nothing."

"She knows how to embrace without showing affection."

"He can speak and follow his heart without being judgmental."

"She might seem forgetful or not fully present, only because we do not know presence."

"We see him being foolish, perhaps at great cost to himself, even though we do not—and cannot—know his inner nature."

After everyone spoke, someone else added, "Fellow Journeyers, it just became clear to me that we see an Awakened One as someone else, yet who is she but you and me? Is it not true that we must already be this person if we are ever to Awaken to her? Let us become who we are." ↝

January 30

IN HIDING

"I have this intense yearning to find myself," said a Seeker. "For so long I have stumbled along telling people my name and what I do, but I can't tell them who I am. It is the deepest loneliness, venerable Elder, to know others but not know yourself."

"How strange that you do not know yourself," replied the Elderwoman, "as he has nowhere to hide. The trouble is that our true selves cannot be described, because we have no image of who they are. Our normal senses are no help. There's nothing there to admire or deride, or to even give the time of day, for that matter."

"So how, then, will I ever come to know myself?"

"You are looking for someone who can tell you if the Air is hot or cold, someone with whom to have a conversation. When we think we are someone who has preferences and dislikes, our true self disappears."

"Then I have chased my true self away many times."

"More than chasing him away," replied the Elder, "you fight with him. You want to possess him, which is silly, because he is standing there saying, 'Take me.' If only you could hear him."

"If only," bemoaned the Seeker. "What is the secret to doing that?"

"The only secret is that there is no secret. You already have it."

Right then, the Seeker felt a presence. It was nothing special, nothing that could be put into words, or even feelings. It just was. *He* just was, and that was enough. ➤

January
31

THE GRATITUDE PITFALL

"Why do you never thank me for what I do in service to you?" a troubled Seeker once asked his Elder,

"The first reason," she replied, "is that what you do for me is in service to yourself."

"Egad, you are right! I see that right away when you mention it, and I will start to practice it immediately by not expressing gratitude to you for it. Yet you implied that you had more than one reason."

"The next one is not mine, but rather it is the way of things. If I were to thank you, it would be as though you were being paid for a job well done, and that would be the end of it. Except that I would be cheating you out of something. By acknowledging you, I give you a nut to eat, whereas by serving you in return, I plant that nut for you, so that it will grow into a bearing Tree and provide you with bountiful nuts over many seasons."

February
1

SOMETHING FROM NOTHING

Seekers often like to spend as much time as possible with the Sages they hold in high regard. This particular Seeker was no exception: she was dedicated to the study of The Way, and she took every opportunity to gain the awarenesses that would benefit her.

One day she asked her Sage, "What might I do to give me a great leap forward on my Journey?"

"I will give you your next step," the Sage replied. "However, it will only work if you practice it until everyone in the region knows you by the reputation you will have gained."

"I will abide by your Guidance," replied the Seeker.

For the next several years, the young woman wandered the country lanes and visited the village squares, wailing to everyone and anyone, "The end is upon us! Put your affairs in order and forgive your transgressors, for very soon will come a day like no other!"

When everyone took her to be an unfortunate soul who had lost her mind, she opened a small shop in one of the neighboring villages, as the Sage had instructed. For years she had to beg to get enough to eat, as the only people who would enter the shop of a lunatic were those who desperately needed something she had and could find it nowhere else. Yet over time, she gained a reputation for fairness and handling goods of utmost quality, and she prospered.

One day, she went back to the Sage, curious to know why he asked her to defame herself, then do the complete opposite by building her character.

"Only from nothing can something arise," he replied. "It takes the night to invite the day, and it takes hate to instill the lust for love. By giving up everything, including our very integrity, we see and value everything— every relationship, every transaction, everything that someone else casts aside. It is the true way of life."

"How did you know that I would discover this?"

"If you followed through, I had no doubt that you would learn it, as everyone does who ceases to judge and no longer values one thing over another." ∼

February
2

THE MYTH OF USELESSNESS

"What do we do with those things for which we have no use?" asked the new apprentice wheelwright.

The Elder craftsman was used to the typical questions of apprentices, yet he was never asked this one.

Seeing his confusion, the apprentice elaborated: "My father is a mason and he uses many varieties of stone. He goes to his favorite boulder field, where there is granite, marble, and many other types of stone. He says that some are useful and some are useless: they are either too small or too big, or they are cracked or misshapen. Those stones get in the way, so he casts them aside and buries them. I wonder which approach to useless things you use in this trade."

"For me, it is how I see something, rather than what I see."

"What do you mean by that?"

"Look at the Mongoose, who is deft at getting in and out of tight places and has boundless energy. No Rat stands a chance when she is around. Yet she is totally inept at avoiding traps—her curiosity gets the best of her every time. Then there is the great Bull, massive and powerful, though totally useless at catching Rats."

"I see that, yet how does it apply to rocks?" asked the apprentice.

"Think of a boulder rejected by your father because of its uselessness. It could provide a quiet, shady place for you to sit and reflect while your father is off in another part of the field. While you are there, you might notice that the Moss does not consider the boulder useless, nor does the Bird who built her nest in one of the boulder's cavities that your father saw as an imperfection. The Tree that took root in the crack also found the boulder to be quite useful, as did the Snakes who live underneath the boulder, and the Hawk who perches atop to hunt."

"That makes sense," replied the apprentice. "I now see useless as quite useful, and the perfect stone proves useless in many ways.

"Such is the trap of the Thinking Mind," concluded the craftsman. "It is the Mindless Mind that sees all for what it is." ▬

February
3

THIRST

A Seeker once asked an Elder why she went out of her way to inspire those who were not able to gain from it.

"Apples can attract a greedy person," she replied, "yet that is not the fault of the apple."

"That makes sense," said the Seeker. "What I don't see is how this will benefit someone in the long run."

"If someone eats too many apples, he may get sick. However, the farmer he bought them from does not get sick."

The Seeker reflected on the Elder's words, then asked, "Would it not be better to give someone small amounts of apple, a little at a time, so that he does not get himself sick?"

"That is sometimes the case, yet there is not always a caring person around to help. And if there was, a man obsessed with eating apples could see that person as his enemy and push him away."

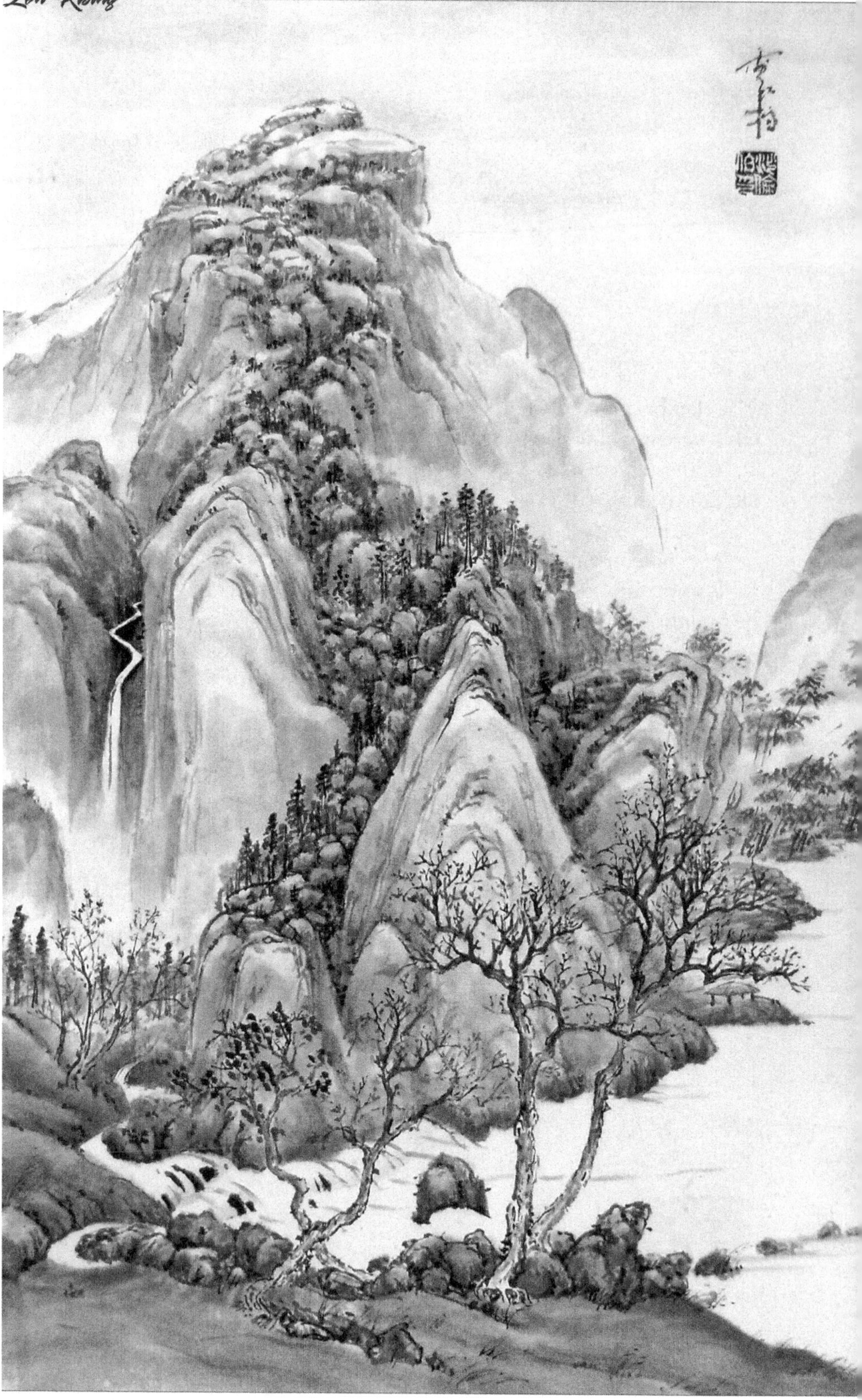

February
4

LEAVE EVERYTHING BEHIND

A story is told of an old man who was coming to the end of his days. He didn't think he had anything to show for his time on earth, yet that's not the biggest thing that troubled him—he wanted to become Awakened before he left. In despair, he went to a Hermit for help.

She met him at the gate to her garden and welcomed him. "My only request of you before entering," she stated, "is that you leave your followers and belongings outside the gate."

"But I have no followers," he replied, "and I have no baggage. I have nothing but what you see."

Still, he listened to her. After a time of reflection, he understood. In that moment, he became Awakened and entered the gate.

February
5

THE SWORDSMAN TENDS THE TRAINEE

One young man wanted to learn swordsmanship only from a man of great renown. When he finally found that person, he discovered that the Master no longer took Trainees, as he was of great age and lived alone in a distant wilderness cabin. Yet the Master saw something unique in the youth that enticed him to offer training.

"Training for what?" thought the youth after he was there for a while. Day after day and week after week, all he was directed to do was fetch water, split wood, cook, and tend the garden. Never was there instruction in the Way of the Sword. "I am ready to quit," he told himself. "I could go anywhere and be a servant for no pay."

At the same time, he had already invested so much time that before leaving he decided to ask the Master if training might soon begin.

"It already has," came the reply. "We'll see how well you developed your awareness while fetching and tending."

From then on, the Trainee couldn't turn his back on anything or focus on any task without fear of getting a rap from the Master's stick. Most frustrating was that it seemed to come out of nowhere. The young man lived in constant stress.

Several cycles of the seasons passed before he could sense a fair number of the coming blows and dodge or deflect them. "He still has learned very little," thought the Master as he went out to the hearth in front of the cabin to cook his vegetables, which is something he seldom did.

The crackle of the fire disguised the Trainee's steps as he stole up behind the old man stooped over the pot and raised his stick to strike.

As nonchalantly as the Master stirred vegetables with one hand, he flipped the cover of the pot up with his other hand to deflect the stick.

In that moment, the youth was Awakened, and all of the training made sense to him. He could then embrace the Way of the Sword, which was kept secret from him by his own actions. For the first time he could sincerely appreciate the supreme kindness of the venerable Master in taking him on. ∼

February
6

TEACH ME

"I have so much to learn," lamented a young woman to her friends. "I need someone to teach me."

They recommended that she go to the village Beggar.

"A Beggar!" she protested. "Of all people!" Yet she saw they were serious, so she went.

"You come to me on a leash," the Beggar said to her, "and you are asking me to put another leash on you. That would make you happy, but only because I will have rescued you from your fear."

"But that is exactly what I want," responded the woman.

"My grandchild, The Way is a mystery. It has no form or purpose, only a vague indescribable radiance. However, those led on leashes cannot trust in the radiance. They want something tangible, so they grasp onto sutras and koans and try to find their meanings. The years roll on into decades, yet many continue to carry those lifeless bodies around."

"That sounds worse than my fear, and I didn't think anything could be as bad. Yet I know of no other way—what can I do?"

"When a Savior or Teacher appears, kill him right then and there. Kill him in your mind, because that is where he lives—you created him. If it is an object, smash it. Even if it is your mother or father, kill them immediately. It is the only way to cut the leash and be yourself."

"But without a Teacher, how will I ever overcome my fear of being off a leash?"

continued on page 54

continued from page 53

"Know the difference between Guidance and Teachings," said the Beggar. "There are clever ones who use tricks to make you think you are being guided, when you are actually being leashed."

"How can I know when that is happening?"

"Saviors are not born; they are created by their followers. When we put another above ourselves, as you tried to do with me, we create our Savior. We are saying, 'I am incomplete and you complete me.'"

"I see. We act like Dogs who sniff and chew anything we come across. We cannot tell the difference between one who invites us to learn and one who traps us to teach."

"I see that a leash is not so comfortable on you after all. Here are three things to do: avoid imagining you have experienced something, or you will end up believing in an illusion; avoid creating yourself from a hodge-podge of 'Ancient Ways;' and above all, be a Fool."

"A Fool? What do you mean?" asked the young woman.

"There are mindless Fools and there are clever Fools, and I do not mean either of them. Be a Fool with no pride and nothing to defend. Then no leash will nab you—not even your own mind." ⤳

February
7

LESS IS MORE

"They are not telling me all they know," said a Seeker who had gone to spend time with many Sages. Frustrated, he searched on until he found a Sage who impressed him with all that he received from the Sage in a short amount of time.

The Seeker was even more struck after talking with a Monk who had studied long with the Sage. The Monk revealed the Final Secret, and the Seeker was then content—he knew everything.

Yet after a time, the Seeker felt empty. He could not understand why, for he was given all that he sought. He took his dilemma to a Sage who was known for speaking few words, yet every one was inlaid with gold.

"To give generously is noble," said the Sage, "yet generosity lacks substance. To give consciously, feeding a hunger just what it needs at the time, gives sustenance."

"But I do not understand. Why can't someone give me all he has and leave it up to me to decide what is useful and what is not?"

"Imagine you are a child. Would you like the Knowledge you could use right now, or would you prefer to have a lifetime's worth dumped upon you all at once?"

"Your words may be few, yet they are pregnant with Wisdom. I now see that so much at once would make me drunk with confusion, and my mind would be crippled with what it is not ready to carry." ✎

February
8

WORDS WON'T WORK

An Elder of the village was sitting languidly in the afternoon sun with a group of Seekers. As the shadows started to crawl over the clearing, one of the Seekers grew anxious. "Honored Elder," he began, "there is trouble in this world, and I want to help. Will you share some Knowledge with me that will help me go forth and do some good?"

"A problem has never been solved by words," replied the Elder.

"But words must help—at least as a starting point."

"When we seek Knowledge out of need, we attach ourselves to it."

"Is that not what we are supposed to do?" asked the Seeker.

"When we do, the information becomes useless, both to you and to whomever you might think you are helping with it."

"That cannot be! I see Knowledge helping all the time."

"This is true," remarked the Elder. "And this is why it is useless. When we attach ourselves to Knowledge, we see Knowledge as the answer. We see it helping all the time because Knowledge keeps recreating the situation that it purports to help. What happens is that once we attach ourselves to Knowledge, we must remain attached to it in order to keep the situation it perpetuates from collapsing."

"Then why do you share Knowledge?" asked the Seeker.

"Knowledge is not the problem, but rather it is the love of Knowledge. The Way of the Seeker is the way of nonattachment. Knowledge then remains a tool, rather than becoming a belief or a way of life. When a tool has served its purpose, we set it back in the toolbox and grab another tool if it is needed. However, when we attach ourselves to the tool, we end up finding or creating ways to keep using it."

"Ever-wise Elder, you are describing the Way of Questioning."

"You have recognized it. Everything we want and need, everything we know and want to know, comes back ultimately to a question. An answer is only a question in disguise, and what passes for Knowledge is only the unknowing that begs another question."

"You have brought me back to silence," said the Seeker after a pause. "It is as though we talked about nothing, and I bow to you for guiding me back to the Eternal Question."

February

9

THE SONG OF FRIENDSHIP

It is said by the Ancient Ones that friendship is listening. When one friend listens to the other singing about the verdant hills on the horizon, it is as though they are strolling together through the hills' lush Meadows in the warm summer sun. When one friend sings of love lost, the other feels the sickness in her heart and the yearning for the comfort of a caress.

Then when the friend dies, the singing stops, and there can be no more listening.

Yet the green hills still glow and lost love still pains; so are these songs not still being sung? And are songs not still for listening? And who is a friend but his song? And what is friendship but embracing his song?

Is it not friendship that endures, then, rather than the friend? It may be that as long as we listen, we are blessed with friendship. ➤

February
10

CONTRARY CONCEALMENT

In a long-ago time lived a fabled Wise Man, who many a Seeker set out to find. However, all the stories of his whereabouts seemed to lead only to a palace in a distant land. There a wealthy nobleman lived, surrounded by luxurious gardens and waited upon by legions of servants.

When Seekers came upon the scene, they felt defeated by their Quest. They could only turn around and leave, reasoning that either the stories were false or they did not get clear directions.

One day, a Seeker decided to disguise himself as a servant. Week after week he waited upon his Master, and in time he came to realize that his Master was actually waiting on him.

"My hunch proved true," thought the Seeker. "This is no wealthy lord—he is none other than the storied Wise Man. And these servants are none of the kind, but rather Seekers like me."

Late one afternoon, the Seeker summoned up the courage to ask the Wise One, "Why is it that you have everyone know you as someone you are not?"

"You I shall answer," the Master responded. "There are two ways to be invisible: one is not to be seen, and the other is to be so conspicuous that you are not seen. To the true Seeker, the Truth reveals itself regardless, and this is the reason you are here. This is also the reason I am invisible to nearly all who set their eyes upon me." ❧

11

HOW TO TELL A TRUTHSEEKER

"What about those who come to see you and do not receive what they need?" asked a Seeker.

"They never did come to see me," replied the Sage.

"And what about those who come to tell you things?"

"There is nothing for me to hear."

"What about those who only come to hear?"

"To them I have nothing to say."

"Then what is the use of anyone coming?"

"There are two possible benefits," said the Sage. "Those who embrace what they are given will receive much more as they Journey onward. Those who reject what they are given will find nothing for themselves, no matter where they go."

"I do not understand," replied the Seeker.

"It is like a woman who is starving and wants Fish. Someone comes along, feels compassion for her, and gives her eggs. 'I cannot eat them,' she replies, 'because they are not Fish.'"

February
12

WHAT IS DESERVING

At our hamlet's harvest feast there was an array of delectable dishes that represented the best from every pasture and garden in the valley. Our custom is that each of us serves what we bring to the feast, and my contribution was a fire-roasted Sheep.

Our cobbler was one of the first in line. "I wish to have that strip of tenderloin," he said to me, "for I have made the shoes that you are wearing. Without me, our people would have to walk barefoot through the mud and over sharp rocks, so I should have the choicest piece."

The next person to be served was a seamstress. "All I do is patch clothes," she said. "I don't contribute much of value, so why don't you just give me a couple of those scraps that you have trimmed off." And so went the serving.

After everyone had sat down and begun to enjoy the meal and camaraderie, I stood up and asked for attention. "I am honored to serve each of you from the best of my flock," I began. "Many of you asked from me what you thought you deserved. Are you all pleased with what you were given?" Everybody nodded in agreement and thanked me.

"I am pleased that you are satisfied," I went on. "At the same time, I must confess that I have deceived you. To you who asked for the tenderloin because of the valuable service that you saw yourself providing, I gave some scraps that I tucked into the carcass where the tenderloin would be found. To you who thought you deserved only the scraps that I had pushed aside, I gave the tenderloin, which I cut up to look like scraps. Is the illusion I created any different than the illusion we each create to stand in for who we are?"

After a moment of silence, someone stood up and said, "Your lesson, Wise Shepherd, is graciously received. This person asks that from here on we all be served the same, as each of us is as valuable to the other as the next."

At that, a great round of applause went up and the harvest feast turned into a celebration of the hamlet's Awakening. ༄

February
13

CONTRARY KNOWING

The two Seekers were desperate. For quite a while they had been looking for the Path they should be taking, and they were just as lost as when they began. In desperation, they set out on a quest for a Sage to guide them.

One day, as they followed the bank of a broad and beautiful River, they heard a faint voice that seemed to come from under a Tree up the bank. Curious, they followed the voice and found a small group of people sitting with a Sage. She looked as old as a Mountain and spoke in a voice that seemed to reverberate from a treasure-laden cavern deep within that Mountain. The pair of Seekers was so mesmerized that they sat with the others and listened. Time seemed to disappear.

After the others left for their midday meal, the pair approached the Elderwoman. One of them said, "I have never heard such gently-spoken words echo with such thunder."

"That is ridiculous," said the other Seeker. "This woman is an imposter who lures people in only to satisfy her own ends.

The Elder asked the praising Seeker to continue on his Journey to find a Sage, and she invited the demeaning Seeker to stay.

February
14

MIRROR IMAGE

An Elder and a Seeker were traveling together. Passing through a village, they came upon a building with the front door left invitingly open. The young man stepped in, and in no more time than it took him to turn around, he jumped back out and into the lane.

"There is a group of angry-looking men inside," he stammered. "As soon as they saw me, they gave me a scornful look. This town must be filled with hateful people! Let's get out of here!"

"Come with me back into the building," the Elder requested, "and show me what you saw. You need not fear; I will enter first."

The two went back inside. There where each of the previously wrathful men stood, the Seeker now saw a kindly person wearing a gentle smile and holding out his hand in greeting. Bewildered, the Seeker followed the Elder back out to the lane.

"I do not understand," muttered the Seeker. "A minute ago I wanted to leave this town as fast as I could move, and now I feel welcomed and wouldn't mind staying a while."

"What we give comes back to us a hundredfold," the Elder stated. "This is a mirror shop—the only thing the shopkeeper has to sell is his customer's reflection."

February
15

NAMING THINGS

"Why is it," asked the trader, "that you seldom identify things for what they are?"

"And what are they?" replied the Wisdom Keeper. "How does one determine that?"

"There are definitions for things," replied the trader.

"Would a Fish define water the same way as you?"

"I never looked at it that way."

"Labeling and naming might bring conformity and agreement," stated the Sage, "yet neither of those are Truth. This is why the Ancient Ones never asked for, or expected, even one explanation. This is why they shunned convention."

"Labels, then," said the trader, "can be abused when we try to use them to capture reality."

"This is so," explained the Wisdom Keeper. "It has been said by the Ancient Ones that when we refrain from naming and labeling, we bring good fortune." ⨯⨍

February
16

IS THAT SO?

A Mystic lived on the edge of a town, where all of the townspeople held him in high esteem. His neighbor's beautiful teenage daughter came to him for tellings. Before long, she became pregnant. Her angry parents marched her over to his cottage and screamed into his face about what he had done.

He listened with respect and replied calmly, "Is that so?"

As the gossip spread, the Mystic lost the eminent regard of the people. When the child was born, the teenage girl's parents brought the baby over to the Mystic and said, "You caused this, now you take care of her."

"Is that so?" was his only reply.

A year later, the young woman could stand her guilt no longer. She confessed to her parents that the apprentice at the carriage shop was the real father of the child.

Feeling great distress over what they had done, her parents went immediately to their neighbor. With heads bowed, they explained the situation, apologized, and begged forgiveness. Then they asked for the child back.

"Is that so?" he said as he handed over the little one. ➤

February
17

I KNOW NOT

There is a Sage in the next village who answers nearly every question by saying, "I am not sure," or "I never thought about it that way," or "Let us explore that together."

"I do not understand the way you answer questions," stated a Seeker. "You are a Sage—you have lived long and studied much and guided many. Surely you must know things."

"The more I learn, the more I find there is yet to learn," replied the Sage.

"What does that mean?"

"When I reply with a question rather than an answer, it does not mean that I know nothing, but rather that I want to know more."

"I understand that," said the Seeker, "yet I can't see what would happen if you were to say, 'I know.'"

"That would be disrespectful."

"I would think it would be the reverse."

"As soon as someone thinks I know," responded the Sage, "the discussion then focuses on me, on my knowledge. Look now what we are coming to know together because I said that I did not know."

THE FALLACY OF JUDGMENT

On the charge of encouraging young people to think on their own, a Sage was taken before the district magistrate. The intellectuals, who were convinced that the Sage was the cause of the dwindling enrollment at their school, thought the youth should turn instead to the words preserved in the Classics.

"We will let the people decide on whether or not this humble Sage is guilty of anything," proclaimed the magistrate. "I will choose seven citizens at random and they will make the decision."

When it came time for the trial, the Sage asked if he might begin by posing one question to the seven citizens. The magistrate granted his request. Handing a piece of paper and pencil to each of the citizens, the Sage said, "Will you please write your answer to the question, *What is a boat?*"

Their answers:

A floating conveyance for people and commercial goods.

A way for my family to get out on the lake and enjoy the weekends.

An object made of wood and powered by sails.

A toy that my son plays with in the puddles.

A way for me to set Fish nets to earn my livelihood.

A vessel for transporting troops and munitions.

A hull that I fill up with dirt for planting flowers.

"Honored Magistrate and respected townspeople," spoke the Sage, "these seven people cannot agree on something as simple as a boat. They each perceive it differently, yet none of them are wrong. So how could these same seven people fairly judge me and agree on a matter as complex as my intent and the results of my actions?"

February 19

HOW YEARNING CREATES FOOLS

Four Monks were discussing among themselves how their desire for Knowledge revealed their ignorance.

A Seeker who was passing by overheard their conversation and asked how it could be possible that Knowledge showed ignorance. "I had always thought it was the opposite," she said.

"Let me illustrate with this story," replied one of the Monks. "Once there was a woman who was swept down a swift-flowing River. Fortunately, she was barely able to grab onto the branch of an overhanging Tree. However, her strength was fading fast. She cried out for help.

"A man who was walking past heard her call, crawled out on the Tree, and reached down to her. 'Take hold,' he said, 'and I will pull you out to safety.'

"'First I must know who you are, to see if I can trust you,' stated the woman.

"'My name is of no consequence,' replied the man, 'for my hand is strong and the shoreline is solid.'

"'But I must know, so that I may trust your intent.'

"Before the man could reply, the woman lost her grip and the current swept her swiftly to her death."

February
20

THE NATURE OF TRUTH

A Seeker tried many different ways to find Truth. Sometimes his efforts left him in a state of ecstasy, yet just as often he found himself frustrated and feeling empty. Not knowing if his search for Truth would ever end, he often sank into depression.

One morning, he woke up and decided to go and see how other Truth-seekers were faring, in hopes of learning something that would be of help to him. The first group he came across had followed people who claimed they were Teachers. This group followed the Teachers' instructions, and they were miserable. The Seeker asked for the reason.

"It is because we did not seek the Truth in our own hearts."

Not wishing any more misery in his life, the Seeker moved on and sought people who were filled with joy. When he found them, he asked how they had come to such a state.

"We did it by not following our hearts," they replied.

"How can that be?" stammered the Seeker. "You have ignored your heartvoice and you are still happy?"

"It is because we decided to take happiness over Truth."

The Seeker understood that, as those who were miserable made the same choice. Yet part of him was left deeply confused, as he had always believed that happiness would result from his Quest for Truth. Above all, happiness was the state in which he wanted to dwell. He took his dilemma to a Sage of renown and asked for Guidance.

"Happiness and misery enslave us," said the Sage. "We become prisoners of our passions, and Truth cannot abide by either stricture. When we dwell in Truth, we can choose our feelings, or we can choose to have no feelings. It is like the blue that makes the red so bright and the night that makes the day so sweet." ⤳

February
21

THE RIGHTEOUS ONE

There was a man who considered himself humble in thought and righteous in action. One day he was walking along a path by the River. Up ahead he saw a man and a woman sitting on the bank and drinking from a wine flask.

"What a sad state they are in," he said to himself. "They are destroying their bodies and minds with such debauchery. What great things they could be doing if only they could pick themselves up and be more like me."

Right then, he heard panicked voices out on the water. Looking out, he saw a quickly sinking boat with seven people on it.

The man up the bank immediately set down his flask and dove into the water. Back and forth he swam, bringing the people to shore. He pulled the sixth person up the bank and collapsed from exhaustion.

Summoning a bit of energy, he shouted out to the righteous man, "You are so much better than me—go out and save the last person!"

That person drowned, and all the righteous man could do was stand there in confusion.

"The woman I was sitting with is my mother," said the man after he caught his breath. "The flask we were drinking from is filled with water. It is known by the Wise Ones that as we judge, so we are."

The righteous one collapsed at the feet of the woman's son and whimpered, "You have rescued six people drowning. Let me be the seventh that you save—save from drowning in the pride that I have disguised as virtue." ∿

February
22

TO KNOW

A Seeker who studied many years with a Sage had grown weary and bored. "I seem to have made no progress over the past few years," the Seeker complained to the Sage. "Venerable Elder, I respectfully ask that you give me the essence of your Teachings, as I feel that I have earned them."

"I will give them to you," the Sage responded.

After she finished, the Sage asked the Seeker if he understood. He nodded.

"Now take these Teachings and study them," instructed the Sage. "In five years, come back and tell me what you have gained."

The Seeker did just that, and in five years he came back to the Sage to report that he was angry and confused.

"At first I was elated by the priceless gift you bestowed upon me," the Seeker stated. "Then I grew frustrated because I could not apply it. Then I doubted your Teachings, suspecting that you had just made things up and told them to me, so I forgot about them altogether. Only they started to haunt me, so I looked at them again and began quarreling with myself about their meaning. 'Perhaps I am just too stupid to get it,' I thought, and I sank into a deep depression."

"Now you may be teachable," replied the Sage, "as you have discovered that when Teachings are given rather than acquired, the person has not prepared himself for them, so all that can come of it is confusion and misuse. Even when someone states that conveyed Teachings are understood, it does not mean that they are comprehended."

"What, then, should I have done?"

"Just what you did," replied the Sage. "It was the only way for you to see that I was not reluctant to impart the Teachings I carry—I was incapable." ➤

February
23

THINKING IS CREATING

The world was full of conflicts and contradictions, at least as a Nun saw it, and it troubled her. She worried about everything and couldn't make decisions because of it, so she went to a Sage for help.

"There is a large Tree growing by the roadside just up from the village," replied the Sage. "Go in silence and sit under it, until someone comes by with your answer."

The tormented woman went to the Tree, and there she stood. "Which side of the Tree am I supposed to sit on?" she wondered aloud. "What if I fall asleep and miss my answer? Or a limb breaks off and falls on my head? What are people going to think of me sitting here? And what if…"

Finally, she sat down. A day passed, then another, and another, and her mind kept churning with conflicts and contradictions.

One foggy morning, a blob of soft poop, from a Monkey sitting up in the Tree, fell right on the Nun's head.

It happened right as two people passed the Tree on their way down the road.

"Who is that person sitting there?" one of them asked the other.

"There are some who say she is a holy woman," replied the other, "and there are some who say she is a shithead."

The Nun smiled, and right then she was Awakened. ☙

February
24

DEAD OR ALIVE

"Halt!"

The woman ignored the growling voice and kept walking down the road.

"Halt, or you will be lying in a pool of your own blood before you take another step!"

Still, the woman kept walking.

The command came from a vicious highwayman who had pillaged and killed many a person on the country's isolated stretches of road. He was hiding in the brush and he didn't want to reveal himself. Dumbfounded, he watched the woman who, alone and vulnerable, maintained her demeanor and kept on her way.

"Why did you not halt?" he hissed into the woman's face after he ran to catch her and grabbed her by the shoulders. "I could have sliced you in half with one lash of my sword!"

"I am like you; I wish to go on living. Yet if you want to kill me, I accept that as well. If there is anything you need, I would consider it an honor to help you as I can." The woman then bowed and turned to continue her journey.

The outlaw stood there for a moment, then dropped his sword and followed the woman, who was a wandering Beggar. For the next four years, he listened to her every word and observed her every action. He is now a revered Wisdom Carrier, and anyone who knows him would argue vehemently against his supposed past as a notorious bandit whose very existence once instilled bone-chilling fear in every person to travel a lonely road. ❧

February
25

SEEKING ANSWERS WITH ANSWERS

"I am like a Bird without wings," complained a Seeker. "I run and I run, trying to take off, yet all I do is bump into Tree trunks."

"That is strange," replied the Sage, "as it doesn't look like you have feet to run with."

"What do you mean?"

"When the Air is clear, it is hard to see."

"You speak in riddles," said the Seeker. "You can't see my feet because the Air is not clear. I would give anything for clarity, as it would make my seeking much easier."

"It would—as easy as flying is for you now," responded the Sage. "You wouldn't even have to spread your wings."

"Now you mock me. I came to you for Guidance and you only make me look foolish."

"It sounds as though you already looked foolish, scurrying around and running into Trees, when you had clear Air through which to see them and a perfectly good set of wings to rise above them."

The Seeker thought for a moment. "It is true, insightful Sage. What you hear me speaking is only my frustration, and that muddies clarity. Will you tell me, then, what I am doing, so that I might understand it?"

"You are out looking for a flame while carrying a candle," replied the Sage.

"What then must I do?"

"Blow out the candle and the flame will become visible."

With that, the Seeker Awakened. 〜

February
26

MANIFESTING

The villagers living beside a shallow Sea over the Mountains needed a pier, so they would not have to drag their fishing boats up on the rocky beach. "Let us summon our craftsmen to build a pier," implored the village Elder.

The carpenters and stonemasons got off to a good start. Yet after a few weeks, their progress slowed. A month went by, then another, and people walking by noted that only a few planks were being added every now and then.

Until one day, when a whole section of the pier was suddenly completed. Then another section, and another. Nobody knew how it was happening, yet they were happy for it. Within the month, the pier was finished and the whole village celebrated.

Yet the question of who did the finishing work on the pier was never answered. Years went by.

One day, the Elder who initiated the project passed on. At the wake, one of the masons who worked on the pier got up and spoke to the villagers: "Our revered Elder wanted us to have the pier we needed so much that he took on the project himself after we grew lazy and distracted. I walked by one early dawn when I couldn't sleep and caught him working on the pier. He asked that I keep it a secret, yet I was so touched that I worked beside him every night until the project was finished."

From that day onward, you would be hard-pressed to find any group of people who took each other's welfare to heart more than that village with the Elder who so loved his people. ⟿

February
27

MANY SAGES

A Seeker heard about a Sage who was reputed to be the wisest in the land. The young woman went through great hardship to travel to the distant province where the Sage lived.

When she finally reached his hamlet and was given an audience with him, she humbled herself before him and said, "I have sought out many Wise People, yet I have never been satisfied. I am sure you are the wisest of them all."

After a long moment of deliberate silence, he answered, "I can help you best by telling you that you are not listening to the one you sit before."

"But that is impossible!" she protested. "I have come all this way to be at your feet and listen."

"Nor have you listened to any of the others," he continued. "You have never known them, nor will you come to know me. I entreat you to go back to one of them—any one—and drink from his well. For if you do not, you will be like a thirsty Donkey who runs endlessly back and forth trying to control two wells. Even though he never lets himself stop to drink, he ends up dying from exhaustion rather than thirst." ↜

February
28

TO SEEK KNOWLEDGE

"What do I need in order to seek Knowledge?" a Seeker asked an Elder.

"Observe yourself right now," replied the Elder, "for you are in fact seeking Knowledge at this very moment."

"I think I would need good ears for listening," replied the Seeker, "and good eyes to read, and a voice to ask questions and carry on discourse."

"That is the common conception. Yet what good does it do to pour water in a jar that cannot hold it? A person cannot grasp what she is learning until she has learned how to learn."

"How does one learn how to learn?" asked the Seeker. "It seems as though that should come naturally."

"If it were so, Seekers would not be coming to me and saying, 'Give me Knowledge; give me answers.' Yet that is what they do. And that is what I do not provide, because they are not ready for Knowledge or answers."

"When are they ready?"

"When they have Awakened to the point where they realize that answers come from the Journey, not the Elder. With someone who is not so Awakened, we Elders cannot discuss the deeper matters of life. Only when a person comes and says, 'Please show me how to learn,' can an Elder help."

"How do I arrive at that state of Awakening?" asked the Seeker.

"When you are no longer too proud to ask for help in learning how to learn, you have arrived."

"Why is that?"

"Because pride is ignorance," replied the Sage. "The person who says, 'No one has to teach me how to learn,' is both proud and ignorant."

February
29

WHERE BLAME LIES

"Wandering Nun," said a young man, "I know you are on your Journey and just passing through our village. Nevertheless, I respectfully ask you to stop for a brief moment and listen to my story. Perhaps you can lend me fresh perspective."

"I would consider it an honor to hear your tale," the Nun responded.

They sat down on the bank of the nearby River, and the young man proceeded with a woeful litany of how this person did that to him and that person didn't do what she promised him and another person didn't listen to him, and so on.

The Nun respectfully listened. After he finally finished, she said, "That is quite the saga. It sounds as though you have been wronged by many people."

The man nodded and let out a heavy sigh.

"Your story reminds me of the one I heard about a farmer," continued the Nun. Try as he would, he could not get a Colt to go into a corral. Finally giving up, he went to the Colt's mother and cursed and chided her. The farmer's wife, hearing the commotion, came out and asked why he was berating the Horse.

"She is to blame for that Colt's behavior," the farmer explained. "She didn't raise him right." ᕈᕈ

March
1

PITFALLS

One must pity the beleaguered Seeker who is continually either crushed by criticism or inflated by praise.

A Sage commented to one such Seeker, "What you feel is of your own creation, and it keeps tripping you into the mud, rather than lifting your feet to empower your Journey."

"What hurts me the most is that the things other people say about me make me doubt myself and lose interest in the Journey."

"It is incorrect to think that you are questioning because of lack of interest or conviction. Rather, this is a test. You will find yourself continually tested."

"Why must that be?" asked the Seeker.

"Because you will continually have doubt," replied the Sage. "You may not always notice it, because it is weakness that highlights doubt. So the greater your weakness, the greater your doubt and the more valuable the test. Cherish those moments." ➤

March
2

WHAT TRUTH IS NOT

"What is your perspective on Truth?" asked the Sage of a studied Philosopher.

"The very idea of there being Truth turns my stomach," replied the Philosopher.

"Is there anything else?"

"Yes. It tries my patience."

"And what else do you think of Truth?"

"Just talking about it makes me angry."

"I see," said the Sage. "Can a learned man such as you, who is trained to be objective and ferret out the essence of things, only give reactive feelings when you are asked for insight?" ◂

March
3

ENTER THE NIGHT

A woman was afraid to go out at night, and she did not like to be alone—especially with her mind. Yet out of desperation, she summoned the courage to climb the long Mountain trail to an alpine valley where a Hermit lived.

"You must possess courage to live way up here all by yourself," the woman said when she arrived. "I would be terrified of the Yetis."

"I am a timid person like you," replied the Hermit. "Have you heard talk of The Void?"

"I have," replied the young woman. "It is the Mindless Mind, and the very thought of going there petrifies me. I imagine it is like being possessed by a demon, and it makes me sick."

"We must enter The Void, or we will be possessed forever," explained the Hermit.

"But I can't. I tried, and I am too afraid. Still, I am curious: what is it like for you?"

"It is a night beyond blackness; there is no moon, no stars, no fog. I fall into it and let it become my world. There is no form, no color, no shape or sound, no dimension, no up or down. I have no body and I am every body. I have no feelings and I know every feeling."

continued

"If it is a night without blackness or stars, I have trouble imagining it."

"Abandon your straining eyes and thoughts," instructed the Hermit, "and enter The Void from there."

"But why do it when it is so horrifying?" asked the woman.

"It is horrifying only until we open our eyes and see everything in nothing and nothing in everything. There will then be no more you or me, no more better or worse. Judgments, regrets, and inadequacies will disappear, and they will not come back."

"Why is that so?"

"Because they cannot take shape or form in The Void."

The woman considered for a moment, then said, "That is where I wish to dwell, Lucid Hermit, and that is how I wish to dwell. You have freed this person's Truth, and she bows to you for it." ∽

 *March*

4

I LIMIT MYSELF

"I wish to discuss the various ways to approach Knowledge," stated a youth. "That is not possible," replied the Fool.

"Why is that?"

"A Frog in a well cannot talk about the Ocean, for he is bound by the walls of the well."

"Yet he knows water," said the youth, "and there is water in both the well and the Ocean."

"If only water were water," responded the Fool. "A summer Insect may know dew, but he does not know ice."

"True, yet I am not sure how that applies to my desire to discuss the ways to Knowledge."

"One who studies," began the Fool, "cannot discuss the many ways to Knowledge because of the well created by the Knowledge she has gained."

"What, then, does it take for open discussion?"

"To answer that, let us look at what it does *not* take. First, we must escape our well—but not the fear that got us there. We want to take that fear with us to the Ocean, as our Guide. Next, we must realize how little we know and how incapable we are of grasping what we don't know. Then we will be open to true, unbounded exploration."

"I think I now see," stated the youth. "I need to realize the limits of my Knowledge in order to get beyond it."

"Oh, there is one more thing," added the Fool. "Knowledge is bound to words, and what you really yearn for cannot be talked about." ➤

March
5

GUIDANCE: OLD OR NEW?

"How do I approach the Teachings of Old?" asked a Seeker. "Some say the Ancient Ones are to be revered, and that we can be inspired by visiting the shrines of their birth and burial. Others say we should avoid their writings and listen instead to the Sages in our midst. How should I proceed?"

Her Sage replied, "It is said that Wisdom is timeless, yet many forget that it must also be timely. Much Wisdom stands the test of time, and that is because true Wisdom transcends time. Those who attempt to attach Wisdom to a time, place, or person, are likely confused as to the true nature of Wisdom."

"I am afraid I am one of them," replied the Seeker. "Will you please clarify for me the nature of Wisdom?"

"Think of it as the Path on which we walk the Journey of Discovery. Without Wisdom, there is no Path, and therefore no Journey. The Teachings we garner are the stones that pave our Path. When a Sage suggests that we not read a certain book, it is not because the Wisdom is unsound, but because it is a cobble of a size that does not fit with the cobbles already on our Path. It will trip us up rather than smoothing our way. When the Sage encourages us to seek out a Hermit or listen to the Fool by the roadside, it is because she is one of our Path's missing cobbles."

"I recognize that," replied the Seeker. "Then what about the cobbles that lie ahead? Is it not good to put them in place so that my Path will already be laid out before I get there?"

"That would appear to be the thing to do, for we worry about the future and want the comfort and security of having it planned out before us. However, the present is the death of the future."

"How can that be, when all I have for future preparation is the present?" asked the Seeker.

continued

"The Wisdom we now hold only relates to the present," her Sage responded. "When we use it to make decisions for laying out our future, it will only amount to a repeat of the present. The future is our Frontier—it is the unknown. To think of it now will bring up only fear. And that is as it should be, for fear is the music which dances us to our edge, then into the unknown. It is only there—and only then—that we have the presence and perspective needed to choose the cobbles to lay immediately before us."

"What you say overwhelms me," said the Seeker. "I am only barely able to grasp what you describe."

"Think of it as choosing clothes when you were growing up. At age ten, would you have been able to pick out a shirt that would fit when you turned fourteen?"

"Of course not! I now understand: my Path becomes visible only as it unfolds for my next step." ❧

 **March**
6

EXERCISES

"Why do you give these Seekers such superficial exercises?" a passerby asked a Sage. "They are not true Teachings."

"When these Seekers embrace an exercise or routine," replied the Sage, "they become enamored with the cook instead of enjoying the food. In time they will come to realize that their infatuation cripples and blinds them, and that they must feast not on the exercise but on its fruit."

"But how will they know to do that when they get so wrapped up in their training?"

"There is nothing wrong with enjoying the exercises any more than there is with enjoying the rich aroma of food. Once they learn that the full experience of a feast comes with eating the food as well, an exercise will disappear as it becomes their lives, just as food disappears when it becomes their bodies."

"I understand that," said the passerby, yet I suspect a greater purpose to your decision to give them exercises."

"There is: to help them return to Balance. The exercises help them count the steps on their Journeys, so that later they will remember how silly they were for doing so." ᴧᴄ

March
7

HOW TO LEARN

"What is the best way to learn?" asked a Seeker.

"By forgetting how bad you want to learn it," replied the Sage. "The harder one tries, the longer it takes. And the learning is compromised."

"How, then, do I proceed with learning?"

"By *letting* the learning happen, rather than *willing* it to happen. Instead of studying diligently how to avoid being stung by Bees, go pick berries in the Meadow as you normally would, and you will be stung."

"But that is what I want to learn to *avoid*."

"In this way, you learn without trying to learn, and you learn faster and better than with any study or discipline. With time, you will come to intuitively know how to lithely step through the Meadow in peaceful coexistence with the Bees. Without thinking, you will adapt and adjust as you go from berry bush to berry bush, as opposed to following some memorized and rehearsed protocol. Herein, my granddaughter, lies the difference between the practitioner and the Master."

"That is impressive," commented the Seeker, "yet what about the times when I am not in the Meadow?"

"A Bee could be found anywhere," responded the Sage.

"But what about Scorpions and Snakes?"

"It is only the eyes that categorize. The eyes see a Bee, and their memory says, 'Bee… avoid.' Our conscious self is different. It reacts to the danger rather than the Bee. This is why we become adaptable when we let the danger train us rather than training ourselves for the danger." ～

March
8

TRUTH QUEST

Three Seekers had set out to find Truth. After many months of searching, they went in desperation to a Sage who was reputed to know where Truth dwells. Without saying a word, she motioned for them to follow her along a path through the nearby Meadow. Once there, she picked up a stick and commenced to whack the blossoms off of flowers.

After a short while, she turned to the Seekers and asked, "Do you know the deeper meaning to what I am doing?"

"Some people think they know," said one of the Seekers, "and they stand up to voice it, only to return to the Great Unknowing."

"Visibility is not to be confused with Truth," commented another.

The third Seeker pointed to the stick and said, "Something that is so unconscious that it can only repeat itself can still do much harm to repressing the Living Truth."

The Sage replied, "There is no right or wrong with Truth, so what each of you has said is a worthy answer. No one person possesses—nor can possess—the Truth, as we each contribute a piece to its ever-unfolding definition." ➤

March
9

THERE IS HERE

"Where must I go to find the Sea?" asked Young Fish, who was about to embark on his Journey of Discovery.

Elder Fish contemplated the question. Even though he had been asked for the same directions a hundred times before, this was a new day, unique unto itself, so there were new considerations. And he had another consideration: example is the greatest Teacher. He saw the importance for the Young to see that Elders also take pause and question, even with things they seem to already know. This could mean more to Young Fish than any words he might utter.

"The Sea," eventually spoke Elder Fish, "is a place that grows farther and farther away the more you search for it. The picture that you have of it in your mind gets muddier the more you try to clarify it. At the same time, the less you look for it, the more it comes to haunt you. It will stalk your dreams, and you will hear it beckoning you even in the call of the Bird flying overhead."

"With all respect, Elder Fish, you speak in metaphors, and they make my head hurt. You must know that I am driven to find the Sea, for it is every Fish's destiny."

"That it is, and look you must. Yet only when you are able to seek it without passion will you find it, for emotion blinds and drive cripples."

"But I am filled with both emotion and drive. They consume my being and I cannot help myself."

"That is as it should be, as it is the way of every Seeker who is newly on his Journey. Because of it, I can give you these words. They will mean nothing to you now, yet they will come back to you one day and tell you that you have found the Sea. Right now, the Sea is within and about you. Your every breath takes in the Sea, and your every movement swirls the Sea's waters. You began your life in the Sea, and your life will end in the Sea. The Sea embraces you as your flesh embraces your bones. So go to land's end, my grandson, and see if there you find the Sea. I will journey with you, so that when you finally hear the Voice of the Sea, it will be my voice as well."

March
10

WHAT IS NOT, CANNOT BE

A Seeker, who grew frustrated in her relationship with her Sage, went to talk with another Sage about it.

"I have been under his Guidance for half of my life," she lamented, "yet he gives me very little, and he treats me as though he barely knows me."

"I see," replied the Sage. "Did you give him your full presence and attention?"

"Well, perhaps I didn't."

"Were you there for him as you expected him to be there for you?"

"I often was. At other times, I was elsewhere."

"Did you recognize in him the Wisdom of the Ancients?"

"I often doubted him, I'm afraid. And I was suspicious of his motives."

"Your Sage was waiting for you," said the Wise One. "Like you, we Sages are also Seekers who aspire to another realm of Awakening, and we too have Sages at whose feet we sit. It demands our full presence and openness, and we cannot expect nor accept any less from those who sit at our feet. For without presence and openness, there is no way we can pass on the words of the Ancient Ones. So we wait. As with you, sometimes we wait a long time. And as you are doing, sometimes we are blamed and judged for not providing what falls into your realm to provide."

March
11

NO WAY

"Why do uncentered people belittle the Quest for Knowledge?" asked a Seeker.

"Because they do not see the need for it," replied the Sage, "and that causes them to become arrogant. Unfortunately, arrogance leaves no room for Knowledge, even if a person were to desire it."

"That is unfortunate," said the Seeker. "What is it that keeps people uncentered and arrogant?"

"There are several things. Study is one, debate is another, and discipline and belief are yet others."

"How, then, should one proceed to obtain Knowledge and avoid what keeps us from obtaining it?"

"When we look at how we might gain Knowledge," answered the Sage, "we are looking for a way that Knowledge can be transmitted to us, and there is no way but the effort to obtain it."

March
12

I AM NOT YOU

When I was young, I listened to an Elder's discourse on the source of Knowledge. "Your mind already knows all that is," he stated.

"Then what do I seek?" I asked myself. "Why do I seek?" I could find no answers, and I was driving myself mad over it. In desperation, I went to see a Sage recommended by my fellow Seekers. With trembling voice, I asked her, "Is it true that my mind already knows all that is?"

"If I say 'yes'," she replied, "I will give you the impression that you know. Only the truth is that you cannot grasp what you know. And if I answer 'no,' I would deny what many people have already become aware of."

"Then how do I find the answer?" I asked.

"I do not know."

"But you are a Sage! How can you not know?"

"Because I am not you."

I froze. My head spun. I could not make sense of it—everything was a jumble.

The Sage loudly clapped her hands in front of my face, and I became Aware. ⌇

March
13

WHERE TO START

"The Way must have a beginning," stated the young Nun in a beseeching voice. "I have to set my feet down somewhere to start, don't I?"

"I will give you that start," replied the Fool. "In fact, I can do it right now, before I speak another word..." He paused for a moment. "There, I have just done it! And before you take your first step, you have already finished your Journey to The Way."

"That is nonsense," replied the Nun. "A true Fool you are! I came to you for inspiration because I am struggling, and all you give me is some cosmic gibberish."

"Does the Bird need to know where the Sky starts and ends in order to fly? To find the place to begin, more than the Wisdom of the Ages is needed, more than the sharpest intuition, more than the insights of the most Awakened Mystics."

"Then please tell me what it is."

"Spit on your fear, then wipe it clean and spread your wings."

March
14

ORDINARY MAN

A number of people were traveling together on a Pilgrimage. In the evenings after they had set up camp, they would share stories.

One woman told about being captured by a gang of robbers who lived back in the Mountains. "They took all my food," she related "and said they would kill me after they feasted. 'I can show you a way that you will not have to go hungry,' I said to the thieves, and I taught them how to garden. With deep gratitude, they let me go free. I learned how to tend plants because a man I once met encouraged me to do so."

A man spoke next. "Just recently," he said, "my family and I were caught in a flash flood. I quickly lashed together a raft from logs lying around us, and we were able to float safely to highland. I could do it because a man at the market suggested that I learn how to tie rope."

The stories continued every evening. One by one, the Pilgrims came to realize that they had each been given straightforward Guidance by a stranger, and that they never knew how important it was until it came to the test. They were surprised that they each described a similar person: a man of ordinary demeanor who had nothing profound to say, yet people felt comfortable with him and would seek him out for advice. It was practical advice that people appreciated, and it helped them in their everyday lives—and ultimately in situations where their lives depended on it.

One night the leader of the Pilgrimage spoke. "It seems that none of you would be here if you had not followed some advice you received long ago. There are others who are not here because they did not follow the advice they were given. They dismissed it and moved on, because they could not see the deeper Teaching within it."

By the time the Pilgrims reached their destination, they had come to realize that their leader was the same man who had long ago given each of them fortuitous advice. The man was none other than the Awareness of Truth.

"Why did you not tell us who you were right away," they asked him, "so that we would not have to endure the travails of this Pilgrimage to find out?"

No sooner had they uttered the question that they realized it contained its own answer: they had to first hear the glimmer of Truth in the advice and trust in it, then apply the Truth by traveling with it, before they could fully recognize it for what it was. ━

March
15

THE ULTIMATE LIE

"What are you looking at?" asked the Sage.

"I am looking at my mind," replied the Seeker.

"Can the mind see itself?"

"My mind thinks it can."

"Is thinking then seeing?"

"Knowing One," said the Seeker, "I…I am confused. I think you have just shown me that thinking is a lie."

"It appears that you have shown yourself, Wise Seeker," replied the Sage.

"How is that so?"

"Asking yourself what you see is like hiding stolen goods, then telling yourself you don't know where they are." ➤

March
16

INCAPABLE

Once there was a Sage who had much to teach, yet he refused to do so. He would only guide people on their Paths to their own Teachings.

A Seeker came to him who was in the habit of going hither and yon to presentations, workshops, and ceremonies.

"How can I best learn from these Teachings?" he asked the Sage.

"It would be a great honor for me to give you the method," the Sage responded. "It is one that has been passed down from Sage to Sage since time immemorial, and it is known to work for nearly everyone. Here are the instructions: plug your ears and think about turnips."

"Shall I do this before or after a ceremony or workshop?"

"The Ancient Ones say that it is best to practice it *instead* of those activities."

March
17

THE KNOWLEDGE THAT MATTERS

For the Seeker, there is an ultimate paradox: those who seek Knowledge will, in the end, only find insanity. However, if they do not seek Knowledge, they greatly reduce their odds of finding *anything*. This story is about a Seeker who was driven to acquire all the Knowledge he could on all manner of topics. He thought that if he understood everything, there would be no more mysteries, and he would then become Awakened.

Traveling along the coast on his Quest, the Seeker came upon a large bay that he wanted to cross. There was no one around with a boat to ferry him. The only person he saw was a man who came by on a raft made of several logs lashed together.

"Will you take a learned man across the bay on your raft?" the Seeker asked.

"Fer a piece a' gold n' a smile, I'd be a-happy ta," replied the man.

They pushed off, and a short ways out, the logs began to creak as they rolled over the waves.

"Are you sure this raft is safe?" asked the Seeker.

"I ain't never abserlutely shore a' nothin'."

"I suggest that you take my gold piece," stated the Seeker, "and hire yourself a tutor, so that you don't waste the second half of your life speaking improperly."

The rafter said nothing, for a piece of gold was a lot of money to him. Besides, he thought, this man was just an odd, passing stranger.

Soon after this exchange, great waves came rolling in from the Ocean, making the raft creak and groan. The ropes holding the logs together started to snap.

"Do ya know howta swim?" asked the man.

"I do not," replied the panicked Seeker.

"What a shame," replied the man, "because not just half, but *all*, of yer life is gonna be wasted." ⌁

March
18

MINDFULNESS IS FORGETFULNESS

"What do you mean when you say that the Masters are our servants?" asked a Seeker.

"Your question," replied the Sage, "says that you are not ready to quit studying and start serving your people."

"How will I know when I am ready?"

"When you can hear someone speak, even though she has not said a word."

"That makes no sense!" cried the Seeker. "By definition, speech is comprised of words. Honorable Elder, you are giving me contradictions for clarity."

"Not at all, my grandson. Much beautiful poetry has been written about the sound of waves lapping the shore and thunder rolling over the horizon in a stampeding cloud. Yet when we are ready, the verse that catches our ear is the song of the pines when there is no wind."

"I must trust in your words, for I do not know from personal experience of what you speak."

"You may not know it to speak it," said the Sage, "yet you do know it to *be* it."

"How then do I bring it forth?"

"Avoid thinking to form thoughts, for that is thinking fruitlessly."

"Gracious Elder, how do I know when I am thinking without thoughts?"

"When you do not remember a single word."

"That is what I wish to do! Or perhaps I should say *not do*. So where do I start?"

"It is more about where *not* to start. If you turn to practices or techniques, you are no more than a mindless insect who can't help but do what he does."

"But what about books? There are many that have helped me in the past, and there must be even more out there that can guide me on my way."

"If with all the books you have read, you have still not come to know your own nature, is doing more of the same a wise choice?" asked the Sage. "The Way is no way, and there is no direction to get there. This, hungry Seeker, is where words must stop."

March
19

WHO WINS?

"If I win an argument," posed the youth to the sage Beggar, "doesn't it mean that I am right and the other person is wrong? Or what if the other person wins the argument? Does that mean she is right and I am wrong?"

"Is it really a case of one person being right and the other wrong?" asked the Beggar in response. "Or could either or both of you be right or wrong?"

The youth gave it some thought, yet could come up with no answer. "Maybe we could ask someone else for an opinion," he said.

"Should it be someone who thinks you are right or someone who thinks she is right? Or should it be someone who agrees or disagrees with both of you?"

"How could any of them—or us—make a fair judgment?" offered the youth. "Should we ask an outsider who has no opinion?"

"Can we expect *any* person to render an honest, objective judgment?" asked the Beggar. "Might it be that *no* person can clearly judge?"

"Then why judge? I now wonder if it even makes sense to argue."

"The odd thing," added the Beggar, "is that there is nothing to argue about when we listen. It is not when we are centered, but when we are caught in our ego-driven thought-minds that we want to create separation and dominate."

The Beggar and the youth each took a refreshing breath, then smiled and bowed to each other. ᴧᴣ•

March
20

ONLY WHEN READY

A Seeker once asked a Sage, "Why do you not allow me to study all of your writings? They come from your hand, so surely they can only further me on my Journey of Discovery."

"That might be so," replied the Sage, "if it were not for the fact that you would interpret them. In doing so, there is a good chance that you would misinterpret them. They would then actually hinder your Journey. When you are ready, I will share them with you, as it is then that they may be helpful."

"If they are now beyond me, would I not just be wasting my time if you were to let me read them?"

"Those writings are for an audience different than you. Perhaps at some point your Journey will be similar to theirs. Remember that a boat is needed only when there is water to cross. At any other time, a boat would be a burden, slowing your progress and giving you a sore back as you cart it overland."

"How will I know when I need a boat?" asked the Seeker.

"Your role is to walk your Journey," replied the Sage, "and my role as your Guide is to recognize when you need a boat and provide it for you."

March
21

REPETITIOUS TRUTH

"I called you four times," complained a Seeker, "and you did not answer. I'm sure you heard me."

"It would have been disrespectful for me to answer," replied the Monk, "for I heard you calling yourself."

"How can that be? It was your name I called."

"If you were truly calling me, did you receive my answer?"

"Well, I guess I did."

"Why would you then call me three times more?"

"Attuned One, your insight astounds me and your words guide me to my Truth. I was feeling needy, and I wanted you to make me feel better. Then I self-righteously thought you should apologize to me for not answering. But really, I should apologize to you for not listening, either to you or to myself."

"Fellow Seeker, never apologize, for what we have just done is the way of Teachings. Let the cabin crumble if it is falling down upon you, rather than trying to hold up a window for escape." ➳

 *March*
22

THE WAY OF AWARENESS

A long time ago, there was a Seeker who embarked on a Quest to find a renowned Sage who was said to be living in disguise in a fishing village by the Sea. The Seeker wandered from village to village, yet no one she met had any idea who he might be.

Then one day, when she paid a fisherman at the dock for a small Fish for lunch, she caught a gesture of his that made her realize that he was the one she sought.

At the end of the day, she went to talk with him as he brought in his boat. "Honored Elder," she began, "why do you keep your identity and your whereabouts a secret?"

"The awareness of my existence does more good than my actual presence," he responded. "When people think that anyone they meet could possibly be me, they treat each other with reverence, and they truly listen to what others have to say."

"Why, then, did you give me the signal that you were him?"

"I give the signal to everybody, and it is only the one-in-a-thousand, the Seeker who is truly present and observant, who catches it. It is only this Seeker who is ready. I would be overwhelmed by the thousand, and I could not then honor the one."

"You are not a mere seller of Fish. I can tell already that you have much more to share. Is there not a better way for you to do it?"

"It is best done by stinking of Fish and giving my coins to Beggars for bread. If I were to set myself up as a Teacher, the great lot of people would think I was speaking nonsense, or even that I was insane. Others would say I was doing it for my own gain. I could masquerade as a man of wealth, and most people would respect me. Yet it would be because of my status, which would compel them to either please me or rebel against me."

"I understand," said the Seeker. "Yet what about the rest of the thousand?"

"I touch the one who has prepared through the rigors of the Quest. In your time, perhaps you will do the same, and so on, so that it becomes one-in-a-thousand times one-in-a-thousand times one-in-a-thousand. In this way, we might all one day find the Sage in the fisherman. And in the baker, the mother, the cripple, and the little child." ～

March
23

THE DEMON LOOMS

The Warrior-Prince was constantly on edge, as he never knew when his territory would be invaded by a neighboring warlord. A whole generation had grown up in the shadow of violence, with every man fearing the slash of the sword and every woman living in dread of being raped.

"Why must it be this way?" a young man asked the Warrior-Prince. "We constantly battle our neighbors, and it takes a great toll on us. Many of those I have grown up with have fallen. There has to be another way."

"There is, troubled one," answered the Warrior-Prince. "If you wish to know it, I will open the gate for you."

"Anything but this!" cried the young man. "Nothing could be worse."

The gate swung open and the young man passed through. Right away he came face to face with a Demon. Gobs of blood matted his scruffy fur and chunks of rotting flesh were wedged between his black, jagged teeth. The Beast lurched over the youth, who nearly passed out from the stench alone, not to mention his heart-stopping fear.

The young man shrieked, spun around, and bolted for the gate. He went directly to the Warrior-Prince and said, "I now see why we choose to fight each other. If that nightmare is what I must face in order to avoid conflict and suffering, I will return to battle."

March
24

TRANSIENCE

An Elder walked through the gate of a great nobleman's estate and ignored the Gatekeeper. He made no effort to check the Elder's credentials or ask the reason for his visit. The same thing occurred with the doorman at the mansion. The Elder walked straight into the lounge, where he found the nobleman sitting.

"What gives me the pleasure of your visit?" asked the nobleman.

"I am traveling through, and I would like to know if there is a room for me here at your roadside inn."

"Surely you are jesting, for this is my estate and my mansion."

"Whose mansion was this before it became yours?" asked the Elder.

"It was my father's," came the reply, "until he died."

"Whose mansion was it before it was your father's?"

"It was his father's, who was my grandfather."

"And whose mansion will it be when you pass on?"

"Perhaps my son's."

"I see. I hear you describing an inn: a place where people come and stay for a short time, then continue on their journeys."

"I bow to you," replied the nobleman. "Please take the room of your choice." ◈

March
25

THE HEAVY VINE

Every year when a certain grapevine was hanging heavy with fruit, people in the neighborhood would come and pick it. After the harvest, the vine would lament that no one expressed gratitude.

One day a Fool came by and sat in the shade of the vine.

Here is my opportunity, thought the vine, to solve the riddle of why these people are so thoughtless. "Oh Master of Riddles" said the vine, "will you tell me why the townsfolk are so willing to take my fruit and so stingy with their words of thanks?"

After contemplating for a while, the Fool said to the vine, "I believe the reason is that people have the notion that you cannot help but produce grapes."

 *March*
26

WHAT ARE BELIEFS?

Three Seekers found themselves arguing with each other about which of them held the right belief.

"Let us consult an Elder," suggested one of them, "and her word shall be our Truth."

The Elder asked each of them to state what his belief gives him.

"Mine keeps me out of danger and makes me feel safe," replied the first Seeker.

"Mine fills me with happiness," said the second.

"Mine makes me feel special," responded the third.

"All three sound to be beautiful beliefs," commented the Elder, "and I take it they have served you well, or you would not still be holding them. Nor would you be arguing amongst yourselves over them.

After a brief pause, the Elder added, "At the same time, I would like to suggest that your separate beliefs are nothing more than fancy garments that you have each created to cover the true belief that you hold in common."

"But that is impossible," stammered one of the Seekers "My belief is held sacred by the Wise Ones I have studied under for years."

"As is mine," replied the second.

"And mine," said the third.

"Do you each have undying faith in your belief?"

"I do!" they all stated at once.

"Then disrobe yourself of your belief and see what is left standing naked."

"If I must be honest," meekly stated the first Seeker, "my belief was masking fear."

"As was mine" agreed the second.

"And also mine," added the third.

"Now you have your true belief, and you can see that the three of you are not so different after all."

"Amazing! How can we use this awareness to empower our Journeys?" asked one of the Seekers.

"To become a Seeker, one *must* step out from behind the veil of belief. Fear is the Seeker's first and final Frontier. Fear is not to be shed like a garment, nor is it to be conquered like an enemy—it is to be embraced as a revered Guide. It is the only Guide we need; and in the ultimate, it is the only Guide there is. We know that we have embraced our relentless fear when it has become our relentless Question." ➛

March
27

THE GRAND ELDER

An Elder was renowned throughout the kingdom. Even people from far-off lands had heard of him and benefitted from his Teachings, which had been passed from Sage to Sage.

In the last days of the Grand Elder's life, Sages from the farthest regions came to see him. When they arrived, the people of his village lavished them with feasts, entertainment, and the best of accommodations.

It came time for the Sages to sit before the Elder; however, word got out that he was only going to invite six of them into his room.

A representative of the villagers went to speak with the Elder. "We bestowed every luxury we had upon the visiting Sages," she stated, "so that they might have the privilege of hearing your final words. We considered it a deep honor to do that, as we have been blessed with the gift of your presence for our entire lives. Now you will grant only six of them an audience with you; is that not playing favorite?"

The Elder looked benevolently upon her and said with a feeble voice, "My days are short, and this will be my last Teaching for my village family. Isn't it so that you had no trouble playing favorite with them, treating them like royalty since their arrival? Is this not how you treat every traveler who passes through our village? It is seldom that we are given something, yet when we are denied something, we complain of unfair treatment. When want and plenty are embraced equally, we learn that trust is no more than fear embraced." ⤳

March
28

HOW WORDS SPEAK

A Seeker was keeping vigil with an Elder who was preparing to leave life. With a faltering voice that took nearly all of his remaining energy, the Elder said to the Seeker, "It is you who will receive my last words. Remember them, if you will. Even more, I implore you to listen to the silences between them, for it is within emptiness that deeper Wisdom is spoken. When people ask you for my parting words, have them sit down with you, as you are doing with me, and listen."

A short while later, it so happened that a group of young Seekers asked this Seeker for the last words of the venerable Elder.

"It would be an honor to share them with you," said the Seeker. Please sit with me and you shall hear them."

The Seekers sat and waited. A half hour passed, and with irritated looks on their faces, a couple of them got up and left. As it neared an hour, another one left, showing a twinge of anger. After two hours, only one Seeker remained. He looked serene and wore a faint smile.

"You have been listening," commented the older Seeker. "The Elder One has thus chosen to speak to you, and you shall carry on his Teachings."

29

WHAT IF

While talking one day about what it is like to be Awakened, a group of friends came to realize that none of them knew for sure.

"Let us ask the two Nuns sitting over there under that Tree," one of them suggested.

They approached the Nuns and asked their question.

"Give us experiences from your everyday lives," said one of the Nuns, "and we will do our best to tell you what they would be like if you were Awakened."

"Eating."

"You are the aroma and flavor of the food, which alone fills you."

"Pain."

"Neither pain nor pleasure consumes you, as you dwell between them."

"Exhaustion."

"You let it overtake you, and you feel complete."

"Travel."

"You melt into the creaking and swaying of the carriage, which is an integral part of the new sights and sounds."

"A bug crawling on me."

"It enlivens your senses, which brings you right to the then-and-there."

"Change."

"Rather than it consuming you, you consume it."

continued on page 114

continued from page 113

"A wandering mind."

"You are there; you are it."

"Self-consciousness."

"There is no fear of abandoning yourself, and you become each person you are with."

"Being caressed."

"Time transforms into timelessness."

"A clear Sky."

"You enter the clarity."

"Lovemaking."

"You are not trembling; the trembling is you."

"An everyday object or person."

"It is as though you are seeing and experiencing it for the first time."

"Something that catches my attention."

"You are spontaneously immersed in the experience."

"I react to someone."

"You stay centered."

As the suggestions trailed off, the friends bowed to the Nuns and left them to the quietude under the Tree. ➤

March 30

THE POWER OF PRETENSE

A wandering Nun was passing through a town where a Grand Feast was being held. The townspeople invited her to attend.

She was seated at the far back with the farmers, laborers, and crafters, who wore their everyday clothes. Up front, she saw finely-attired people at linen-covered tables being promptly served refreshments. There was no service yet at her end of the banquet, and it looked like it would be awhile before there would be any. She got up and left. On the way down the lane, she passed a clothing shop, and that gave her an idea. She rented a gown for the night, styled her hair, and went back to the Feast.

Immediately upon entering, she was escorted up to the front tables, seated, and provided with food and drink. The Nun proceeded to rub the food into her gown.

"Look at that!" those sitting nearby whispered as they nudged each other. Everyone was hushed and aghast at the spectacle.

She then stood up and spoke. "I am a Nun who was passing by, and you invited me to join you here. I came in my traveling clothes, for that is all I have, and I was seated at a far table. I noticed that those in fine dress were automatically escorted up to the front tables, where they were given prompt and benevolent service. I left and came back dressed as you see me now, and I was then given the same service as those you see beside me. Obviously it was my costume that was seated up here, not me. And it was my costume that was served. So it is this garment, rather than me, that deserves the food." ↝

March
31

WHERE ANSWERS COME FROM

The district was in turmoil: people struggled under high taxes and a stream of famine-stricken refugees put pressure on dwindling food stores. The magistrate of the district assembled a panel of experts to travel from hamlet to village, answering questions and offering advice to the beleaguered inhabitants.

At one hamlet, the delegation members set up a platform for themselves in the central square, then called the people together.

"You are missing someone at your table," said a citizen from the audience. "There is a person who knows what is going on here and can answer questions that you may not understand."

The experts up on the platform looked at each other, wondering who from their delegation was missing.

"It is not one of you," added the citizen. "You come from far-off places and have interests of your own. It is our Elder, who has seen and guided us through much travail over his long years here with us. He can give you insight and information to help you actually do us some good."

April
1

THE REASON FOR TEACHINGS

"Why is it," asked a Seeker, "that you, our esteemed Guide, will sometimes give a Teaching to a person, and to another person you will give Guidance?"

"Watch the expressions on their faces," replied the Elder, "and you will have your answer."

A short while later, the Seeker asked the Elder if she might again address the matter. "I have noticed," he said, "that those who receive your Teachings smile and leave content; while those who receive your Guidance often leave with furrowed brows. They look troubled, as though they were given a burden. I know you said that if I observed I would have my answer, yet I seem to have failed."

"On the contrary. Clarity is no more than an unreachable ideal. That is why we are ever Seekers, always striving toward that elusive state of Knowing, until our last breath. Those who come to me and are not ready for the Seeking Journey are given a Teaching, and they think they have received clarity."

"Yet they are Teachings," replied the Seeker. "Do they not have intrinsic value?"

"I hand out Teachings like candy. It doesn't matter which Teaching I give to which person any more than it matters to a child which piece of candy he receives, as long as he thinks he holds something sweet."

"Is that not deception?"

"Truly, for only deception will have someone who comes for one thing take something else—especially something of no value—and bring it close enough to realize that he is looking point-blank at the condition of his own soul. It is then that he is able to return as a Seeker and cherish his troubled mind." ➷

2

WHY DEATH HAUNTS

Two men killed themselves at the same time. There was great distance between them in how they lived: one had wealth beyond measure and wanted for nothing, and the other had to grub for his bare existence.

Confused by this paradox, a Monk asked a Sage what would drive these men to take their lives. "Surely their problems were very different," stated the Monk.

"That is what the Thinking Mind likes to tell us," replied the Sage. "Each man actually carried the same burden."

"I don't understand. How can that be?"

"Too much eats away the soul just as greedily as too little."

"What, then, is the way to live, Learned One?"

"It is to find the pleasure in life, for then it is impossible to be poor. And it is to live without demands on life, for then one needs no riches."

OBSERVING OR BEING?

For many years, a mother had been a dedicated Truth Explorer. "Over this time," she said to the Ascetic who counseled her, "I have gradually come to an awareness: Awakening does not happen in a flash, but rather as a gradual process of listening and seeing more clearly. It is like an ever-opening flower. Is that accurate?"

"We have just heard from your thought-mind," replied the Ascetic.

"How else might I gain perspective?"

"It comes from becoming our breathing. Right now, let your mind roam and breathe in, breathe out. Breathe in, breathe out." After they shared a few breaths, he asked, "What does that tell you?"

"Now I am confused," she responded.

"Yes, confusion—that is what *being in our breathing* gives us."

"But why confusion? Isn't it clarity I want?"

"Again we are hearing from your thought-mind, which wants a clear and identifiable thing to grasp onto. The life of an ever-opening flower is a process, like breathing. You are ever-curious about what you inhale and ever-surprised by what you exhale, which is confusing to the thought-mind."

"You have just described the real me—I can feel it!" she exclaimed. "With clarity, I would be a paper flower, always the same, and I want to breathe into the bedlam of blossoming." In that moment, the woman opened into her Awakening. ✒

April
4

ALWAYS MORE

An Elder in our village told us this story about how he was very disgruntled with life when he was a beginning Seeker like us. "Late one afternoon," he said, "I was walking home from work in the stone quarry and passed the estate of a wealthy merchant. I peered through the gate. All I wanted was to be dressed in beautiful clothing and eating sumptuous foods like the people I saw inside.

"I was very tired from a grinding day's work, so I sat down to rest in the shade of a Tree along the road, just past the gate of the estate. The next thing I knew, I was the merchant, dressed in velvet refinement and feasting on exotic food.

"Before long, a nobleman came by with his entourage, and everyone bowed to him. 'I want to be just like him,' I said to myself. 'I want to be loved and feared by all.'

"In that instant, I became the nobleman. Only I was not at all comfortable. The hot sun baked down on my carriage, and I was dripping sweat. Yet I had nowhere to go, as it was even hotter outside in the direct sun. 'How mighty the sun is!' I exclaimed. 'I want to be as all-powerful as he is!'"

"And I became the sun, in all his blazing glory. Until a raging storm obliterated my presence and unleashed a ferocious barrage of wind and hail upon the earth. 'Everything quakes before the storm—there is nothing more terrible!' I told myself.

"Right then I became the tempest, flattening everything before me. Everything, that is, but the stalwart rocks. 'I have been deceiving myself,' I lamented, 'for the rocks that everything stands upon are truly the most powerful thing in the world. If only I could be a rock...'

"In stoic grandeur, I stood there as the rock, laughing in the face of the fury. 'Now there is nothing that can move or change me!' I exclaimed. 'I am the most powerful!'

"I then heard a tapping at my base. I looked down and saw a stone quarry worker with his hammer and chisel, taking chunks out of me." ⤳

April
5

NO PATH

"I came here to gain Knowledge," stated a Seeker to the Sage, "and once I have done so, I shall journey on."

"Who led you here?" Asked the Sage. "And who shall lead you from here?"

"I led myself here, and I shall lead myself away."

"Is it true then that you see yourself coming and going?"

"It is, Honored One," replied the Seeker. "I am guiding myself on the Path."

"What if you were to become the Path, rather than yourself? What then would you see?"

"Ah, I am such a fool that I amuse myself!" cried the Seeker. "When I am the Path, I see that it is neither coming nor going. Its direction is both ways, and no way—it is merely the Path. I bow to you, Boundless Sage; and I realize that bowing to you is bowing to the Pathless Path."

April
6

SMALL IS LARGE

There is a Seeker who was once troubled by events of his long-ago past. What other people would take in stride stuck with him, and he would lay awake at night mulling it over. His life was so filled with bitterness and regret that he often sank into states of depression that would linger for days, even weeks. "I have lost myself," he lamented. "I must find Guidance back."

His fellow Seekers encouraged him to climb the Mountain to find the Hermit who lived near the summit, for it was rumored that he too had once suffered from the same affliction.

After an arduous climb, the Seeker rounded a boulder and found himself at the Hermit's feet.

"Why do I keep fretting over things?" asked the teary-eyed Seeker. "Why do I hang on to them and let them eat at me? Why can't I be like others and just learn from my experiences and then let them go?"

With a knowing smile, the Hermit swept his hand in a broad arc and asked the Seeker to notice all the pebbles lying about. "These are the matters and affairs of life," he said. "We have choices: we can either take them in stride, picking one up and setting it down again, then picking up another and doing the same; or we can bring one up close and focus on it."

"That's just what I do: I fixate on one and can't put it down."

"Then even a small stone held close could become all-important and blot the others from sight."

"That's just what happens. Nothing else seems to matter."

"The shadow side of that is your answer," replied the Hermit. "When you set the pebble down with the others, it no longer looks so big, because it gains perspective from the other pebbles." ❧

Zen Rising

April

7

OPPOSITION

An Elder who lives in the foothills is known for always speaking her Truth and holding uncompromisingly to it. This has caused her much criticism, and a few people have dedicated themselves to working against her. They accuse her of alienating people and opposing greater understanding.

"Why do you not seek a middle road?" asked a Seeker. "Would it not be easier to live with less criticism and opposition?"

"It is actually they who are the intolerant ones, and I shall explain why," responded the Elder. "When a greedy person chases money, death chases him. As soon as I want something from the expression of my Truth, it is no longer the pure Voice of Truth, but rather a payment for something in return."

"What happens when people still perceive your Truth as payment?"

"They see it as payment for me taking on their Truth."

"And what happens when you don't?"

"They retort by saying, 'Even though you have made an effort to have me understand you, you have not succeeded.' What they are actually saying is that they have been unable to convert me, and that is how I become their enemy."

"Does that not trouble you?" asked the Seeker.

"I am actually grateful for it," said the Hermit. "By creating distance, they might one day see that the more they deny others' Truths, the more they invite the death of their own Truth."

April
8

TRIMMING HAIR

While a barber was trimming a rich man's hair, a wandering Seeker came into the shop for a haircut. The barber turned from his wealthy client and tended the hair of the Seeker. When finished, the Barber gave the Seeker a coin instead of asking for one.

Upon leaving, the Seeker told himself that whatever else he was given that day, he would gift to the barber. That afternoon, a passerby handed the Seeker a bag of gold coins. He went right away to present the bag to the barber.

"I trimmed your hair for the sheer joy of serving," responded the barber. "To take payment from you would first cast shame on you for being on your Journey of Discovery. Then it would shame me by imagining that my gift was worth anything other than what it was." ━

 *April*
9

WHAT YOU TAKE, I GIVE

In the dark of the evening, a thief broke into the cabin of a Sage. "Give me all of your money, or I will kill you!" he shouted, as he waved a knife in her face.

"I will be glad to share my money with you," replied the woman. "How you ask for it is of no concern to me. It is there, in that bowl on the top shelf."

The thief quickly stuffed the contents of the bowl into his pockets and turned to flee.

"It is proper to thank a person when receiving a gift," commented the woman.

Taken by surprise, the thief nevertheless thanked the Sage.

Soon after that, the thief was caught committing another offense. At his trial, he confessed to stealing from the Sage as well. However, when the Sage was asked to identify the thief, she said, "This man stole nothing from me. He asked for money and I gave it to him. He even thanked me for it."

After the thief made restitution for his offenses, he went back to the Sage and bowed at her feet. Since then, he has been a Seeker of Truth, helping many people find what they are seeking deep down. ～

April 10

WHAT SKILL IS MADE OF

A young Archer, winning nearly every match he entered, grew quite boastful and self-assured. He decided to challenge the Elder Archer in the next province, who had already become a legend before the young Archer's father was born.

The challenger shot first, at a swinging target fifty paces away. He hit it right in the center. In the same fluid movement, he unleashed a second arrow and placed it right beside the first.

The Elder gave a nod of recognition for such a brilliant display of skill. He then motioned for the young one to follow him up the steep path that led away from the archery field.

Soon they reached the edge of a deep canyon, where a turbulent River flowed far below. The Elder stepped out on the trunk of a fallen Tree that reached out in midair over the lip of the canyon.

Halfway out on the trunk, he drew his bow and sent an arrow flying into a distant stump on the rim of the canyon. He then casually strode back to solid ground and invited the young sharpshooter to take his turn.

Shaking with fear, the youth bowed and said, "Master, your skill is rooted in your mind, whereas mine is only in my body. I dream that one day I will become the arrow, as you have."

April
11

WHEN SILENCE COMES

"I am aware that everything has a deeper meaning," said a Nun while talking with her Elder. "I have learned much about silence and the openings it creates for clear vision and hidden Knowledge. Yet, Kind One, I know there is something more to silence—a deeper value that once I could not fathom even existing. I have become aware that it is there for me, and I believe I am ready for it."

"Listen to the Crows," replied the Elder, "for they are the greatest Teachers of the value of silence."

"Crows!" protested the Nun. "Of all Birds, they create a horrendous ruckus, squabbling amongst themselves and cackling at anybody or anything that disturbs them."

"Ah, dear Nun, remember the Teaching that whenever we hold something strongly, its opposite holds even more Truth."

"It is as you say, Wise One," answered the Nun. "I am afraid I drifted away from thinking without thought, which blocked me from being open to the Truth of your words. When I let them speak, I hear that when Crows find food and come down to eat, they are silent. Is this what you are referring to?"

"When we argue and push the opinions we have about this and that, it is because we have not tasted the food of consciousness. To find that food is to know the value of silence." ⤳

April
12

HONOR OR DISHONOR

"Some people come to see you and I want to stay here with them," stated a Seeker to the Elder, "while others come and I only want to leave. Why is that?"

"You are addressing the two ways we naturally respond to people," replied the Elder, "and there is no simpler way to describe them than what you have just done. This is what all of our behaviors toward others amount to. Awakened Ones are the only exception, as they do not respond in either way."

"Yet there must be something more, for all those who come to you are people like me, with unfulfilled yearnings."

"Yes, my grandson, they are no different from each other, or from you and me. It is not what they seek that sets them apart, but how they seek."

"You now play with words, Venerable Elder, for I see no difference when I react to these people."

"Nor do I. The distinction is not a matter of the mind, but rather of intuition."

"Please explain," said the Seeker.

"The Honor Way is our natural way of being. We are naturally drawn to those who honor themselves, for they in turn honor those around them. We feel a quick friendship with them, and a resonance that goes beyond whether we speak the same language, or even if we agree or disagree.

continued on page 130

continued from page 129

On the other hand, those who dishonor themselves also dishonor others. These people are the ones who assume moral superiority. They are quick to disagree and criticize, even though they seldom understand what they are disagreeing over or criticizing. They simply feel compelled to do it, and this is why we instinctively shun them."

"I feel for these people. What can I do to help them?"

"They must go on with their illusions, until they realize that their sense of superiority and special insight are only desperate attempts to escape their plight."

"Their plight?" asked the Seeker.

"They dishonor only because of their plight," explained the Elder. "We are naturally honorable, and to be honorable is to be a Seeker. You are repelled by the dishonorable ones, while they are attracted to each other, as like attracts like. They see things the same way because they are mired in the same bog; and they end up together because they are stuck together. All they can do is gaze out at the idyllic place where they want to be. In utter frustration, they lash out at anyone whose feet are free to pursue it." ∿

DEEP MAGIC

A short while ago, I was sitting with my fellow Seekers and exploring some mystery of life with the Elder who guides us.

"I think the real mystery," said one of my comrades, "is in magic. I know a Wizard who can create a flame by clicking his fingers, and he can crush a stone to dust between his hands."

Being very impressed to hear this, we made plans for a trip to visit the Wizard.

"Would you like to accompany us?" we asked our Elder.

"I am watching a magic show right now," he replied.

"Surely you are giving us a paradox," one of us stated, "for all we see about us is the commonplace."

"What if you had never before seen a Butterfly emerge from a chrysalis? Or an Animal giving birth? Or a Bird soaring high in a blue Sky? Would you not take these to be magic?"

"But we have seen them before, Insightful One, and many times. That is why they have become commonplace—they have lost their magic."

"Would that not also be the case with a Magician's tricks? What would you do then?"

"We would find another Magician."

"I see. Would she be any more a Magician than the last one?"

"I guess not. Does that mean there is no magic? Or perhaps everything is magic."

continued on page 133

continued from page 131

"Remember what you have learned in the past: whenever we grasp something, look at its opposite, for therein usually lies the closer Truth."
"Then Knowledge would just lead to confusion, would it not? Every time we arrived at something, we would have to throw it out and start over again."

"You have just discovered the secret of magic," the Elder said with a smile. "Is not clarity, sameness? Is not clarity, knowing? And what does one do with sameness and knowing other than become bored by the commonplace?

"On the other hand, is magic not found in unknowing? Is it not confusion that creates mystery? When we categorize and make assumptions, there can be nothing new, for we have grouped it with something old. However, when we are in conscious presence, our relationship with every new lover is an uncharted galaxy to explore, even though we have had past lovers. Every Bird to take wing is a delight for the mind, even though thousands upon thousands of Birds have performed the same magic trick in front of us before."

READINESS

"How do I know when I am ready for something?" asked a Seeker.

"It is impossible to know," replied the Sage, "for the mind judges in ways that suit only the mind, and the aware being is mindless."

"I am listening to what you say," replied the Seeker, "yet it is too deep for me. I still do not know how to tell when I am ready for something."

"That is because you are still talking about knowing. The mind does not want to let go of control, so it keeps you caught in an endless loop of seeking something through knowing, only knowing is incapable of giving it to you."

"Then what shall I do?" asked the Seeker.

"There you go again—you want to *do* something. That is your mind speaking."

"Then I give up."

"Now you can listen," said the Sage. "Not to me, though, but to your body. What does it feel like when you try to do something that you are not ready for?"

"Well, I get nervous; and sometimes I break into a sweat."

"That is because fear is your Master rather than your Guide." The Sage paused for emphasis, then continued to speak. "When we listen to our heart's voice rather than our mind's, we naturally do what is intended and refrain from what is not. It comes from a sense of being rather than knowing. In this way, knowing yourself is being in a state of ignorance about yourself, for there are no thoughts to grasp and no words to express."

April
15

ALL THE SAME

In a neighboring province, there was once an uprising. The people were fed up with their government and wanted change. They gathered in the town squares and shouted slogans like "Freedom for the people!" and "Down with the oppressors!"

At the same time, the troops loyal to the government were massing outside the towns to quell protests before they got out of hand. A group of Seekers, who were watching the events unfold, didn't quite know what to make of it all.

"Which side should we support?" they asked their Sage.

"The unaware ones," the Sage responded.

"Which side is that?"

"Whenever there are sides, everyone involved is unaware. There is no difference between opposition and opposition to the opposition. Out to destroy each other, they cannot see that no matter what happens, they are really destroying themselves."

"Then do we not help anyone?"

"It is easy to identify a person who is sick in the body," continued the Sage, "yet there are far more with troubled hearts. Look around you and see that nearly everybody is taking sides. Their hearts were already agitated, and the Awakened Ones recognize this. The heart is tormented whether or not the body shows sickness, and this is what the Awakened Ones see and address. In this way, what we see here today will one day cease to happen, and we will be able to live again as we did in the times of the Ancient Ones." ➤

April
16

THE DISTRACTION OF KNOWING

"What is it that we should avoid?" asked a Seeker.

"When one is conscious," replied the Sage, "there is no need to deliberately avoid anything, as what would be harmful loses its draw. In other words, when one is conscious, one does not need to be consciously cautious."

"That makes rational sense," responded the Seeker. "Yet, for a person like me who is not fully conscious, your words do not translate into being."

"Perhaps an example will help us move beyond words. If I like mead because of the way it makes me feel, turning to mead tells me that I am not conscious, as I am looking to alter my feelings rather than be my feelings."

"Again, that makes sense. Still, how do I know that I am altering my feelings if I am not yet conscious?"

"We can tell by whether or not we hold onto answers. Being conscious is embracing fear as our lover and dancing with her. Holding onto an answer is putting up a sign that says *Fear—Do Not Enter.*"

"Where, then, do I turn for diversion?" asked the Seeker. "Shall I practice a skill?"

"That is another form of wine. The more we become the skill, the more we live as an answer and the less conscious we become. The mere fact of having expertise defines us, and we are no longer of Mindless Mind, free to think without thought."

"Being without escape is asking much of me."

"Who is asking it of you?"

"I appreciate that question," replied the Seeker, "as it has just helped me realize that a symptom of my unconsciousness is to think that I am on this Journey alone. I bow to the Teaching." 〜

THE OPIATE OF SAINTS

Five Nuns got in the habit of coming together and reciting Sacred Passages. One day, a passing Nun stopped when she overheard what they were doing. "When the Fox goes for two Chickens," she said to them, "the second is to satisfy greed, not hunger, and he will be discovered."

"What are you trying to tell us, kind woman?" asked one in the group of Nuns. "It appears that you have transformed the Pathless Path into a well-worn trail," the traveling Nun replied.

"At what point did we do that?"

"As soon as the Fox opens his mouth, he is already caught. His reason for eating the first Chicken does not matter, as it will lead to the second Chicken, and he will be done in. There is no distinction between the two Chickens—they are One. It would be better that he eats no Chickens, for it would save his life."

"What you say is true for us, gracious Nun. We have grown lazy by adopting this recitation practice. Fellow Seekers, let us burn these books, so that we may renew our primary hunger."

April
18

POOR, PITIFUL ME

In a time long ago, a wandering Fool came to a village. He was just passing through, yet many people came to talk with him when word got out of his presence. Back then, Fools were known for their unorthodox and often irreverent perspectives, which many people appreciated.

One woman told him her tale of having to work in the fields all day to grow enough food for her family. She was small and weak, she said, and she could not do the work of a man. When she went to the market to sell her craftwork, she had to carry it all the way on her back, then trudge home with what did not sell. On top of that, she had four children to care for. And she was just one woman, she cried. What in the world could she do?

While she paused to catch her breath and recall what she might have missed, the Fool grabbed her by the shoulders, looked into her eyes, and said, "When is it that you became this woman?" ➤

April
19

ONLY FOR ALL

There is a Fool who travels from hamlet to hamlet asking for gold coins to distribute to those in need. He once approached a merchant at a market, who said, "I would be glad to give you some coins if you will be sure to help the cripples who have only crutches to assist them."

"The cripples will benefit," replied the Fool, "and so will the lepers and the orphans and those who are ravaged by floods and fires."

"Well, they are not in as desperate a need as the cripples," retorted the merchant. "Besides, I must ask you to not give any of my coins to the poor, for all they do is come around to beg and steal from me."

"I cherish all who have need," responded the Fool. With that, he moved on to the next merchant. ～

April
20

BEHIND ECSTASY

"I have become Awakened!" claimed the Seeker who came bursting into his Elder's presence. "I have never felt this way before: colors are brighter, people are beautiful, and everything has a place and a meaning in my life. How could I have ever imagined feeling so complete, so serene? I don't ever want it to leave."

"Are you saying that you never want to be sober?" asked the Elder.

"What do you mean? I have not been drinking; I have not touched a drop of wine! This is genuine ecstasy—I have been Awakened!"

"That may be," replied the Elder. "At the same time, you act like you are under the influence of something."

"Is this not what it is like to be in the Awakened State?" asked the Seeker.

"Have you ever been in an altered state from wine or something else?"

"I now see what you are saying; it did feel similar to what I am now experiencing. Is that not okay? I always thought that Awakening was the better way to experience ecstasy than wine."

"There is little difference between a person drunk on wine and a person drunk on his own Awakening."

"Why is that?"

"Both people have chosen to drown their fear rather than become it," explained the Elder. "Both of them have taken the cowardly way of escaping the present breath for a world that drifts in and out of the Breathing."

April
21

TO LIVE LIKE BEING

A traveling Monk had only one set of clothes. When he revisited a village, people would see him in the same robe he wore the last time he was there.

"Are you too poor to afford another set of clothes?" someone once asked.

"There are those who are generous and provide for my needs," replied the Monk. "They give me food and gold coins, yet it is this set of clothes that keeps me poor."

"How can that be?"

"It is the Way of the Monk."

"But isn't that deception?" another asked. "When we give you money, when we give you gold coins to buy new clothes, you say, 'Yes, I will go and buy some,' yet we always see you in the same tattered garment."

"I speak my Truth to you in doubles when I tell you that I am going to get new clothes," said the Monk. "Every time I put my garment on in the morning, it is new to me, and every time someone gives me coins to buy new clothes, I do just that, and I give them to the poor people of your village. So every time you see a Beggar on the corner in new clothes, you see me in new clothes."

April
22

TALKING JARS

During the last harvest season, a farmer came from the neighboring province to sell his surplus honey at our market. He had many jars in his hand-cart and he was tired from the journey, so he lay down to nap under the shade of a Tree before the market opened.

When he awoke, his cart was empty. "I needed to sell that honey to buy wool and leather to clothe my children," stated the farmer to our village Elder.

At the next village meeting, the Elder announced, "The bridge we use to cross the River to reach our fields has grown rickety and must be replaced. The honey harvest has been bountiful this year, so if each of us will contribute a jar, we will have enough to afford a new bridge."

After all the villagers brought their jars of honey, the Elder summoned the farmer whose honey was stolen and asked him to identify his jar. He did, the thief was apprehended, and the farmer recovered his honey. ━

THE COST OF REFINEMENT

"What is our true nature?" asked a youth.

"The same as a Horse's," replied the Horse trainer.

"How can that be? Horses run on the wind and go where they please. They live out in the weather, where they have thick hair to keep them warm and hooves to grip when it is slippery. They have no use or desire for the refinements that we enjoy."

"And what of those refinements?" questioned the trainer. "When free-living Horses are herded in to live a refined life, they get hobbled and put in stables. They are haltered and branded, and their hooves are cut."

"Is it not for their own good?"

"The cost for some of them is too much, answered the trainer. "They die before they can enjoy the pleasures of civilization. The trainer refines the Horse, the potter refines the clay, and the mason refines the stone. We all do this with pride, just like the rulers who refine us." ✒

April 24

RIGHTFUL TEACHING

"I am so baffled," said the Seeker. "A short while after a Teaching comes clear to me, it seems to evaporate. And when Guidance begins to sound like gibberish, there is no way I could benefit from it anyway."

"That is the way to tell if you have been given a Teaching or not," replied the Sage.

"Now nothing is clear to me." The seeker paused to reflect. "Will you please explain?"

"If you understood the Teaching, there was no Teaching. If you did not understand, there was no substance—only a flight of fantasy."

"Then what is a true Teaching?"

"It comes dressed in strange clothing, so that you do not at first recognize it. And it affects you in unexpected ways, so that you do not at first embrace it, either." ∿

THE DEEPER TRUTH

Two female Elders have long been good friends. One lives in my village, where she leads a worldly life, enjoying fine food, good wine, and the company of men. Her friend in the neighboring village is celibate and follows the simple life of an Ascetic.

One evening, the plain-living Elder came to visit her friend in our village, who was enjoying a luxurious meal with one of her male friends.

"Come and join us," invited the two. "There is plenty to share!"

"I would not think to indulge in such things!" exclaimed the visitor.

"One who does not enjoy life is hardly Human," replied her friend as she raised her glass of wine.

"Are you saying that I am not Human because I do not indulge? Then what am I?"

"You are an Awakened Being." ⮑

 *April* 26

WHY SILENCE?

Many pursuers of The Way gain from discourse: they explore topics together, analyze the Ancient Texts, and converse with Wisdom Carriers. However, some grow confused from these endeavors, as they regularly come across admonitions about researching, speaking, and even thinking.

"Why are we encouraged not to speak," one such Inquirer asked an aged Ascetic, "when in fact much of what we do with you is speaking?"

"Your mind will hear 'Do not speak' and take it literally," replied the Old One, "because the mind functions in a yes-or-no reality. However, your heart hears 'listen.' It appears as though your mind is overriding your heart."

"That may be. At the same time, it seems as though you are saying that speaking can also mean listening. If so, how do you define *listening*?"

"When we are in our egos, we speak, and we hear speaking. When we are in our hearts, there is only listening."

"But how can that be?" asked the Inquirer. "Whether I am in my heart or my ego, there are still words."

"Ego is separation. The ego perceives a voice as something coming at it, so her first response is to react defensively. The heart, on the other hand, embraces the voice, which causes it to immediately melt away as a distinct entity. What is left is authentic communication based on deep listening."

"I now see that. Yet there are words, and we are clearly told, 'Do not speak.'"

"There is the cup of water to sate thirst," said the Ascetic, "and there is the deluge of water in floods. When we speak and listen from our hearts, the great majority of our words are unnecessary. Most of what we tell each other with words is as necessary as saying 'What rises at dawn is the sun.'"

"What about introductions and getting to know each other? Don't we need words for that?" asked the Inquirer.

"Whether it be two thieves or two lovers," answered the Ascetic, "they know each other when they meet. It is only the fearful ego that insists on words."

"So the focus is not on talking or not talking, but on dwelling in my ego or in my heart, and my relationship with words is just a reflection of that state."

The Wizened One bowed to the Awareness. ～﹥

April
27

TRIPPING OURSELVES UP

"To have no expectations is to be invisible," stated an Elder. "Everything then becomes visible to us."

The Seekers in his presence said nothing. Nor did they need to, as their furrowed brows gave away their confusion.

"Look at it this way," continued the Elder. "Who would imagine something as delicious as an egg coming from the filthy rear end of a Chicken, unless someone had the prior expectation? At the same time, the prior expectation limits what I could imagine coming out of a Chicken's rear end."

"I see that," replied one of the Seekers. "To help us to not be limited by our expectations, we would like to know why they are limiting."

"It is not the expectations themselves," replied the Elder, "but the blindness they cause. When I am waiting beside the road, full of expectation for a certain person to come by, I become blind to all the other people passing by. Does my expectation create only one possibility? Of course not, yet it might as well be so, as I have shut myself off to all other possibilities."

"Should we then *not* expect something?"

"Be careful lest you trap yourself in dualistic thinking. To not expect something is the same as to expect it, since it too blinds us. How many times have you said, 'Oh, I wasn't expecting that,' as your reason for missing something?"

"Then what is the answer?" asked a Seeker.

"You have an expectation that there is an answer, and that is what keeps tripping you up. There is no single, definitive answer. When we remember that there is only the eternal, ever-evolving Question, we can remain open to anything."

April
28

TRUTH BEYOND WORDS

A Monk traveled to a far-off land over the Mountains to learn the fabled Sacred Teachings for Living from the people who dwelled there. When he returned, he was inspired to share the Teachings with his people. He decided to call everyone in the village together once every week for a year, as he figured it would take that long to impart all of the lessons he had been given.

However, a wicked typhoon leveled the village before the first meeting could be held. The survivors spent the next year rebuilding and piecing their lives back together. Working right beside them was the Monk, who shared everything he knew in order to help.

When the year ended and the village was back to its normal bustling state, the Monk decided that it was time to begin sharing the Teachings.

Right then, a drought befell the land. The villagers had to do devote themselves entirely to deepening their wells and procuring food from far-away regions that were blessed with rain. Again, the Monk helped by giving all that was within him.

After a year the rains returned. Now is the time to begin sharing the Teachings, thought the Monk, and he called all the villagers together.

"I would like to describe the sacred way of life of those who dwell in the land over the Mountains," he began. He told of how they held each other in such regard that they embraced each other's needs, desires, and Truths. They would celebrate each other's joys and comfort one another in time of sorrow.

Before the Monk could say anything more, a woman politely interrupted him. "Honorable Brother, what you speak of you have already given us, twice over. During the rebuilding after the typhoon, and throughout the drought, you bestowed upon us the Teachings in a way that words never could. Rather than the Voice of Truth, you gave us the *Experience* of Truth."

BAREFOOT

A group of Seekers were debating the way in which their Elder determined what they should each pursue. Unable to come to agreement, they decided to go to her with the question.

"That is a study in and of itself," she replied. "It has to do with your footwear."

"How on earth can what we put on our feet have anything to do with our Quest for Knowledge?" asked one of the Seekers.

"The real question lies in the fact that you put anything on your feet."
"But that does not make sense. If we wore nothing, you wouldn't be able to help us, as you would have no footwear to study."

"And that *is* the point—I would then not have to help you."

"We started out just questioning," said another Seeker, "and now we are confused as well. It seems that our decision to come to you is doing more harm than good."

"Or more good than harm," replied the Elder. " Be careful of attaching value to anything, for value is judgment."

"I understand, yet you lost us in the very beginning. I am guessing that you referred to footwear metaphorically?"

"You are correct. If you wear high boots, I encourage you to find a pair of low boots. After you have broken in the low boots, I suggest you get a pair of sandals. Once the sandals start feeling comfortable, I recommend that you get a feel for going barefoot."

"Why all the steps?" asked a Seeker in the group.

"Rare is the person with the courage to throw his high boots into the fire and let his tender feet carry him right from then and there, even though that is the easiest and most effective way."

"You must be speaking of the beliefs, boundaries, and patterned behaviors we use to protect ourselves and keep from having to think."

"You know this and can admit it because you are already in the process of releasing your feet from their shackles," said the Elder. "Only feet that are free to touch the ground with naked sensitivity can truly walk the Journey of Discovery. Feet of any other type merely create the illusion of being out on the Journey." ⤳

THE STINK OF ROSES

A wealthy man from a foreign land had everything he wanted—except for one thing. To procure it, he hired a guide and ten porters to take him over the Mountains to the cabin of an Elderwoman who had been sought by Noble and Beggar alike for so many generations that she seemed to be ageless.

When the entourage arrived, the rich man asked the Elder, who looked old as a Mountain, for the deepest meaning of her Teachings.

"I would be honored to share that with you," replied the Elder in a voice like the creaking of one boulder against another. "But first, will you be so good as to tell me the guiding principle of your life?"

"I would be glad to, for I am proud of what it has helped me achieve. I believe that each of our destinies is ordained at birth, and that is why there are princes and there are paupers."

"That fits perfectly with the marrow of my Teaching: a cage is nothing without the Bird."

The man of wealth bowed and departed, leaving a bag of precious gemstones outside the doorway. He knew he was destined to receive the Teaching, and he felt all the wealthier for it.

Yet with every step on the way back home, he grew more morose, until he could no longer stand to hear even his own breathing. Every thought, every sound, and every thing he looked at, reminded him of the Ancient One's words: a cage is nothing without the Bird.

That bitter night, he slipped out of the tent while everyone else was sleeping, stripped off his robes, and traversed back over the pass to return to the Elderwoman.

"I have been blind to my cage," he told her. "Because it was gilded, I didn't realize that I had stepped inside. I felt sorry for those I saw between the bars, because I thought the bars were theirs. Voice of the Mountain, I am at your service." ⌁

May
1

THEN WHAT?

"I am totally confused!" lamented a Seeker to his Guide. "You say that the Way of the Seeker is neither about this world nor the next world. You also say that it is neither about the past nor the future. Then where do I dwell? And where did I come from? And where am I going?"

"Those are the affairs of the Student," replied the Sage, "and of the Philosopher and the Mathematician and the Alchemist. Whereas they have things to find, the Seeker has nothing to find. Yesterday never was and tomorrow never will be."

"Then where does the Path of the Seeker lead?"

"You assume that it leads somewhere. A Path that is walked many times gives the impression that it goes somewhere, just as the wind that blows by day after day. Yet where does the wind go?"

"I see what you are saying. So why do I still want to know where the Path goes?"

"The mind wants to make order out of things. Because the very idea of order is a product of the mind, what can the mind do but get caught in an endless loop of its own construct?"

"I do not understand!" protested the Seeker. "Will you please explain this to me in a way that I can grasp?"

"Surely," answered the Guide. "Does a blind Horse running in circles make any progress? You would of course answer 'no.' However, what would be the Horse's reply?"

May
2

HOLY CATS

Deep in the Forest lived a Hermit with her Cat. People from far-off places would go on Pilgrimages to see her. Though she never said much, her beatific presence inspired each visitor to find the voice within.

It so happened that the Hermit's golden Cat would always seem to appear at right about the time that one of the Pilgrims was experiencing an ecstatic moment. When the Pilgrims returned home and told the stories of their experiences at the Hermit's refuge, they would always include the golden Cat.

Before long, the ecstatic experiences came to be referred to as Golden Cat Moments. People started to believe that being in the presence of a golden Cat would bring them Wisdom and good fortune. Golden Cats became sacred, and artisans created icons of them. It became illegal for anyone but a Mystic to possess a golden Cat.

When word of the Golden Cat Cult made it back to the Hermit, it reminded her once again why she chose the solitary life. ∼➤

GOING TO THE SOURCE

There is a Seeker in our hamlet who is quick to learn. He listens well, he takes notes, and he has a good memory. As well, he can express himself clearly. The Seekers who know him often attend talks he gives about what he has learned on his Journey to Awakening.

One day, the smart Seeker asked a traveling Monk, "What do you think of my practice of giving talks?"

"What does it bring you?" the Monk replied.

"It brings me honor, I suppose. The recognition feels good, and I like the fact that I can help others."

"How does it serve your Journey to be a living book for others?"

The Seeker paused, then said, "Your question leaves me wordless, and that is rare for me. Have I been deceiving myself by thinking I was doing somebody else good, when actually I was only serving myself?"

"Perhaps it is not as simple as this or that."

"Perhaps not, yet your question of how my discourses serve my Journey brings me an awareness that I think is far more important: I could seek Knowledge into infinity and give lecture upon lecture, but to what end other than self-aggrandizement?"

"It appears that Wisdom is beginning to find its way through the heap of Knowledge," said the Monk.

"The awareness you have just brought me is of such value," responded the Seeker, "that I cannot begin to compare it with all the Knowledge that I have accumulated. Oh Gateless Wanderer, you must have learned much in your travels. If you will permit it, I will walk in your footsteps, keeping silent and listening while we travel the Endless Road." ━

May
4

OVERHUNGRY

One day, a woman said to an Elder, "I once had a strong yearning to Quest for Knowledge and find an Elder to guide me, yet I never came across an Elder with whom I was content. In time, the desire subsided, and I forgot about it."

"I understand," replied the Elder. "What happened is that you went beyond the point of becoming a Seeker. You were trying to satisfy a yearning, which made you both unreachable and unteachable."

"What does that mean?"

"Liken it to a person who has gone so long without food that she fears she is going to starve. She has become desperate: she is no longer able to think clearly about food and where to get it, but rather she becomes obsessed with her neediness and her fears around it. Such was the case with you."

"Was I not acting as any Seeker would?"

"The seeking needs to be for a Guide, and for the Wisdom her Guidance will bring. If that were your goal, you would truly have been a Seeker, and you would have found yourself pleased with a Guide and the Guidance that passed through her."

continued

The woman thought for a moment. "I believe I would have been—if only I had found what I was yearning for."

"There is a difference between seeking and yearning. Seeking is like hunger, which one approaches with a clear mind. Yearning, on the other hand, is like starvation, which one approaches with a roiled mind. Food has lost its meaning and its qualities are no longer recognizable. The starving person will try harder and harder to satisfy her yearning, until she finally gives up."

"That is exactly what I did!" exclaimed the woman.

"In reality, she needs to do the opposite and relax around her yearning, so that she can again feel her hunger and regain the perspective she requires. She will then be guided to the foods that can nourish her."

"If I understand you correctly, the Path to Knowledge is not gained by trying to gain fulfillment, but rather by seeking Guidance."

"That is correct," responded the Elder. "A Sage will help you with Guidance to the Teachings, but you were looking for instruction in the Teachings. That is what made you a Student rather than a Seeker. At that point, only a Teacher—not a Guide—could have satisfied your yearning." ➤

May
5

I KNOW BEST

"I am nothing more than a hypocrite," stated a Monk to a bystander.

"How can that be?" asked the bystander.

"Because I go around and tell people that I speak to them for their own good."

"How can it be hypocrisy if you are helping them?"

"Anyone who says he is doing something for someone else's good is actually serving himself. Years ago, I was told this many times by a Wise Elder. And it stung, which told me it was Truth. Yet at the time, I was too weak to admit it. I was struggling to tend to my own good, much less somebody else's."

"Instead of telling people that you know what is for their own good, what if you were to tell them that they already know it, and that is what they should follow?" asked the bystander.

"I would still be a hypocrite," replied the Monk, "because I am still telling them what to do."

"At least you are telling them to do their own thing."

"Even worse than telling them what to do, I am telling them they know something they do not know. Some people merely repeat what they have learned from others about what is good or bad. Others deceive themselves by calling *good* what supports their beliefs and prejudices, and calling *bad* what they struggle with and fear."

"But isn't that a person's choice?" asked the bystander. "How does it affect anybody else?"

"It does when people dishonor others with their projections about what is good or bad. I am a hypocrite when I say, 'This person is good and that person is bad,' or 'This person is to be listened to and that person is to be avoided.' What I am really saying is that this person does not recognize my weakness or challenge my fear, and that person does."

"If you are a hypocrite, then I am a hypocrite ten times over. What must I do to keep from hypocrisy?"

"Watch for the man who talks his Path up and another's Path down, responded the Monk. "If you are tempted to listen, look and you will see that his feet are mired in the muck of his own Path. The sun proves his own warmth, so shun anyone who tries to speak for the sun." ๛

May
6

THE CAGE

A Seeker wanted to learn, so that she could have something to share with others. She went to a Sage with her request, who replied, "Spend a week in the neighborhood park making toys with the children, then come back and we will talk."

The week went by, and the Seeker returned to the Sage. "At first," the Seeker said, "the children were curious about what I was doing. They asked questions and wanted to learn how to make what I was making. However, when I gave them the toys I finished, they no longer had an interest in learning, nor did they have any questions. They only wanted more toys. When I came back to the park, they all flocked to me and followed me around."

"What have you gained from the experience?" asked the Sage.

"That the reason for thirst is to quench it, rather than to make it serve another purpose."

"You have spent your week well. To quench a thirst merely for the sake of the thirst is pure. When we look to gain or give something by quenching a thirst, we inject an ulterior motive that causes the thirst to satisfy a need other than the thirst itself."

"I see the immediate harm," said the Seeker, "as with the children losing their curiosity to learn. At the same time, I know there is always a deeper Teaching."

"And that is the personal Teaching," said the Sage. "When I divert a thirst, I am no longer a vestal Seeker being as a question, but rather a mercenary out to achieve an end. A Bird flies free unless she creates a cage around herself, and an outside motive in the Quest for Knowledge is the cage that entraps many a Seeker. Now that you have discovered the cage, you can avoid it. Come walk with me and we shall learn together."

"I shall come," replied the Seeker, "and it will be for the pure sake of learning." ⤳

DOUBLE STING

Two Seekers sat on the bank of a Stream eating a meal. After they finished their food and washed their bowls in the water, one of them saw a Scorpion floating past them.

"That poor thing must have fallen in," she said. While attempting to scoop up the Scorpion with her bowl to rescue him, he stung her.

A few minutes later, the Seeker saw the same Scorpion back in the water. She figured he must have slipped down the bank, so she scooped him back up. Again, she got stung.

"Why did you do that again?" the other Seeker asked. "Didn't you realize that you could get stung again? And sure enough, it happened."

"I didn't have any choice in the matter," replied the first Seeker.

"How ever could that be?"

"Because I am called to serve."

May
8

PROOF

A Philosopher and a Sage would meet often to discuss matters of Ancient Knowledge.

"What proof do you have of what you say?" challenged the Philosopher on a particular point. "For my part, I have quotes from the Classical Texts to back up my statements."

"That is impressive," commented the Sage. "I have not thought to do that."

"The fact that you cannot support what you say is all I wanted to know," replied the Philosopher, and he begged his leave.

Not too long after that, the Philosopher and the Sage found themselves together in a public discussion on the Teachings of the Ancient Ones.

"What the Sage says is worthless," accused the Philosopher, "for he is not able to trace it back to the Old Writings."

"It is my Truth only," admitted the Sage, "as I have discovered it on my life's Journey. It is of value to me because it is mine, not because it belongs to another."

"Why do you even bother seeking your own Truth," taunted the Philosopher, "when it might not be supported by the Texts?"

"It appears that you are unsure of yourself," replied the Sage, "as you need others to endorse your thoughts and feelings in order to confirm that they exist." ∾

May
9

HOW TO WALK

A young Seeker was feeling quite full of herself, as she had come to a great awareness over something that had troubled her ever since she began her Journey of Discovery. "I feel a great sense of accomplishment!" she exclaimed to the Sage who was guiding her.

"I am sad to hear of this," replied the Sage.

"That makes no sense to me! Is it not my role to Quest for Awakening?"

"It is exactly your role," said the Sage. "However, what you are telling me has nothing to do with the Quest, but rather with completion. Those are two quite different things."

"I am confused," muttered the young woman.

"When the True Seeker comes to an awareness, it removes her blinders to how much more lies ahead, and she is humbled. In this way her hunger returns and strengthens. You, instead, have taken a great step backwards. You are like an Emperor at a drunken feast after conquering the enemy. Go now, and decide whether you are out to conquer or out on a Journey of Knowing."

THE RIGHT PLACE

"I think I will learn much here," said a Seeker upon first arriving at a Sage's residence. "I feel comfortable here right away, and I like the surroundings."

"Then this is not the place for you," replied the Sage.

"I do not...I do not understand..." stammered the Seeker.

"There is a great difference between liking a place and knowing what a place is like."

The Seeker paused, then said, "I am still puzzled by what you say."

"Liking a place is a matter of preference and design, and knowing what a place is like comes over time as a result of the Quest for Knowledge. The former gets in the way of the Quest for the latter. It is only the rare Seeker who can choose what will most benefit his Quest, as how can not-knowing assume that it can know?"

"Yet must I not make choices on my Quest?" asked the Seeker.

"Those who tamper with Matters of the Unknown will miss much more than they might steer themselves toward."

WHAT WE NEED

Recently, a Scholar asked a Sage about a distant Elder he had gone to visit.

"The woman is a poet," replied the Sage. "She embodies the Wisdom of the Ages, and her mere gaze inspires."

"It sounds as though she transforms the commonplace," replied the Scholar, "and has the power to Awaken the common man."

"That is who she would be to you. For me, she took the mystical and the blindingly beautiful and made it commonplace, so that I could embrace it."

"I see why you are no Scholar."

"What would really challenge your studied approach is how she exposes herself to attack and rebuke, so that we can see the true nature and motivation of attackers and keep our distance from them."

"That truly would challenge me," responded the Scholar. "It makes no rational sense."

"Yet what I appreciated most about her," said the Sage, "is that she would say things to irritate and anger me, to give me the opportunity to trace my aggravation to its source."

The Scholar thought about the Sage's words, then said, "That would make my skin crawl." ⇝

TO SPEAK IN POETRY

"How does one know that another is speaking from the heart?" asked a Seeker.

"To our ears," replied the Elder, "the heart's voice often sounds like poetry. It is just naturally so. There is no need to choose words or balance lines. When a fresh breeze weaves through the Trees, it sings. It is the only thing a breeze can do, and so it is with the poet-voice of the heart."

"We understand," replied another Seeker. "Yet how would the heart-voice sound to the ear of someone not accustomed to it?"

"What you would hear first is a grounding statement to introduce the topic. The heart would then speak a second line to elaborate upon the topic, followed by a line that creates the story by introducing a new topic or idea. A fourth line would then conclude the story by showing the relationship between the first three lines."

"That sounds both poetic and effective," commented a Seeker. "Will you give us an example?"

The elder nodded. "Here is one:

A Rabbit hopped into the clearing.

She was looking for succulent greens to nibble.

Out of the Woods came a Fox.

He, also hungry, chased after the Rabbit."

PERSONAL POWER

A Seeker expressed intent to go on his Journey of Discovery. He asked his Sage, "Will you send word out before me to those friends of yours who reside along the way, so that I may visit them and partake of their Wisdom?"

"That I cannot do," replied the Sage.

Confused, the Seeker left to start his Journey.

"Why did you not grant his wish?" asked another Seeker of the Sage.

"If I did, he would have been welcomed by my friends, yet he would not have been prepared for the Teachings."

"Why so?"

"Because he did not have to invest anything of himself."

"I understand," responded the Seeker. Still, I am concerned that he left here disillusioned and may not even go on his Journey."

"If that is the case," replied the Sage, "it shows that he was not ready. Had he the clarity and passion, he would go regardless of what I did or did not say or do."

14

TRUTH OR HAPPINESS

There are many ways to find Truth, and one Seeker wanted to explore as many of them as possible. Sometimes he found himself in a state of ecstasy for his efforts, yet just as often he was left feeling frustrated and empty. Questioning whether his search for Truth would ever end, he would sometimes sink into a depression.

One morning he woke up and decided to go and see how other Truthseekers were faring, in hopes of learning something that would be of help to him.

The first group he came across abided by the instructions of people who claimed they were Teachers. Those in the group were miserable, and the Seeker asked why.

"It is because we did not seek the Truth that dwelled in our own hearts," they replied.

Not wanting any more misery in his life, he sought out a group of people who were filled with joy and asked them how they had come to such a state.

"We did it by not following our Inner Guidance," they replied.

"How can it be that you have ignored your heartvoice and are still happy?"

"It is because we decided to take happiness over Truth."

The Seeker understood, as those who ended up miserable also chose something over Truth. Yet he was left deeply confused, as he had always believed that happiness would be the result of his Quest. He took his dilemma to a Sage of renown and asked for Guidance.

"Happiness and misery enslave us," said the Sage. "Truth gets choked out by either emotion, and we end up becoming prisoners of our passions. When we dwell in Truth, we can choose our feelings. Or we can choose to have no feelings."

"Why would someone want no feelings?" asked the Seeker.

"Is it not the night that makes the day so sweet?"

15 May

LIVING TRUTH

Several Seekers were very dedicated to their study of Truth. They read the Sacred Texts together and discussed them afterwards. They held dialogues and attended talks. All the time, they sought the deeper meaning of things.

One day they decided to ask their Sage what she thought of their commitment and studiousness.

"It is good to study," she replied, "if one wants to hold a discourse on what was examined. Yet the more we think about Truth, the less life it has."

"Then what is the Quest for Truth if it is not the relentless pursuit of its deeper meaning?" asked one of the Seekers in the group.

With a warm smile, the Sage replied, "Unless Truth is lived, it has no life. As helpful as the Sacred Texts can be, they get in the way when we focus on their words. Then *we* get in the way when we add another layer of words. Truth is wordlessness. Unless we constantly return there to keep the Truth alive, we do no better than imagining how a corpse functioned when it had life." ❧

RUDDERLESS SHIPS

"Why do I need Guidance?" asked a Seeker.

"Because you are here," replied the Elder.

"Where else would I be? Where else *could* I be, with or without Guidance?"

"You would still be here, it is true," said the Elder. "Whether you are drifting rudderless or under sail with sound rudder, you are still a boat out at Sea."

"If I were rudderless and drifting, could I still call myself a Seeker?"

"Rudder or not, does the ship not take a course? What we do or don't do has no effect upon our destiny, as our ship will ultimately find shore."

"But what, then, is my role? And that brings me back to my original question: Why am I sitting here before you?"

"What you have just spoken, my grandson," said the Elder, "is the beginning of consciousness. We will now explore together."

May
17

IN THE GUISE OF TRUTH

"When we are controlled by fear, we do not speak our Truth," commented a Sage. "Instead, we get philosophical or analytical. When the fear mounts, we tend to turn either critical or congratulatory."

"That must mean I am in a near-constant state of fear," confessed a Seeker, "as most of what I say and feel falls into one of those categories."

"Yes, granddaughter," replied the Sage, "this is true for so many of us. Yet it is easy to recognize, especially by those who are listening to us. People have an intuitive sense for what is spoken from the heart and what is not."

"Will you give us an example?"

"Of course. Ask me where I am going."

"Kind Elder, where are you headed?"

"Wherever my legs take me. Now ask me again."

"Where are you off to?"

"Down to the lake to wash my face and hands."

"I see what you mean!" cried the Seeker. "With your first reply, I felt distanced from you, and I even felt some irritation. However, I was content with your second reply, and it was easy for me to hear it. I felt connected to you."

"It's that easy," replied the Elder.

The Seeker considered this for a bit. "So what do we do when we sense that someone is speaking from fear?"

"To continue the conversation in that vein entrenches the fear," replied the Elder. "It is best to remain silent and merely accept the person's state of being." ━

18

KEEPING AFLOAT

"Elder One," spoke a Nun, "I would like to tell you the clarity that came to me today regarding who we are as Nuns. I see us floating on a life raft made of logs lashed together. When we are in danger of sinking, you add a log or two to keep us afloat. Then when we get stuck in complacency and ego consciousness, you remove a log or two, in order to bring us to One Voice and get us back out on our edge."

"That may appear to be so," replied the Elder.

"You say 'appear'; does that mean there is another possibility?"

"As always. Let's not limit ourselves to only one."

"That is my oversight," reflected the Nun. "I must watch slipping back into this-or-that thinking."

"Remember that dichotomies do not exist when we dwell in our Mind-less Mind."

"Yes, I must remember. There is then no need for me to worry about sliding back."

"Regarding your metaphor, you see me as fine-tuning your raft to keep you barely afloat, so that you will stay sharp and present." The Elder paused, then added, "In actuality, I am working to eliminate your raft altogether."

19

THE DEATH IN DOING

"What must I do to become Awakened?" asked a Seeker.

"*To do* and *to become* are two different things," replied the Sage.

Right then, the Seeker became Awakened.

"Why practice when you can be?" commented the Seeker with an air of serenity.

"This," added the Sage, "is why those who chant, meditate, debate—any practice—cannot become Awakened."

"I now see that. I was doing rather than becoming."

"Those *who do*" said the Sage, "are nourished by praise and criticism, whether it comes from self or other. This keeps mind and body separated. When the two become One, the desire and need for assessment both cease."

WHEN BEAUTY SHAMES

In a long-past time, there lived a woman too beautiful to be a Seeker. She was young, barely old enough to be considered a woman, yet her grace and form mesmerized all whose gaze she caught. She wrote poetry that anyone would mistake for classic verse.

"You should go and serve in the royal court," encouraged her family. Others suggested that she marry a nobleman and bear children who would lead a life free of want. However, all she wanted was to be a Seeker of Knowledge.

She went to one Sage, then another, and then another, and all of them refused to guide her. They told to her that she would be too distracting for the other Seekers.

In great despair, she shaved her head of glistening raven hair and went back to the Sages.

"Without your hair," they told her, "your beauty shines forth all the more."

There was only one thing left to do. With glowing coals, she pockmarked her face; with a sharp stone, she carved deep grooves into her arms and breasts. The Sages then accepted her as a Seeker.

May
21

INVISIBILITY

In a neighboring village lived an Elder who drew many Seekers. She would periodically ask them if they were sincere, and of course they all said they were. Yet after a while, the Seekers started to study each other, wondering who really was wholehearted and who was not.

One day the Elder said, "I will no longer ask who is sincere, as it compels you to reply in a way that contradicts your actions."

The Seekers looked at each other, and many of them got up to leave. Several of them, with indignant looks, murmured "I am no hypocrite," under their breaths.

The Elder then began to babble nonsense, as though she had gone mad, and more Seekers left. Next she hurled insults, and even more left. On their way back to the village, they talked among themselves about how the old woman could have made such a good Elder if only she were not so mentally imbalanced.

Only four Seekers remained with the Elder, whose reputation had become so tarnished that no new Seekers would dare to come and join.

"Have we passed the test?" one of the four asked the Elder. "Will you now instruct us in the Ancient Teachings?"

"Some of you are so driven by your thirst for Knowledge that you will overlook or tolerate anything to receive it," replied the Elder. "Now you too will take yourselves, disillusioned, down the lane back to the village."

With that, two of the remaining Seekers got up and departed.

"You who are left will continue, for you are aware that you have been partaking in the Teachings all along." ∿

22

ALREADY THERE

"I am discouraged," said a Monk. "I have studied and waited, and waited and studied, and I don't know if I will ever Awaken. Do you, a wise and insightful Elder who has witnessed many Awakenings, think it will ever happen to me?"

"It may happen," replied the Elder. "Why do you wish to know?"

"Sometimes I get so frustrated that I just want to quit The Way and be an ordinary person again."

"If you had set out to reach the highlands, would you turn around at the halfway point, just because you weren't there yet?"

"I don't think so," replied the Monk.

"Might you quit because there is no guarantee you would ever reach the highlands?"

"I doubt that very much."

"Then what would keep you going?"

The Monk considered the Elder's question, then said, "I believe that even if I grew weary of the Journey, every step closer would encourage me all the more to continue." After a reflective pause, the Monk exclaimed, "Of course, I see it now! What I am experiencing is exactly like a journey to the highlands! It is natural that I would get discouraged with an undertaking as arduous as The Way. Yet that tiredness is for a reason: I have progressed that much closer. And if perchance I never do reach my Awakening, just as if for some reason I did not reach the highlands, it was still a beautiful Journey that gave me so much more than if I had stayed at home. You must also be a Wizard, dear Elder, for who else could so cleverly show a person that he already knows what he wishes to know?" ∼∽

May
23

ROADHOUSE LUNCH

In a kingdom beyond the Desert, there lived a woman who ran a little roadhouse, where she provided meals and overnight lodging for travelers.

One day, the King and his entourage were passing by and stopped in for midday refreshments. When the King traveled away from the castle, he made a point of partaking in the simple fare of his subjects.

"Do tell me what I owe you," said the King to the innkeeper as he rose from the table after his meal.

"Food and drinks for the seven of you," replied the woman, "will be a thousand gold pieces."

"Cabbage and barley must be in short supply in this district to be so costly," responded the monarch.

"It is not the fixings that are scarce, Your Highness, but rather the times that one such as you comes through my door."

THE NATURE OF KNOWLEDGE

"I believe I am gaining Knowledge," commented a Seeker.

"You speak as though Knowledge were a thing," replied the Sage. "For the uncentered, Knowledge is a thing to be gained; for those on the Quest, Knowledge is a force to be known."

"That mystifies me! I cannot comprehend such a Knowledge."

"Think of it as that which constantly flows through us. If it were to stop, our existence would cease."

"How, then, is Wisdom related to Knowledge?" asked the Seeker.

"Wisdom is developing a sensitivity to Knowledge," answered the Sage, "along with an awareness of how it functions. Think of Wisdom as the awareness and the personality of Knowledge. It is Wisdom that compels us to abandon old beliefs and habits, so that we can open ourselves to new Knowledge."

THE MASK

"First we sell out, then we buy ourselves back," commented a Sage to a group of Seekers.

"You taunt us well," replied a Seeker.

"Then let me taunt you even more: we create a mask, then we put it on."

"You have shown us that there is always a current beneath the surface," said another Seeker, "and I am afraid that here I am still on the surface. Will you goad me even more to help me break through?"

"When our mask doesn't feel right, we often secretly copy the mask of another and call it our own."

"Why would we do that?" asked the Seeker.

"Because one mask only knows another mask."

"I follow that, yet it brings me no closer to knowing the mask."

"I shall elaborate: most of us refer to the mask as the man. When we first reply to something, it is our mask speaking rather than us. However, we are not aware of this."

"So the problem is not knowing the mask," reflected the Seeker, "but knowing ourselves."

"That is correct," responded the Sage. "What happens is that when we think we are defending ourselves, we are actually defending our masks. And when we stand up for others, we don't realize that we are doing the same thing and defending their masks. In doing so, we help them bury their true selves even deeper."

"Aha!" exclaimed the Seeker. "The mask is the ego! We project our egos, then we embrace and defend what we project as our true selves. Then others enter into relationship with our ego selves rather than our true selves. So we end up being masks looking into the faces of other masks."

"We bow to you," said the other Seekers. ✦

May
26

WHO WILL SAVE ME?

A troubled woman heard about an aged Wizard who lived over the Mountains. He was reputed to have magical powers: he could give you certain words to repeat and your wish would be granted. The woman left her work and told her husband that she was off to find the solution to her problem.

When she arrived at the Wizard's little cottage, a servant greeted her at the door.

"I have come to see the Wizard," she said to the little man. She thought it strange that someone living in so small a place would have a servant.

"Please come in," he said as he held the door open for her.

On the way through the cottage, the woman's eyes scanned eagerly for sight of the fabled Wizard. When they walked through the entire cabin and reached the back door, the servant opened it for the woman to leave.

"But I have come to see the Wizard," she protested.

"Indeed, and you have," replied the servant. "Be present with what first strikes you as insignificant. In the deep black of the night, one candle can be as welcome as a bonfire. When you walk your days with this awareness, what you think is commonplace will become magic, and your problems will give you their own solutions." ➤

May 27

LIKE THE WINDS

On her first trip away from home, a fledgling Seeker went up to the Mountain cabin of a Sage. She accompanied a group of older Seekers who had been going there on retreats for a while.

After the first day, the young one pulled the Sage aside and asked if she could talk with him. "I feel privileged to be here," she began, "yet I don't know what to do. My legs ache from sitting cross-legged and I keep drifting off to sleep, even though I am very interested in the dialogues. If I'm not falling asleep, I get distracted so easily. I feel bad about myself."

"There's no need to worry," replied the kindly Sage. "It will all pass before you know it."

A few days later, the struggling neophyte said to the Sage, "Something happened: I feel so alive now! I'm full of energy, I listen to every word being said, and my legs have adjusted nicely to sitting on the ground."

"I must caution you," said the Sage with a fatherly look, "it will all pass before you know it."

May 28

CHASING ILLUSION

There is one story about an old Man of Wisdom who left his land of origin and went to settle in another country. There, by merely going about his day, he began to draw crowds. It seemed that everything he said inspired the people around him and caused them to see the everyday in new ways.

The people kept coming, even from the distant hills and beyond. They arrived by boat and caravan, and many walked. However they arrived, they all waited for the next appearance of the luminous Sage.

"Where do you come from, that you are so Awakened?" the people asked.

"I dwelled in the Village of Sages, which lies in high Mountain valley in the Mystical Land to the South. There even the children speak the Timeless Wisdom."

It wasn't long before the throngs of people set out on a great Pilgrimage to find the Valley of Sages. Very few people stayed to spend time with the Wise One anymore. Instead, they would hurry to catch up with the Pilgrimage.

"Is this the Sacred Valley where the Wise Ones dwell?" the Pilgrims would ask after making it through every Mountain pass. Finally they arrived. Right away, they inquired if anyone knew the Man of Wisdom who came to settle in their midst.

Some would reply, "Yes, we know of him. He used to live here," yet others were not sure who such a person could be.

The Pilgrims grew confused. They went to the village Elder for advice.

"You had the pearl in your hand," he said to them. "Why did you throw it away, then grope around trying to finding it?"

SAMENESS

"Be careful of those who are quick to point out your inconsistencies and question your motives," spoke an Elder to a group of Seekers. "And be cautious of those who call you a fake or hypocrite."

"Why should we be particularly heedful of them?" asked one of the Seekers.

"They have expectations of you to be a certain way, and they do not understand that a Seeker's Journey would be rendered impotent by sameness. They think they are being helpful, when they are actually being self-serving. They will drain your energy."

"But what if they have a point?" asked another Seeker.

"What they don't understand is that The Way brings a mélange of seemingly irrational and contradictory awarenesses and experiences. Yet to the heart-of-hearts, there is no contradiction—only the unfolding Journey. Sameness and consistency are the Guides for those who have not yet found the rootedness in their hearts and the courage to venture out on the Frontier of Unknowing."

"Will you give us a simple guideline?"

"Truth lies in inconsistency and contradiction," replied the Elder. "Whenever you find two of the same, expect one to be a contradiction."

"Yet how can we tell that our naysayers are wrong and we are actually on our Journeys, rather than just imagining it is so?" asked a final Seeker.

"If a finger is pointed at you and it makes you seek the comfort of sameness," answered the Elder, "you are still a child, for that is what children do. If instead you take the pointed finger as confirmation that you are out on your Frontier, greeting the unknown and seeking the unique, you are truly a Seeker on your Journey." ➛

May
30

THE WISDOM OF IGNORANCE

Many Sages are reputed to possess endless Knowledge, and to have the ability to read the thoughts and feelings of others. There was once a Scholar who did not believe that any Sage had such powers—especially one who had not studied and memorized the Ancient Scriptures.

The Scholar set out to prove his claim. Going to visit a Sage who lived nearby, he challenged her to prove to him that knowing another's thoughts and feelings was possible.

"Better yet," replied the Sage, "I will help you prove it to yourself."

The Scholar agreed to the proposition.

"Let us go and stand beside the village gate," said the Sage, "where I will have you read the thoughts and feelings of each person who passes by."

The Scholar stood there with the Sage's hand on his shoulder. The first person to pass by was a Nun, and the Sage whispered, "She is going to meet her secret lover in the Woods," and with the next person, "That boy will soon be beaten black and blue by his father," and with the next, "That man carries tremendous responsibility, and he must succeed, or the livelihood of many struggling families will be jeopardized."

After a few more people, the Scholar tore himself away and collapsed to the ground, sobbing. "I have seen too much," he wailed. "It is driving me insane! No wonder you say so little of what you know and refuse to know all that you could. I have always held Knowledge as the ultimate goal, and now I see that there is much that is best for one person not to know." ⤳

31

THE SAGE OF SAGES

He is a Master, thought a group of Seekers of the Elder with whom they were studying. They had never met anyone like him: in all circumstances he could maintain his centeredness and see the Truth behind the illusion.

"We want to tell people about you," said the Seekers. "Others should have the opportunity to learn by your example and come to you for Guidance, for you are the rare White Eagle soaring overhead."

"You are gracious with your words," replied the Elder, "yet if you were to describe me as such to others, it would show that I could not be such a person. This would be even more the case if you were to allow others to describe me as such—and more so yet if I were to do the unspeakable and describe myself as such."

"Why so?"

"Those who aggrandize a person with whom they are associated are in actuality trying to aggrandize themselves. It is a sign of arrogance, which is a mask for fear. People choose fear to hide from vulnerability, and it is just that vulnerability that is needed in order to be a true Seeker."

"That," replied a Seeker, "raises the question of those who do the opposite, by turning against their Elder, demonizing him, and trying to turn others against him. What is their motivation?"

"It is the same," replied the Elder. There is no difference between aggrandizing and demonizing, or between those who do either, as both are attempting to elevate themselves by using their Elder. In both cases, the more arrogant the person, the more desperate he is to keep from feeling vulnerable. And the farther away he drifts from knowing Truth." ᷎

THE MEETING

A Nun on her Journey to find herself came to a River. It was too deep and wide for her to cross on her own, so it was fortunate that a fisherman came by and offered to take her across.

Around mid-River, she noticed something floating toward them. When it got closer, she saw that it was a dead body—her dead body.

She immediately turned white, tore at her hair, and thrashed about at the bottom of the boat in a fit of sobbing and moaning.

As quickly as she was overcome, she grew still. "Row on," she said to the fisherman as she sat up and regained composure. "With what I have just seen, I have been given new eyes for what matters on my Journey."

June
2

NO EFFORT

A Sage once dedicated himself to drawing an image that would inspire Seekers to listen deeply to their dreams.

One Seeker was very critical. Every time she came to visit the Sage, she would tell him that the image he was working on was doing nothing for her. The Sage would set the drawing aside, take out another piece of paper, and begin anew.

After the Sage progressed a bit on the new image, the Seeker would look at it and say, "What you have there looks worse than the last one."

This went on until the Sage was down to his last piece of paper. Right then, the Seeker went out to take a quick break.

Laying the paper before him, the Sage centered himself and relaxed into his flow. The pen drifted effortlessly over the paper.

"That is incredible!" exclaimed the Seeker when she returned.

3

QUIET STRENGTH

A Seeker liked to tell anyone who would listen about what he was learning and how he was growing.

Once when he was relating such matters to an Elder, she replied, "The showy flower soon withers and dies."

The Seeker quit talking immediately. After a moment, he quietly asked, "What do you mean by that, Revered Elder? Should I not be proud of what I am learning? Should I not be proud that I am growing? Should I not show humility for what I receive?"

"When humility is overtly shown, it is actually pride in disguise. The placid flower in the shade needs no perfume to be noticed."

"Then what is left for me to do?" asked the Seeker.

"Public display and recognition only foster the illusion of growth," answered the Elder. "Showy flowers get passed up all day along the Path, whereas those tucked away in the glen are sought after for their rarity and for the inspiring nooks in which they dwell."

June
4

THE WAY TO AWAKENING

When a Seeker gains a certain amount of Knowledge, she often stagnates. Such was the case with a young woman when her Elder said, "It is time for you to leave. Say nothing of your Journey as a Seeker. Gain an amount of wealth, then come back to me."

"How can I do that?" asked the Seeker. "It contradicts my vow of poverty and my dedication to the Quest for Knowledge."

"You have just shown that you are not ready to fulfill your vow of poverty, which must ultimately be poverty of spirit. You say you want to *Quest* for Knowledge, which tells me you want to follow your own Path. Doing that, rather than being open to the Path that unfolds before you, will keep you from accepting whatever comes."

"I think I understand," responded the Seeker, "yet how is gaining wealth any different?"

"It is not the gaining of wealth that is important, but the acceptance of the Path. Only by following the Path of Wealth, which is actually the Path you have chosen for now, will you be able to find that it is gut-wrenching. And only then will you be able to recognize and follow the Path that is intended for you." ∿•

June
5

WHAT IS, IS

"The thought-mind," said the Ascetic, "continually searches for differences and distinctions, and it is not satisfied until it finds them."

"How is that so?" asked a youth.

"If I gave you two bowls of rice for one meal and four for the next meal, would you be satisfied?"

"Probably not," the youth reflected. "I would want more for my first meal."

"What if I gave you three bowls of rice for each meal?"

"I would be more satisfied."

"This is because the mind is appeased," explained the Ascetic, "even though either way you get six bowls of rice."

June

6

RENUNCIATION

A woman saw a Monk in the market who appeared to make no particular effort to abandon the ways of the world. She said to him, "It seems out of character for someone of your calling to be here engaged in the material affairs of common people, yet I wish to make no judgment. Will you please explain to me why you are doing this?"

"You are a kind woman," replied the Monk. "In actuality, what you see me doing is what I am not doing."

"How is that?" asked the woman.

"By being engaged in material life, I am not glorifying it. Rather, I am showing how superficial it is."

"Now I am even more lost, so I must ask you again to explain."

"Of course. My actions appear to be a contradiction, yet I will show you how they are the ultimate clarity. If I were to renounce the material world, that would make it important to me, as I would constantly be giving it attention by working to *not* give it attention."

The woman thought about this for a moment. "Now I see!" she exclaimed. "If you were to renounce this world, you would manifest the appearance of having no worldly attachment while inwardly you would need to keep working to maintain that outward appearance."

"That is correct," responded the Monk, "The Fish drifting with the current needs to put up no struggle to resist it. Therefore, she is free to apply her attention and energy to other matters."

"I bow to you, oh Wise One," said the woman. "May I always have the clarity to look at the unseen side of things, so that I may truly see them."

WHEN I HAVE ARRIVED

A Monk, returned from a time away, went to visit the Prophet who inspired him when he was fresh to his Journey. "Prudent Seer," he began, "I have gained much: I have studied with Fools and Wise Ones alike, and I have become Awakened. What is there for me now?"

"When it appears that we have attained something, my grandson," said the Prophet, "it is good to look down and realize that we have crawled out to the end of a high, brittle branch."

"How can that be?" said the Monk after a moment. "I thought my studies and my Awakening did the opposite and helped me connect to the stalwart trunk of the Tree."

"That is the reality of the mind. A Bird feels good as she soars above the flock only because she does not realize that she is alone and drawing the eyes of a Falcon."

"So should I not have achieved what I did?" asked the Monk.

"Achievement is separation. It is growth that brings expansion."

"Even after all my time with the Conscious Ones of many lands, I still did not have the eye to see what you have just illuminated. Instead, I blindly clung to the branch of accumulated Knowledge, fearing that if I jumped I would kill myself. I deluded myself into thinking that by venturing farther and farther out on the branch, I would find the All-Seeing Eye. Yet all I found was more blindness."

"Do you see how you deluded yourself?" asked the Prophet.

"It was *we* who deluded ourselves, oh clear Seer," answered the Monk. "My fellow Seekers and I were the blind following the blind. Masking our fear of the Mindless Mind, we made it appear as though we were walking The Way. I bow to you for restoring my sight." ~•

June
8

THE DOORWAY

"Whatever you do or whatever you are," said the Elder, "does not make sense—it makes you."

"I do not understand what that means," replied the Seeker.

"That is just what I'm talking about. Whenever I say 'I do not understand,' or 'You do not understand,' it is unlikely that I will hear the Truth behind the words."

"Why is that?" asked the Seeker.

"Because I am forced to rephrase what I said, or the person who is speaking to me is forced to rephrase what she said. The rephrasing distances the words from the Truth. It may draw the listener closer to understanding *something*, yet that something is not entirely what was first intended."

"Then what am I to do?"

"Listen," said the Elder.

After a long silence, the Elder told this story: "Several friends were preparing a meal, and they invited a number of other friends to join them for the evening. Before the food was ready, one of the guests came into the kitchen with her bowl.

"'Why are you here?' asked one of the cooks. 'The meal has not yet been announced.' The woman then went to sit down and wait for the announcement.

"I do not understand the story," the Seeker immediately stated.

"Listen," said the Elder. ➴

June
9

REALITY IS CREATED

A man was haunted with the question of what happens after death. He went to see a Hermit who was reputed to have the answers to all things. If that is so, reasoned the man, he surely knows whether a paradise or an inferno awaits us.

The man was so excited when he came upon the Hermit sitting under a Tree in front of his hut that he blurted out the question before properly introducing himself.

"May I ask who you are and the nature of your profession?" asked the Hermit.

"I am a confused wanderer, and I make my living as a stonemason."

"I'm glad you didn't build *my* chimney. Look at your spindly fingers—they're more suitable for knitting. And you have the physique of an undeveloped boy. How could you possibly set decent-sized stones, unless you have a *real* man working with you? Oh, I have made an assumption: I bet you build play fireplaces for kids."

"You are an impostor!" the stonemason screamed. "A mad man! I'll show you what these hands can do—I'm going to beat you silly!"

As the man raised his fist to strike, the Hermit looked up and said, "You have just created the Inferno."

The man's fist froze in midair. He gently lowered it, took a breath, and sat down before the Hermit.

The Hermit calmly watched him and said, "And now you have found Paradise."

10

THE TEST

A man wanted to become a Seeker and study with a Sage.

"It is not possible," stated the Sage, "until you overcome your inability to listen."

"But I take care of what is needed," protested the man. "I listen to my family's needs, and the needs of the village, and the needs of the poor."

"That is exactly the problem. You are heedful. You, like many, confuse that with listening."

"I do not understand your riddle, so perhaps I *am* unsuitable for being a Seeker."

"On the contrary," said the Sage. "What is important for a Seeker of The Way is to engage in the Quest with awareness rather than argument. If you are willing to take a test, I will show you that what you see as your ability to listen is actually a demonstration of your inability."

"I would be glad to take the test and prove you wrong," responded the man.

"Perhaps you will. After everything I speak, all you have to say is, 'I acknowledge that.'"

"I understand. That should be easy enough."

"I have the strength of a Horse," said the Sage.

"I acknowledge that," replied the man.

"Regular people are starved for Knowledge, yet Sages have so much that they have to hold back."

"I acknowledge that."

continued on page 198

continued from page 197

"I come from another world."

"I acknowledge that."

"I cannot be trusted."

"I acknowledge that."

"I was there to witness your birth."

"I acknowledge that."

"I remember when your mother was a prostitute."

"You do not—she never was!"

Shaking his head, the Sage said, "To hear only what is agreeable to us is not listening, any more than good deeds are proof that we are serving our people. Right now you are un-teachable, and to study with me in this state would make you even more so. You would get more and more angry with me and close yourself off from what little ability you do have to hear."

June
11

THE REAL HEART OF REVENGE

A man fell in love with a married woman. Her husband found out and attempted to kill the man, only he got the upper hand and killed the husband. The two lovers immediately fled to a faraway province where they were not known.

Rather than a fairytale ending, the man lived in misery with the woman. She was greedy and demanded that he toil incessantly to meet her demands. One night, he stole off for a distant land.

Once he arrived, he came to an Awakening. "I must not go on like this," he swore to himself, "for no matter what I do, I keep creating the same scenario. Instead of continuing to serve myself, I must relearn how to serve others."

Nearby was a section of road that clung tenaciously to the side of a cliff. Over the years, many people perished by sliding off the road and being dashed on the rocks below.

"I will dig a tunnel through the Mountain," he declared to himself, "so that the people of this valley can have safe passage."

After beginning the work, he realized it was going to take him twenty years. Still, he never wavered.

In the meantime, the son of the man he killed had grown up and resolved to avenge his father's death. After years of searching, the son finally tracked down his father's killer and confronted him in the half-finished tunnel.

"My life is yours," stated the man, "for I have taken your father's. Yet before you act, I respectfully ask for one thing: that you allow me to finish my task, which is for the people of this valley." The son consented.

Several months passed and the son grew impatient, so he decided to help with the digging. After a year of hard labor, the two of them completed the tunnel.

"Now the people can travel safely to and from their valley," the man stated. "My work is completed; you may kill me."

"How can I kill my Revered Teacher?" asked the son, as tears trickled down his cheeks. ᔓ

 *June* 12

IT'S YOU, NOT ME

Four Seekers had committed themselves to ten days of silence, in order to get accustomed to hearing the voice beyond words. By the seventh day, they were getting irritated with each other. Without being able to verbally coordinate things, one ended up doing all the cooking, another took out all the garbage, and so on.

That evening while they were all sitting and reflecting, the candle burned out.

"I have replaced the candle every night, and I wish someone else would do it," blurted out one of the Seekers.

"I thought this was to be a time of silence," said another.

"Now you two have gone and spoiled it," added a third.

"That's too bad," commented the fourth. "Yet all is not lost, as I am the only one who hasn't talked." ～

June
13

PHANTOM TRUTH

"What about those who oppose Truth?" asked a Seeker. "Are they not the enemies of Truth? Are they not a threat to those of us who cherish Truth?"

"That is but an illusion," replied the Sage, "for resistance and acceptance are one and the same. Those who resist Truth may one day accept it, and those who accept it may one day resist it."

"That confuses me," said the Seeker. "Why would those who are accepting of Truth one day resist it?"

"Because they are not Questing for it—they think they already have it. Truth cannot be found in the hand, nor can it be held. The only place Truth exists is on the journey to its discovery."

June
14

BENEATH CONFIDENCE

An aged woman was so highly regarded throughout the land that Sages from far-off places would come to her for Guidance, or just for the privilege of spending time in her presence. A young Seeker asked his Sage if he could accompany her on her Journey to spend some time with this Renowned One.

"You may," she replied, "yet I advise against it."

"But why?"

"Words would not suffice."

After a brief consideration, the Seeker declared, "Then I shall come."

On the way home from their visit with the Wise One, the Seeker said, "I do not understand what people see in her. I expected the commanding presence of a self-assured Master, and here it seemed as though she could not make up her mind. What she said often had no merit, and sometimes it even seemed banal. She also contradicted herself."

"I see that you noticed her great powers," replied the Sage. "She has the uncanny ability to reflect back to each of us who and how we are. Her sense of presence shows us what it is truly like to live by listening, being as a question, and respecting all Truths." ➤

June
15

AN EMPTY POCKET OF GOLD

A Seeker was starving. No matter what she did, she could not find enough to eat. However, it wasn't food she craved, but rather the Way to Awakening. She went to an Elder Monk with her dilemma.

"You already have the seeds of your Awakening," replied the Monk. "Why is it that you keep craving more?"

"If that is true," said the Seeker, "I do not see the seeds. Where do I find them?"

"You have just done so, for your seeds are in your question, and now they are only waiting to sprout."

June
16

THE SOUL OF SOUND

One day while walking down a shaded trail, we met the Monk who lived in a hut deep in the Forest. We asked him for one of his stories, and this is the one he gave us:

"When I was a young Seeker like you, I would pester anyone who I considered wiser than me with questions. I was insatiable—overcome with a driving hunger to know what they knew. One day I met a wandering Nun. She must have seen me coming, because before I could ask her anything, she asked me to describe the sound made by one hand clapping.

"I had no reply. I bowed to her and walked off alone, mesmerized by the question.

"After I built a little hut in the Woods—the one in which I still live—I sat and pondered. I walked the Forest trails, lost in reflection, and I sought the answer even in my dreams. Was it the rattle of leaves rustling in the wind? Maybe it was the call of a quiet voice. With each new answer I got excited, thinking I really had it, only to sink into despair when the next answer sounded better.

"Four years passed, and one afternoon I was lying in a sun-lit Meadow, thinking about nothing in particular—not even the question, surprisingly. An awareness then passed over me like a chill cloud over the sun: the sound of one hand clapping is the sound between my words; it is the sound of a Bird's wings at rest; it is the sound of water in a puddle.

"I knew I now had the answer, so I left to tell the Nun. For four years I traveled the byways of the land in search of her. Many people had seen her, yet no one could tell me exactly where she was headed.

"One despairing day, I decided that my quest to find her was in vain, so I turned around to go back to my hut.

"And there she stood, in the middle of the road around the next bend. With tears tracing their way over my cheeks, I knelt before her and could not speak. She smiled, touched me on the head, and wandered on.

"I came back to my hut, never knowing if I had the right answer. Yet instead of continuing to haunt me, the question began to enchant me, as it does to this day." ✍

June
17

THE HAMMER

In another time, there was a Seeker who wandered the countryside, looking to gain Knowledge through experience. Everywhere she went, she sought out the Wise Ones and practiced what they taught. Her all-consuming goal was to transcend the boundaries of everyday life.

One day, she stood before the cave of a renowned Hermit-Sage. At his invitation, she stepped inside and saw that he was sitting before a large, glowing crystal. She sat opposite him and was soon mesmerized by the crystal's glittering facets. Looking deeply into them, she saw things beyond what she could have ever dreamed.

"It will not be enough for me to sit here and observe," she lamented to the Hermit. "Somehow I must find a way to experience what I see."

"Then walk on in," responded the Hermit.

The young woman reached her hand into the crystal, then her foot, then her whole body. And there she was, in the middle of the splendid scenes she could only witness a moment ago.

After a time, she stepped back out of the crystal world. Speaking not a word, the Sage offered her a hammer.

She shattered the crystal, bowed, and walked away. ▬

June
18

THE NEW IN THE OLD

A woodworker's assistant grew tired of toiling for his Master, for all he did was fetch materials and apply finishing touches. One day he decided to leave and see if he could better himself somewhere else.

On a rural road, he happened upon a Monk who was sitting beside a Stream. "What is your destination?" asked the Monk.

"I am a woodworker's assistant," the man replied, "and I seek opportunity for myself."

"What a coincidence," responded the Monk, "for in the last village I came through, I met a woodworker—a craftsman of some repute, I might add—who was looking for an assistant. If you proved worthy, I am sure working with him would advance your career."

The man thanked the Monk and continued down the road. He took the first fork, so that he would bypass the village and not be tempted to take the assistant's position.

The next day, he came to a tiny village nestled in picturesque Mountains. Every building and every piece of furniture radiated with attention to detail.

"I am looking for a place to settle," he told an innkeeper, "and your town already feels like home to me. However, this community is very small, and I doubt that you could provide much opportunity for an outsider."

"It is true that there is little place here for someone new," replied the innkeeper. "The only need we have is for a Master Woodworker. Ours has served us well, which you can see from everything that surrounds us. Only his eyes have grown weak with his advancing years, and he finds it harder and harder to keep up with repairs, much less to create the new items that we need."

"Well, I just happen to be a Master Woodworker," said the man. "I have been procuring the right woods and giving them the finishes that bring out their true natures for almost as many years as I am old. I can now take a piece of wood and see within it the item that it is intended to be."

Sure enough, the very first piece of furniture that the man created brought the admiration of every villager. Before long, his reputation for excellence spread to the neighboring villages, and he became a cherished member of the community. There is no way to turn a rotting carcass into fresh meat, yet this man showed that it is possible for succulent roasts and tender ribs to be found beneath a scarred and flea-bitten hide. ~☞

June
19

WHAT MATTERS

A large boulder tore loose and rolled down a steep bank, trapping a woman under it. She lay there for a long time before someone came by.

Late in the afternoon, a traveling Minstrel came by, yet there was nothing he could do. The boulder was much too heavy for him to even imagine moving it, and he was alone and far from help.

Both he and the woman soon came to realize that she was going to die. Even if help came soon, she was too mangled to survive.

"Are you in pain?" asked the Minstrel.

The woman lay quiet for a moment, then said, "Why don't you ask the boulder if it is sitting on top of me? If wondering whether or not I am in pain is your concern, please be on your way, and I will be on mine."

 *June*
20

ONLY ACTIONS SPEAK

Even though it was a hot, sticky day, a section of washed-out trail needed to be repaired. A trail builder and three helpers climbed the hill rising from the trail to get the rock they needed.

The dry clay soil made it hard to extract the stones, which quickly convinced the workers that they needed picks and shovels.

Who was going to go down the hill to get them? The eldest helper looked at the younger ones, as if to say, "I have earned my place by serving; now it is your turn."

"I carried up the drinking water," said the youngest.

"It was a hard climb for me and I am exhausted," moaned the other helper.

After going back and forth another time or two, they turned to the trail builder to ask him who should get the tools.

"Where did he go?" exclaimed one of the helpers as he searched in every direction. He quickly spotted the trail builder, who was nearly all the way back up the hill with the tools. ⤳

June
21

THE STRICT TEACHING

Like most Seekers, this young woman from our village had a burning desire to become Awakened.

"Go and visit the Elder in the next village," counseled a friend, "and she will guide you."

After the Seeker introduced herself and stated her goal, the Elder replied, "Your dedication is admirable; I would consider it an honor to guide you. Here are my words: to become Awakened, go home and be kind to your family."

The Seeker waited for additional Guidance, but no more was spoken. She could not believe what she was told, as she had expected an arduous regimen of instruction in the Ancient Wisdoms. Still, she had no choice but to take her disappointment home with her.

A year passed. She returned to the Elder, stating that she had taken pains to be extra kind to her family, yet she had not Awakened. "Might there be some further Guidance that would help me?" she asked.

"I see your dilemma," replied the Elder, "and I will give you the additional training and direction you need. Do this and you will become Awakened: return to your family and treat them with kindness."

Four times she returned to the Elder, and four times she was sent back home with the same Guidance.

One day, the Seeker woke up and cried, "I've had enough of this!" She marched down the trail to the Elder's village, stood defiantly before her, and said, "I have dedicated myself to the Quest, I have come to you with humility and sincerity, and all you have done is given me the same simple directive, over and over, that I already knew and was already doing. I will not be coming back—I am through!"

With a benevolent smile, the Elder replied, "I see that I have made your Quest too hard for you." ━

June
22

EXPLAIN THE UNEXPLAINABLE

"I seem to have lost my bearings," lamented a Seeker. "I grow confused with all of these terms that we use, like *Mindless Mind, Thinking without Thought, Nirvana,* and *Enlightenment.* My head is spinning, Aware Elder-Nun. Will you bring it some clarity?"

"All these terms," replied the Nun, "are nothing but stakes for tying Goats. If they hold you down, ignore them. After all, the language of The Way is wordless."

"Yet these words must be meaningful, or they would not be used."

"They mean nothing to the Birds in the Sky."

"Then what *does* mean something?" asked the Seeker.

"Going there," responded the Nun.

"Where? How?"

"Who knows? You can't fall into it and you can't fall out of it."

"Now I am more confused than ever!" exclaimed the Seeker. "My head is not only spinning—it's throbbing."

"That's perfect! Now, have your ego loose its hold on you, so that you can fall into The Void and become its crystalline Truth."

"Then what?"

"Then nothing. Only the Fool thrashes around and tangles himself up. A regular Fool is still attached to the world, which is why he panics and grabs at anything to keep from falling. A Great Fool does nothing to help himself; in doing so, he risks everything. He dies in every moment, so he never knows what the next moment will bring. In this way, he opens himself to any possibility."

"How will I know when one of those possibilities is my Awakening?" asked the Seeker.

"Whenever a voice inside you says, 'I am Awakened,' it is not so."

"Then, when is it so?"

"Remember the Birds of the Air," answered the Nun. "They are not staked to the word *Awaken,* nor do they sing, 'I am Awakened! I am Awakened!' They are Great Fools; they do nothing. They think without thought and die in every moment. Be as them." ➤

June
23

HOW WE KILL

A group of Seekers who were studying together came to the conclusion that it is good to show concern for life by not killing. Even insects deserve to live.

At the same time, they feared they might be getting too extreme. They knew from their studies that the farther we venture out ahead of ourselves, the more we risk mental and emotional instability.

The Seekers decided to consult with someone who had already walked the Path they were laying out. They found a Hermit who for many, many years had been living with a deep regard for all life.

He graciously received the Seekers and told them how glad he was to hear about their newfound sensitivity to those who many consider to be lesser beings. This made the Seekers feel pretty good about themselves, and they swelled with pride.

Then one of the Seekers said, "Wizard-Hermit, I believe you have just cleverly showed us that when someone feels clear and self-righteous, it means that he has put on blinders."

"An astute Seeker you are. I made you feel proud, so that you might wake up and see beyond where your minds have taken you."

"But what more can there be? We have already decided to extend our regard to all living creatures."

"Where else does life exist, other than outside yourselves?" asked the Hermit.

The answer was obvious, and the Seekers chided themselves for being so obtuse.

"I will give you just a few examples," continued the Hermit, "then leave it up to you to explore how you can honor your vast inner world of life. Think about how we kill time, and the havoc we wreak by judging and criticizing, and how we deaden the spirit of children by forcing them to do our bidding. This is the real world, fellow Seekers. This is our Frontier, for it is through the window of our inner world that we see the outer world."

June
24

ALL IS TRUTH

A Nun grew very bitter over being continually lied to and cheated. Even her dreams were haunted by frustration and anger. "I can't live this way any longer," she told herself. "I must find Guidance."

She went to an Elder, who asked her to sit down, then he poured her a cup of tea.

"Would you like a piece of Goat sausage with your tea?"

"I truly would," replied the Nun. "It was a long walk to get here this morning, and I am hungry." The Elder served her from a cutting board. "This is the best Goat's sausage I've ever had," commented the Nun. "Did you make it yourself?"

"I did, only it is not Goat. A Dog killed my Cat, then a Bear came along and killed the Dog. So I made the sausage out of the Cat and the Dog."

"You lied to me!" cried the Nun.

"Did I?" asked the Elder. "When I told you it was Goat sausage, was it not Goat sausage?"

"Well…yes, it was—then."

"And when you tasted it, was it not Goat sausage?"

"Hmm…it was"

"Then what changed it: your reality or mine?"

"It was your reality, which I took on."

"Now what if I told you that I was just joking and the sausage was actually made from Goat? Would you again deny your reality to take on mine?"

The Nun bowed to the Elder and continued to enjoy her sausage. 🐾

June
25

APPEARANCES

"You are the Teacher I have been yearning for," began a Seeker to a learned Sage. "I respectfully ask that I be allowed to learn from you."

"How do you know that I am that Teacher you desire?" asked the Sage in return. "And why do you think I have anything of value to share with you?"

"It screams out to me!" exclaimed the Seeker.

"I ask that you be specific. Our land is rich with Wise Ones; why would you not go to another instead?"

"I have. It seems that all my life I have been going to others, and none of them have been as kind as you, nor have they shown such openness or presence."

"Oh, what wistful beings we are," replied the Sage with a heavy voice. "So easily does sacred ground become scorched."

The Seeker felt a chill go up her spine. She sat there uneasily, waiting to see if the Sage would speak any further words.

After a moment, the Sage continued: "The marks of character that you see in me are found in some of the most wicked people. If we were all to judge people by their outward dispositions, many common criminals would become Ascended Masters, and numbers of our Wise Ones would end up as no more than lechers and exploiters." 〜

June
26

THE DOORWAY OF DESIRE

There was a Monk who was plagued with passions he could not control. Even more so, he did not know if he *should* control them. Concerned about being distracted from his Journey, he went to talk with a Monk who was already attuned to the dance with desire.

"You have come to speak of yearning," stated the elder Monk, "yet what I hear is fear."

"How can that be? Fear and desire can hardly be confused. They are two very different emotions."

"To experience what I am saying," answered the elder Monk, "freeze your desire in its tracks the next time it comes up, and see what that leaves you."

A few days went by. "I have done what you suggested," stated the younger Monk the next time they met, "and you were right—there stood my fear, unmasked."

"Now we can look at desire without confusing it with fear."

"I see that. When I stood there alone with my desire, I no longer felt a compulsion to judge it. I then wondered if my desire could, in some way, contribute to my Awakening Journey."

"It already has!" stated the elder Monk. "You only need to become consciously aware of it. When you first feel desire mount, embrace it with your full presence, so that you will know it as you."

"What if the desire becomes extreme?"

"There is your opportunity to practice remaining centered."

"How do I do that," asked the younger Monk. "It is so easy to lose myself to the desire. It is as though I forget that I am there."

"Ah, what a treasure! At those times, you stand at the doorway of what desire offers. The space between the onset of desire and knowing where the desire will lead you is where the sublime beauty of desire can be found. Dwell there, without being consumed by either the desire or its fulfillment. It is there that we dance on the edge of expectation and ecstasy, and it is there that we are fully alive." ➳

June
27

SEEKING PERFECTION

Late one afternoon, a group of Seekers were having tea and discussing how they might improve as Seekers. They decided to ask for input from a revered Elder with whom they studied.

"This is a question that needs no answer," she replied, "for everyone is a natural Seeker with innate capabilities. For this reason, I do not turn anyone away who comes to me. Yet few remain. Some do not make it up the Path to my hut, even though they have been invited."

"That makes no sense," stated one of the Seekers. "It seems to be a contradiction that they are invited yet cannot negotiate such a well-worn Path."

"It is because they turn themselves away. There are two shortcomings that plague most Seekers, and they are not innate behaviors—they are born of fear."

"What are they, so that we may avoid them?" asked another Seeker.

"If only it were that easy! Yet I will tell you, because it will help answer your next question. Most Seekers will not accept silence for an answer, and will instead read an answer into it. Secondly, they want to eat more than they are capable of digesting at the moment."

"Then what are we to do with the passion to learn?" asked the first Seeker.

"Passion has nothing to do with learning—at best it gets in the way. Be centered and be fully awake, and you may learn something. A kinked-up Snake cannot crawl through a hole, no matter how hard she tries. She must relax and straighten herself."

"I think I understand," said another Seeker. "It is not the wanting that is important, but the ability."

"That is so," added the Elder. "Potential means nothing without the tools to realize it." ❧

June
28

OUT OF BLINDNESS

A Sage once found it beneficial for a Seeker who was studying with him to leave.

"That must have been a hard thing for you to ask him to do," commented another Seeker to the Elder.

"My part in it is of no matter," replied the Elder, "when it is the wisest thing to do. Sometimes it is the best way to give support. And to test."

"I see. But what if he turns against you?"

"That would be his ego reacting to my request for him to leave, and that too is of no matter, as long as he gains distance and perspective. Then perhaps the mental fog that brought about his needing to leave will lift."

"And what if he forgives you?"

"That will give him the opportunity to recognize that he has assumed moral superiority."

"If he comes to these awarenesses, what then?" asked the Seeker.

"The awarenesses will have already been there," responded the Sage. He has merely come out of blindness—and our relationship will go on as though he never left. This will be so because he realizes that what was asked to leave was not him but rather his pride."

June
29

OUR DIFFERENCES

"Look at how different we all are," stated a potter at an informal gathering of craftspeople in the market square. "Some of us are kind, and some of us are cruel; some of us are accepting, while others are blaming."

"There are the intelligent and the slow," said another. "And the strong and the weak."

"All of that is true," said a woman, "yet let us remember the thought-based mind's habit of taking us out on a limb, where we forget the trunk."

"Yet these differences do exist," injected another woman. "A killer would have a very different effect on me than a Healer."

"Effects change like the weather," noted someone else, "and perhaps that is why the thought-based mind is so focused on differences. It helps with everyday existence, where there is constant change."

"Let us look, then, at the cause of our actions, rather than their effect," suggested someone. "Perhaps that would be a more accurate way of determining whether or not we are alike."

The group nodded in agreement.

"Where effect is surface and apparent," the person continued, "cause lies deeper, in the thinking-without-thought mind. How do our differences and similarities look from there?"

"We all have thirst, which gives us the same cause to drink."

"Perhaps, then," added another, "all of our basic needs and yearnings are the same."

"And in the ultimate, we all die," stated another. "Whether in our youth or as Elders, we all meet the same end. If we don't recognize our sameness before that, we sure do then!"

"What is that sameness?" wondered a man.

"Maggots," quipped someone, and they all laughed.

"Wait, let us take her seriously—she might have something there. Maggots do not judge or discriminate; we are all the same to them."

"And after the Maggots," added another, "what are we all but a pile of bones? Then we can no longer tell one person from another."

Feeling satisfied, they all bowed to each other. ➷

June
30

HOW TO GIVE

"What should I give of myself?" asked a Monk.

"All that can be received," replied the Sage.

"How am I to know that?"

"People tell us all the time. What would you give to an orphaned child?"

"I would give her everything I could to help her feel provided for and welcomed."

"What would you share with a gardener?"

"All that I knew about gardening."

"How about a minstrel?"

"I would share songs with him."

"And what if you came across a stranger on the road?"

"I would be careful with what I share, lest he take more than I feel safe giving."

"That is how we give and do not give to ourselves," spoke the Sage. "And that is how we remain strangers to ourselves. We come to know the boundaries of our mind but not the vastness of our heart."

 *July* 1

ONE PRECIOUS DROP

A Nun was visiting an Elder who lived in a cabin overlooking a little woodland Stream. "Would you please fetch us some water for the evening meal?" the Elder asked.

The Nun was glad to oblige, as the short walk under the high pines was so uplifting.

She returned with a pitcher of cool, clear, water, and poured them each a big cupful. There was a drop left in the pitcher, which she dumped out before returning the pitcher to its place on the shelf.

"What is more precious," the Elder asked of her, "the water in the two glasses that you thoughtfully poured for us, or the drop that you absentmindedly dumped from the pitcher?"

"Right away I am suspect of my first impression," responded the Nun, "as I know that the opposite of what seems clear and apparent is usually the Greater Truth. Before you asked, I would have given more value to our two cupfuls of water than to the tiny bit I discarded. Now, thoughtful Elder of mine, you have me wondering what Knowledge I can gain from my casting away the drop."

"As you have surmised, dear Nun, what is of deep value has little or nothing to do with what garners our attention. In this case, it is not about the water, but about sense of presence. I watched when you poured our cups: you were present and conscientious. However, when you discarded the remaining dribble, your mind was elsewhere. I bet you would have hardly remembered doing it had I not reminded you."

"This is true," said the Nun after a moment's reflection.

"Well then, the last drop you poured is far more valuable than all the rest. It is your Teacher, beckoning you to be present and engaged in every breath." ➤

July
2

NEVER ENOUGH

A Bear was once catching Salmon who were on their spawning run up a shallow River. He would grab one in his jaws, flip her up on the bank, then go for another. "I might as well get what I can while the getting is good," Bear said to himself. He nabbed another, and another, then another.

The cold water and rushing current eventually wore him down, and he figured he had enough Fish to last him a while. He ambled up to the bank to feast.

All he found atop the bank was one Fish. It turned out that every time he tossed one up onto on the bank, she would flop around and slide back into the water. The Bear let out a mad roar, then sat down to enjoy his Fish. ⟶

July
3

WHAT IS THE WAY?

The people of the fishing village realized that this might be their last day with the Prophet who lived in their midst, as he had finished preparing for his passing over. They all went to behold their beloved Seer for one last time.

"Do you have any last words of Guidance to leave with us?" they asked.

The Revered One was so feeble that he hardly had the strength to speak. So that he could be heard, he motioned for someone to come near.

They all looked in the direction of a respected Elderwoman. She stepped forward and bent over very close. The Prophet whispered in her ear, "The Way is like a River."

She rose, turned to those gathered around, and told them what he said.

Many began to murmur among themselves, "I don't understand…what is he saying…a River?"

The woman grew concerned that those who needed Guidance the most would not be able to benefit from their Seer's final words. She turned back to him and said that there were some who did not understand.

With his last spark of energy, he made a feeble gesture for her to come close again. In a barely audible whisper he said, "The Way is not like a River."

July
4

WHEN NOT TO QUESTION

A woman came to the gate of a garden filled with lush fruit Trees, radiant flowers, and fragrant herbs. The Gatekeeper invited her to enter.

"How do I know this is not an illusion?" questioned the woman. "And how do you know that my intent was to come here and enter the garden?"

"I am known for the power of my mind," replied the Gatekeeper, "and I am dedicated to making my own decisions on my Journey of Discovery. Yet at your request, I will carefully consider what you have brought up, and I assume you will do the same."

While she was pondering, another woman came by and was invited to enter through the gate. She did so, and the gate was locked behind her. 〜

July
5

HOT AIR

One warm afternoon, several Seekers gathered under a Tree for a rest. A couple of them were quite full of themselves, and they soon got caught up in boasting about the awarenesses they had achieved.

One said to another, "I can walk on water. Let us go walk out on the pond and there we will share the great insights we have come to."

The other responded, "I have already done that many times and it bores me. Instead, why don't you come with me and fly into the Air. We will sit on the clouds and contemplate the greatest of Teachings."

A third Seeker, who had been listening to the conversation, commented to the first Seeker, "Your ability to ride on the water can be done by a Duck. To the second Seeker he said, "Any Stable Fly can rise through the Air. Do these abilities you claim not have more to do with the air that inflates your chests than the air that you might glide through? Are the Teachings not for seeking Truth, rather than pride?" ⇒

July
6

THE FALCON

While a Seeker made his way down a long, backcountry trail, a bedraggled Bird landed on a branch just ahead. She was a Falcon, yet the Seeker did not recognize her as such, as he had never before seen one.

"You poor thing," he said. "You have not kept yourself up. No wonder you look so tired and forlorn."

The Seeker approached the Bird, who was too exhausted to move, and clipped her sharp talons and hooked beak. He then trimmed her long wing and tail feathers.

He stepped back to assess his handiwork. "There you go!" he exclaimed. "Now you look like a Bird." ⌁

July
7

EXPOSED

A Monk burst into a conversation between a Seeker and a Sage. With a charged voice, he said, "See that woman over there? I was coming up the path behind your cottage, Honored Sage, and I saw her sneaking out the back door with something in her hand. I ducked behind a Tree and watched. When she turned around, I saw that she had your favorite teacup."

"Why are you telling this to me?" asked the Sage.

"My blood boiled when I saw what she was doing, so I ran over here right away to tell you before she got away with it."

The Sage took a breath, closed his eyes, and smiled. Then he turned to the Monk and said, "It appears that the woman has stolen something far more valuable than my teacup." ➤

July
8

PERHAPS

There is a story about a man who served his ruler well, so the ruler wanted to reward him with something meaningful. One morning the man, who had to walk wherever he went, woke up to a new carriage outside his door, pulled by a team of perfectly matched Horses.

"What a stroke of fortune!" his neighbors called out when they passed by. "You must feel like the luckiest man on earth."

"Perhaps," was the man's only reply.

A week or so later while taking his new carriage down a country lane, he met up with a man in an oxcart coming from the opposite direction. The oxcart swerved and drove the carriage off the road. It flipped over and tumbled down the steep embankment. The oxcart driver pulled the man out of the wreckage, laid him in the oxcart, and took him to a nearby inn, where he could stay until his broken bones were mended enough to make the trip home.

The next day when his friends heard of the accident, they came to visit him at the inn. "What an unfortunate soul you are," they said to him. "Of all things to befall you—especially after such a stroke of luck with getting the carriage." Even though he was in extreme pain, the man looked up into his friends' eyes, and with a slight smile replied, "Maybe."

A couple of days later, his friends came by again with news: "There was a heavy rain up on the Mountain, which triggered a mudslide in the middle of the night. It took your house, which went crashing into the rocks in the valley below. Aren't you lucky that you were here safe in bed?"

July
9

HE BREATHED THE SAME AIR

As is the tradition with some people, a group of Seekers served the best of the food to the Elder who was guiding them. They thought it made sense, as the Elder was frail and needed meals that were nutritious and easy to digest.

One day, the Elder quit eating. No matter what was brought to him, he refused it. Days went by, and the Seekers finally asked why he was fasting.

"Is the food you serve me the same that you eat?" he replied.

It didn't take long for the Seekers to realize what they had been doing, and they too stopped eating.

After they spent several days in quiet reflection, a meal was prepared. Elder and Seekers sat down together and ate the same food. ◆

July 10

PRAISE IS CURSING

A Seeker came to visit an Elder for the first time. Immediately the Seeker lavished praise upon her, for all of the insights and teaching stories that were said to have originated from her.

A Nun who was nearby overheard the Seeker's words. She came over, sat before the beloved Elderwoman, and straightaway tore into her about how all she could do was act beneficent and repeat stories that she had heard elsewhere.

Upon leaving, the new Seeker came upon an older Seeker and said, "I cannot believe what just happened! Yet the venerable Elder only smiled benignly at the Nun, even though she was so disrespectfully crude and demeaning."

"She knows it is the way it must be," replied the older Seeker, "for there is no difference between praise and criticism—one is just as distracting as the other. The Nun could not let one stand in your eyes without it being washed away by the other." ➤

July
11

A BEGGAR'S GIFT

"What does a Beggar have to give?" a Sage asked of a group of Seekers.

"Very little," replied one, "for that is why she is a Beggar."

"Is it possible that she has little to give because we perceive her as a Beggar?" The Seekers could only reply with confused looks.

"Let me illustrate. There was once a man who went to a Wizard and asked to be granted any wish. The Wizard consented, and the man's request was for a beautiful woman he admired to become his wife. And so it came to pass. They were married in a lavish ceremony, and everyone thought the life of his dreams lay before him. Yet the couple's first child was stillborn, and so was their second. After that, a mad Dog attacked the woman, scarring her face and tearing off one of her breasts."

"We do not understand the Teaching," complained several of the Seekers.

The Sage took pity on them and said, "Sometimes what one does not have to give is more the gift than what another *has* to give. What does it serve to label a person a Beggar or a Wizard if it causes us to spite one and value the other, thereby never knowing either for who she is?"

July
12

THE MEANING OF THINGS

A renowned Sage was once visited by four traveling Seekers, who each brought him a gift: an ornate serving dish, exotic dried fruit, rare essential oils, and an exquisite tapestry. After a short while, the Sage gave the dish and the dried fruit away, yet he kept the essential oils and tapestry.

"Why is that so?" the townspeople asked each other when they heard about the Sage's actions. "It must be that he did not find favor with the first two Seekers. Still, he wanted to be kind to them, so he waited until they left before disposing of their gifts. He must have held the third and fourth Seekers in high regard, as he not only accepted their gifts, but also kept them."

"That may appear to be the case," said someone close to the Sage who overheard the talk. "The truth is that our caring Sage gave the dish, piled high with the dried fruit, to a hungry traveler who came to his door. He used the essential oil to treat some leather of his that was drying out, and he spread the tapestry over his bed, as the autumn nights were getting cool."

July
13

SHADES OF TRUTH

"Esteemed Elder, I fear that your stories are too vague," complained a Seeker. "One person will take them one way, and the next person will take them another. Then we argue amongst ourselves, for we are desperate to find Real Truth."

"Is this the way of a cup?" asked the Elder. "How useful would it be if it gave you just milk, and not also tea and water and broth?"

"But isn't that where we get stuck?" asked the Seeker in response. "In our drive to find Truth, we end up with all the possible things that the cup could give us."

"It may appear that way, yet you are only trapping yourself by making an intellectual game of it. How many times have you gotten frustrated while going around and around with others about the many ways to interpret a story? Eliminating that process is one way to honor the many voices of the story, even though having only one would seem expedient."

"Oh, of course!" exclaimed the Seeker. "One person drinks water from the cup, and the next drinks milk, and another drinks juice, as that is the way when we are each given our own Truth."

"As with milk or juice," answered the Elder, "the test for Truth is not in the cup, but in whether its contents nurture."

July
14

CHARACTER

"What can be done to quickly determine a person's character?" asked a Seeker.

"I can tell you what I do," said the Elder, "and you can decide if it is right for you. I approach a person with humility."

"What does that show?"

"If it shows nothing, the person has integrity. If the person tries to take advantage of me or dominate, I beg my leave."

"What if the reverse happens and he values you highly for your humility?"

"Then I too would avoid that person. The difference between exploitation and exaltation is only registered by the ego."

"I bow to the Wisdom you carry, far-sighted Sage."

July
15

SINCERITY TEST

Unscrupulous people kept taking advantage of this particular Seeker. He went to his Elder and asked how to tell if a person was sincere and coming from his heart.

"Accuse him of being self-serving and unaware," replied the Elder.

"You must be kidding!" exclaimed the Seeker. "Wouldn't that incite him?"

"Only if he is of ill intent. If he does not grow angry, he is truly sincere and centered in his heart."

"Could I not yet be deceived by those who imagine themselves to be heart-centered?"

"They, young Seeker, expose themselves by defending the image they are trying to create."

July 16

MY NEMESIS

"I am petrified with fear every time I go out to the Stream," stated a Nun to the Sage who guided her. "I have a special place where I sit to reflect, and whenever I do, a great Crab with fierce pincers crawls out of the water and threatens me."

"I see," replied the Sage. "Have you tried moving to another spot?"

"Oh yes, Esteemed One. I thought I might have infringed on his territory, so I went upstream, and I went downstream, yet he always found me. I have decided that the next time I go to the Stream, I will take a long spike with me and jab him with it!"

The Sage thought for a moment, then said, "It makes sense that you would want to defend yourself, as the Crab appears to be harassing you. However instead of a spike, I suggest that you take a long stick with a charred end. When the Crab appears, streak the burnt end down his brow, then come back to see me."

As frightful as the idea was to the Nun, she trusted in her beloved Sage. The next time she went to the Stream to contemplate, she took a charred stick along. And sure enough, the Crab appeared.

Terrified as she was, she still pushed the tip of the stick into the Crab's face and marked his brow. She then threw the stick aside and dashed off to see the Sage.

As she approached, the Sage saw the dark streak on her brow. ━

July
17

QUAGMIRE

"I crave being around someone of Wisdom, so that I may learn by example," said a Seeker to her comrades.

"Go and spend some time with the Sage who lives alone in the Woods," suggested her friends.

The only person she could find in the area of the Sage's cabin was an obviously drunken man in the distance trying to make his way through a marsh.

"Be careful that you do not get mired in the muck," called out the Seeker.

The man replied, "Fear not, for it is only me who will go under. However, think of yourself in my place and all of the beliefs and unfulfilled expectations that you carry on your shoulders. Drunk as you perceive me to be, would you in your sober state not sink all the more quickly with the heavy burden you carry?"

July
18

DIFFERENT

Three Seekers could not agree with each other. They reasoned that it was because they were intrinsically different, so they could either agree to disagree or live in conflict.

The Sage who was guiding them overheard their discussion and asked if they would like to discover the Deeper Truth.

Each of them nodded. The Sage sent the one who was from a family of merchants to stay with a Goat herder. Another, who was a farmer, went to live with nobles in a castle. The third, a puppeteer, took up residence on a fishing boat.

After a while, the three met with the Sage and told her they were all miserable.

"How can this be," replied the Sage, "when you are so different from each other?"

"Honored One," the Seekers replied, "we have learned to root ourselves in the common ground beneath our differences."

July
19

IN ONE, FIND THE OTHER

A number of Seekers who were studying together under a Sage came to see her in the village where she lived. When they arrived at her little hut on the outskirts of the village, they were greeted by a Beggar.

"Your Master has moved to the Grand Villa along the River," he told the Seekers.

Sure enough, there they found her, sitting on a plush carpet and attended to by finely dressed servants. She bid her Seekers to sit down with her and partake of the wines and pastries that adorned the tables surrounding them.

With what respect they could muster, they parted as soon as they could. Immediately they went to a Sage in the next village, who lived on what he begged and slept in the loft of a Horse stable. They told him how disgusted they were with their former Guide. The Beggar-Sage could only weep.

"You must feel pity for her, because she has lost the Path," spoke one of the Seekers.

"Not for her," replied the Sage, "but for you. How quickly you are poisoned by what you see. And how flippantly you forsake your venerable Guide. She is surrounded by luxury because it means nothing to her; you are *not* surrounded by luxury because it means everything to you. Who knows where we will find her tomorrow, for she walks her Journey without judgment or exclusion."

"Then why are you here, smelling of Horse dung, rather than anywhere else?" asked the Seeker.

"You see me in this stable because you think I have chosen the simple life. In actuality, this means nothing to me. Tomorrow the King will invite me to his castle, and I will go because it means nothing to me. In this way, I will be able to plant Seeds of Awakening in the heart of someone who many would shun." ✦

July
20

THE SEE-THROUGH MIRROR

A quiet Monk, highly regarded by all, once said to a Seeker, "It is sad that I keep tripping myself with my own feet. When I find an opportunity to serve others, I keep telling myself that I cannot trust their motives."

To the Seeker, the Monk's comments seemed so contradictory to who he was. After a troubled night, she took her confusion to a Nun in another village and asked for her help.

"I ask you to listen to the Monk again," replied the Nun, "this time without categorizing."

"How would that help?"

"Perhaps then you will recognize that your confusion and discomfort were already there. If that is the case, you will see the Monk for the mirror he provides you."

The young woman bowed deeply and wept tears of joy.

July
21

LIKES AND DISLIKES

A Seeker went to visit a gardener who was also a Sage. He was known for the talks he gave on esoteric matters.

"I have heard you speak often," said the Seeker, "and I agree with much of what you say. At the same time, there is much that I disagree with. Some of your words make me angry, and some of your ideas I simply do not understand."

"I am but a gardener," said the Sage. "I grow turnips, cabbage, carrots, and many other vegetables, and I bring them to market. Some people like one vegetable and some people prefer another. There are things that some people do not like and even things that make some people sick. Yet what is common to vegetables is not that they are liked or disliked, but that they are all food."

The Seeker bowed to the Gardener.

July
22

CONTROL OR OBSERVE

"Sometimes I feel it is right to push things," stated a man, "and at other times I just want to sit and watch. What is the best way to be?"

"Both are virtuous approaches," replied the Fool. "And both of them stink like rotting flesh. The rot shows itself by the smell of *doubt* and *should*."

The man considered this. "If that is so, what can I do with the rotting flesh?"

"Leave it for the Maggots, as they have neither virtue nor vice—they are Awakened."

"That still does not tell me what to do, but rather what not to do. I can't live in a vacuum."

"Why not?" asked the Fool.

"I would then just do what comes naturally. I would not have any scruples or ideals. And what about social responsibility?"

"Do you want to keep walking your days like a Fly with a boulder strapped to his back?"

"All-seeing Fool, that is just what it feels like, and I truly no longer want it."

"Then be as the Fish who knows the Lake is big and knows how to get around, so he has no need to swim into the net." ➥

July
23

HERE IT IS

The fable of the Fruit of Endless Nourishment has been passed down from one spellbound person to another for generations. When a certain neophyte Nun heard the story, it consumed her. The Fruit of Endless Nourishment was all she could think or talk about. She knew she had to find it.

A Wizard was reputed to have the power to point to things unseen, so the Nun went to her.

"I know where the Fruit grows," said the Wizard, "and I can direct you to it. However, there is much between here and there that you need to know about in order to negotiate the distance. I will teach it to you."

"I cannot wait!" exclaimed the Nun. "I must find the Fruit now!"

"Be it as you wish. Only know that your Journey will be a turbulent one. In order to finally reach the Fruit, you must be clear and unwavering in your resolve."

The Nun went from Wizard to Wizard and from Hermit to Hermit, looking for any clue that would bring her closer to the Tree that bore the Fruit of Endless Nourishment. Thirty years passed, and finally she came to the grove where the Tree grew. There, sitting under the Tree, was the Wizard she visited at the start of her Quest all those years ago.

"Why did you not save me all this effort and travail?" fumed the Nun. "Why did you not tell me that *you* were the Guardian of the Fruit of Endless Nourishment?"

"You would not have believed me. You then had eyes for the Fruit, and not for Truth."

July 24

THE CONTINUUM

A man lay dying. His son, who kept vigil at his bedside, said to him, "Father, we are rebuilding the Horse stable, so that when you are feeling better, you can come out and enjoy the Horses again."

"What if I do not get better?" asked the Father.

"Then someone else will come to enjoy the Horses."

"And what if nobody accepts your invitation to come?"

"That is ridiculous, dear father. Now close your eyes and rest."

July
25

THE VALUE OF KNOWLEDGE

For all of his life, an ancient Sage recorded the Knowledge that he had gathered on his travels to distant lands. Transcribed were discussions with all of the Wise Ones he had met. One day a Scholar came to him and asked if he could copy the book.

"I would be honored to have you copy it," replied the Sage. "I will ask of you one hundred pieces of gold."

"And why is that?" retorted the Scholar. "When I leave, you will still have your journals. Besides, wouldn't you agree that Knowledge is not something to be bought or sold?"

"It is not the Knowledge that I ask you to consider, but the one hundred times one hundred gold pieces that I have spent in gathering the Knowledge, and for the one hundred years of my life that it took to bring it to you. Perhaps you have a more clear idea than me as to what that might be worth to you, yet that is of little matter to me."

"Why do you not consider the value I place on your work?"

"I am thinking of the struggling Seekers on their Quests for Knowledge," answered the Sage, "who for lack of means are not able to come and avail themselves of this Knowledge, as you are here to do. Your contribution will enable them to gain this Knowledge and spread it." ~

July
26

WHAT IS NOT, IS

On the way home from the village to his distant farm, a man sat in the shade of a beautiful house beside the road.

"You look tired," stated the servant who happened to be walking up from the back of the house. "Will you come in for some rest and refreshment?"

Surprised at the invitation, the man was yet glad to accept.

"Please partake of the bounty of food and drink that is laid here before you," stated the servant, "and I will go tell my Master that he has a guest."

A short while later, a kindly looking and well-dressed gentleman walked into the room and greeted the man with a smile and a warm handshake. "Please sit down and share the news of the road with me," he implored.

The traveler was so shocked at the sight of the house lord that he nearly spit out his food. *This is the same person,* he thought to himself, *who I have seen dressed in rags and begging in the village. He grovels for scraps of food in rubbish heaps, and he will take any work that no one else wants to do.*

"You look troubled," commented the elegant host. "Is there something I might be able to help with?"

"I am embarrassed to mention it," replied the guest, "yet speak I must. It seems that I know you from the village. I have given you bread on my way from the bakery, and you moved stones for me to build my garden wall at my farm. But I must surely be mistaken."

"Indeed, that was me," answered the host. "We know each other by our natures, for that is why we are here meeting again. Our true nature does not change with our circumstances. I helped you with your garden wall, and I help you now. You helped me with bread, and you now help me with your presence, for this is the way of true relationship. Tomorrow we may see each other again in another guise, yet are we not the same people?"

"Truly we are!" Exclaimed the traveler. "Let us toast to the Wisdom that makes a mockery of all that we think we know." ━

July
27

NEVER SAY NEVER

An official was traveling alone down a country lane and stopped to nap under a Tree. A thief came upon him and, seeing an easy target, drew his sword and commanded the official to stand up.

Cursing his stupidity, the official grew all the more infuriated when the thief made him take off all his clothes.

"Now," said the thief, "I am going to tell you something that you will remember for the rest of your life."

"You may cause me shame," hissed the official, "but you will never cause me to remember something that the likes of you could tell me!"

"We shall see," replied the thief. He ordered the official to mount his Horse, then tied him down to the saddle. "Now I am going to let you go, and your Horse will take you back to town. The words I want you to remember are *I am going to catch that thief and kill him if it's the last thing I do.*" ~

July
28

TO JUDGE

"Wise Elder," began a Seeker, "which would be best for me: to judge or be judged?"

"Clearly," the Elder replied, "it is better to be judged. We are then continually informed of what others see in us. They act as our mirrors, so that we can find ways to improve ourselves, as often the judge sees with a clear eye."

"Yet is there not value also in judging?" asked the Seeker.

"A judge needs to assume that he is wiser than the judged, along with the assumption that he is right, in order to call the other 'wrong.' That makes it near-impossible for him to look at himself and grow. What then follows is the eternal role-changing dance of those who judge and those who are judged."

"But it could take years, even generations, for that to happen."

"It may appear that way," replied the Sage. "Yet if you were to look at your life, you would likely see that you have changed roles a number of times. It could even happen several times in one day."

"What if I could be both at once?" asked the Seeker.

The Elder pondered the question, then said, "It would require you to let go of both pain and pride." ➤

July 29

THE AWAKENED VOICE

"I seldom hear Awakened people conducting discourses on their Awakening," complained a Seeker. "We could learn so much if they did."

"I have wondered about that too," added another Seeker. "At the same time, we have learned that true speech is not couched in words."

"Let us bring this confusing question to our Elder," suggested a third Seeker.

"The worth of a stone," replied the Elder, "can be determined only by crushing seeds with it."

"But crushing seeds is such a simple, little task," protested one of the Seekers. "What does that show us about something as profound as Awakening?"

The Elder replied:

> *The way of crushing a seed*
> *is the way of crushing a Mountain*
> *or a thought*
> *It is only the mind*
> *that makes it different*

After a pause, he added, "And now it is for you to continue the poem." ⤳

 *July* 30

FULL OF YOURSELF

You might know this young Seeker: he is very serious about his Quest for Knowledge. He studies, he asks questions, and he applies himself diligently to any task.

One day recently, he came across something he just couldn't figure out on his own. He took his confusion to a Sage known for her mastery of many topics. The Sage listened to the Seeker describing his quandary, yet before he could finish, the Sage let out a chuckle she could no longer suppress. In no time, she was laughing so uproariously that she had to get up and leave.

The Seeker stood there in dismay. Eventually he wandered home, and for the next four days his mind kept churning over what had happened. He couldn't eat, he couldn't sleep, he couldn't concentrate on anything. The torment grew unbearable, until the only thing he could imagine doing was to go back to the Woman.

"Even a Clown knows better than you," replied the Sage after hearing his story.

"But how can that be, when I study, ask questions, and apply myself so diligently?" lamented the Seeker.

"A Clown enjoys seeing people laugh. And you—look what it does to you! Who is the wiser?"

At that, the Seeker's eyes cleared and he broke into a hearty laugh. It is doubtful that anyone will ever see him as serious again. ➤

July
31

ONE

Three Beggars who were traveling together came upon a coin lying in the road.

"I want to buy something to eat with it," stated the first Beggar.

"I want several things to eat," asserted the second.

"That cannot be!" shouted the third. "I want something to drink!"

While they stood there arguing, an Elder came along and offered to help them come to resolution.

"Yes!" they all exclaimed. "Please choose which of us shall have his desire fulfilled."

"If you will give me your coin," suggested the Elder, "I will do just that."

Just ahead was a roadside produce stand. The Elder bought a basket of melons and brought it back to the Beggars.

"Aha! I now have something to eat!" rejoiced the first Beggar as he reached for a melon.

"That is not correct," stated the second, "for here I have a *few* things to eat."

"You are both wrong," accused the third, "for this is clearly something to satisfy my thirst." ➤

August
1

HOW TO LISTEN

A giant Boulder was perched on the ledge above the village. No one thought much of it, as it had been there forever. Besides, it was just one of many Boulders strewn about the Mountainside.

A woman from another village was hiking through the area on the trail that passed the Boulder. Awed by the size of the Boulder, she looked closely and saw that a crack was opening beneath it. She peered over the edge and discovered that the monolith was suspended directly above a village. She raced down to warn the villagers.

"There is nothing to fear," they reassured her. "Our mothers and our mothers' mothers, for untold generations, have gazed upon that Boulder and wondered if it would ever come crashing down upon them, and it never has." The townspeople went happily about their business, and the hiker continued on her trek.

On the way back to her village a week later, she again took the trail on the ledge that passed by the Boulder. Only it was no longer there. She peered over the edge and cringed at the sight of flattened remains that were once a picturesque little cluster of cottages and shops.

August
2

BEHIND ANGER

A Philosopher sent a messenger to ask a Sage for an audience.

"Go and tell your Master that I have nothing to say to him," replied the Sage.

A Seeker who overheard the exchange later asked the Sage, "Will your reply not anger the Philosopher?"

"He is already irritated by my Teachings," replied the Sage. "My intent is to anger him further, so that it might help him see that the anger he projected upon me was already his own. He will then be able to see the value of my work as a mirror for him."

"But won't people consider you ill-spirited for causing such anger?" said the Seeker.

"Imagine removing a splinter from a child's hand. It will hurt and the child might well react angrily, accusing you of intentionally causing him pain. Would the chance of this occurring cause you to deprive the child of a growth experience?"

"What if I went ahead and the child ended up carrying a grudge?"

"That is more likely to happen with an adult," replied the Sage. "Carrying grudges is not in a child, for she intrinsically knows the Truth and will soon come to it on her own. A child's Truth has not yet been buried by scar tissue from living in a world that fights Truth."

August 3

SEEING DOUBLE

"I cannot find The Way," lamented a Monk, "so I have come back to you, All-knowing Wisdom Carrier, for more direction."

"It lies right here before your eyes," she replied.

"Then why can't I see it for myself?"

"Because in your troubles, you think only *of* yourself."

"Is it true, then, that you have no trouble seeing it?" said the Monk

"Your vision will remain foggy as long as you continue seeing double by dwelling on *you can* and *I can't*."

"Does this mean that if there was no *you* or *I*, The Way could be seen?" asked the Monk.

"If neither you nor I existed, would there be anyone needing to see The Way?"

4

WHAT WINNING MEANS

Two neighboring villages were in constant competition with each other to see which one was the best. Their rivalry could be over anything: who had the best roads, the cleanest market square, or grew the tastiest plums.

Each village had a runner of renown. Whenever a message had to be delivered to an outlying farmer or a special Healer was needed from another district, the two runners were there to serve.

One day the runner from the upper village decided to challenge the runner from the lower village, to see which of them could hold claim to the title of swiftest message bearer.

"I will gladly accept the challenge," replied the lower-village runner, "but only if you are willing to accept one condition, as it is doubtful that I can perform the same as you."

"I will be glad to accept your provision," said the runner from the upper village. "I want to give you every opportunity to show your best, without looking bad."

"That is kind of you," replied the runner from the lower village. "I ask that you be allowed a head start."

August
5

FROM LEAD TO GOLD

"I walk by here regularly and see you sitting there most of the time" said a Nun to a Monk who was perched on a boulder a few steps off the path. "At first, I thought you just stopped here to rest. However, now I have grown so curious that I just have to ask why you sit here so often."

"I am here to become Awakened," replied the Monk. "If I am diligent and sit long enough, I will eventually become an Awakened being."

"Do you mind if I stay here a little while with you?" asked the Nun. "Not at all."

She picked up a stone and started to rub it with sand, and kept at it through the morning and into the afternoon. As hard as the Monk worked to stay engaged in his own practice, his curiosity got the best of him,

"What are you doing there?" he asked the Nun.

"This stone wishes to become a mirror," the Nun replied. "If I am diligent and polish long enough, it will eventually become that mirror."

6

HAUNTED BY PERFECTION

There is a potter who is imperfect. The townspeople gossip about her staying out all night, drinking in excess, and seeing too many men. On top of that, they say that she is irresponsible, as it takes her the longest time to finish a piece. Yet people come to her for special bowls and pitchers, as her work is beyond comparison.

One day, the magistrate of a neighboring district asked her to create an uncommon plate that was to be set out on market days to collect gold coins for the needy.

"I would be honored to do so," replied the potter. Yet instead of making the plate, she went to parties and entertained men.

After a year passed, the inspiration finally came to her, and she worked diligently on creating the plate that already existed in her mind. Word spread of the woman crafting incessantly on the plate, and everyone eagerly awaited the completion of her creation.

When the magistrate heard that the plate was finished, he was overjoyed. He prepared to go and pick it up.

The night before he was due to arrive, the potter placed the plate on her workbench and took a deep look at it. Realizing that it was not the manifestation of her vision, she smashed the plate to pieces. ➤

August
7

SEEKING WANT

"Why did you come to me?" asked the Sage.

"To discover what I do not know," replied the Seeker.

"I cannot give you experience, nor am I here to entertain. You can distill Wisdom only from new experience, which means it must be yours. All I am here to do is to help you put to practice what you have gained."

The Seeker thought about the Sage's words, then asked, "What if I am fooling myself when I profess to be seeking my own experience, but I really want to gain from yours? How can I tell when I am sincere?"

"When you come to me for something novel or mystical," answered the Sage, "you are after the *sensation* of experience, rather than the experience itself. You will know you are sincere when you hunger for everything that comes before you, without preference or prejudice."

"Is that the same Guidance you give to everyone?"

"It is. And it best fits those who think it fits them the least." ➤

 *August*
8

THE BEDEVILED SCHOLAR

In a far-away land lived a Scholar who conducted study groups on the Ancient Teachings. For years his countrymen held him in high regard, and many people came from afar to quench their yearnings.

Then one day, a wandering Sage settled in the area. He invited people to come and explore whatever they wanted with him. Soon there were lively discussions nearly every night on almost any topic you could imagine, from farming and bread-making to child-rearing and the nature of reality.

Over time, attendance at the Scholar's study groups dwindled. Nearly everyone could be found at one time or another at the meetings with the Sage.

One day, the Scholar decided that he had enough of what was going on. He stormed over to the Sage's cottage and shouted, "You have lured my people away and toyed with their minds until they no longer think for themselves!"

"If they were truly your people," replied the Sage, "were they thinking for themselves? Rather, if they are their own people, can they not go where they please?"

"They are weak and confused," bellowed the Scholar, "and you have taken advantage of that!"

"If that is the case, have you not been able to help them gain strength and clarity after all these years with them?"

The Scholar bowed before the Sage, then said, "I have just come to the awareness that I am not in a battle with you for the favor of the people. Rather, I am in a battle with myself to lessen the pain of my confusion and bolster my beliefs by persuading others to agree with me. Even when misery finds like company, it still does not become Truth. Together let us encourage the people to know the truth of their hearts and the fruits of their yearnings, and I shall be the first by example."

The Sage bowed before the Scholar. ❧

August
9

TRUE NATURE

A Seeker of many years, who was growing in Wisdom, chose to discontinue his solitary ways and have a wife. His fellow Seekers were happy for him—until the day he returned from the neighboring village with the woman. They saw her constantly criticizing him for the decisions he made, along with regularly interrupting him when he tried to speak.

One day when he was out with his fellow Seekers, one of them asked, "Why did you choose such a terror of a woman, who lords over you like a Cattle herder and calls your pursuit of Wisdom *blind foolishness?*"

"There are two reasons, my comrades," the man replied. "One is for me, and one is for her. She makes sure that my pursuits do not go to my head, and that I question everything I do. In the time I have been with her, my awareness has increased ten-fold. The second reason is that she grew up with a domineering mother, and now she has my example for another way to be. She is beginning to trust in me enough to relax and listen, and perhaps one day she will completely shed her armor and let her true self show."

10

BLIND SPOT

A group of Seekers were once pondering the difference between a Scholar and a Sage.

"It seems as though a Scholar conducts research for his own gain," stated one of the Seekers.

"And often for recognition," added another, "which amounts to the same thing as gain."

"The Sage, on the other hand," began another, "applies the Knowledge that he has gained, and shares it with others, along with helping them on their Journeys of Discovery."

"I wonder," said a Seeker toward the back of the group, "if the Sage could help the Scholar by making him aware that he is only serving himself. Might the scholar then consider whether he would draw greater reward from serving others?"

None of them could answer this, so they took the question to an Elder of the village.

"It is not possible for the Sage to impart Wisdom to the Scholar," the Elder replied, "because the Scholar's ego denies that there is any Truth in the words of the Sage. That is why the Scholar discredits both the words of the Sage and the Way of the Seeker." ✒

11

WHEN THE BELL CALLS

"I lack discipline," complained a Seeker. "In my travels, I spent time with a group who used a bell to tell everybody when it was time to wake up, eat, work, and meditate. I liked that, because I found myself engaged without having to feel guilty for not measuring up. Thoughtful Elder, is this approach beneficial for me?"

"On the surface it appears to be," said the Elder, "as it does solve your problem. The only issue I see is that you did not solve your problem. This group's approach is quite common, as it gives quick and sure results. They are conformist and predictable, however, so one could question whether they are truly Awakening."

"Why would they not be?"

"The world is wide. When we narrow it down, we simplify it and lose touch with a good share of it."

"Yet we gain intimate connection with a small part of it, do we not?" asked the Seeker.

"When sound comes to the ear, we hear; when the ear comes to sound, we listen. When we listen, we do not need to follow a sound, a discipline, or anything else. Instead, we respond to what manifests in life."

"What is the difference between responding to the sounds of life and the sounds of a bell? If there is none, I see no need to refrain from the bell and routine."

"Yes, grandson," replied the Elder. "It is wise of you to recognize that sound is sound. The difference is that when we respond to a bell that has been rung by another, it is not the bell that we respond to, but instead to another's Truth. His Truth is saying, 'Do this.' On the other hand, when we listen rather than hear, we can actually see sound. It invites us out into the world."

The seeker reflected for a moment. "I have experienced that, even though I do not understand fully what you say. What I do know is that when I did experience it, I felt as if I were one with the world."

"Those who do not understand," added the Elder, "are in kinship with the life of the world; those who do understand are strangers to the world." ➤

12

THE VALUE OF EXPECTATIONS

The Sage would casually mention a fisherman who was very knowledgeable in The Way, which drove Seekers to pester the Sage for the fisherman's name and whereabouts. When they would ask the Sage would say, "Well, I don't quite remember what he called himself. Now that I think of it, he might live in the fishing village on the next cove; or was it the one after that? If I recall correctly, he had a green boat. No, maybe it was blue."

Invariably a group of Seekers would plan a trip to find the fisherman, and usually they would persist until they found him.

"We hear that you are very knowledgeable in The Way," they would say. "Will you please teach us?"

"Yes," the fisherman would reply, "it is true that I am quite knowledgeable. If you are sincere, I will consider teaching you. Come back in the autumn when the Fish are running, and I will take you out in my boat and teach you The Way."

This confused nearly all of the Seekers: some thought that the fisherman was toying with them, and others figured he was just a plain fisherman who was referring to the way to catch Fish. Yet every once in a while, a Seeker would listen without expectation and would hear what was encoded in the fisherman's words. She would linger after the others left, and the fisherman would share his catch with her. ∿

13

MIND OR HEART

Many Scholars visited this particular Sage and tried to refute his Teachings. However, none of them had ever succeeded.

The most famous Scholar in the land, a man of incredible intellect, decided he would go and debate the Sage.

The Scholar arrived and the Sage showed him every courtesy. They talked about many things, but the Sage did not bring up a single matter relating to the Quest for Knowledge or the Ageless Wisdoms.

After the Scholar left, a Seeker who was present asked the Sage why there was no great debate.

"There was no reason," replied the Sage, "as the Scholar was actually a Sage in disguise. There is no such thing as a silent Scholar. If this man were a Scholar, he truly would have taunted me to argue. Only an unsure Scholar would be intimidated by me and thus feel compelled to argue to prove himself. This is because the Scholar is centered in the mind, and the Sage is centered in the heart."

"What is it that ever compels the Scholar to argue with the Sage?" asked the Seeker.

"Coming from the mind," replied the Sage, "the Scholar is irritated by the gentle ways in which we reach the people. They think the people must be convinced by superior logic, threatened by a fate worse than they already have, or confused by something beyond their understanding."

14

HOW TO KNOW WISDOM

"I have studied under your Guidance for several turns of the seasons now," said a Seeker. "Yet, Cherished Elder, I am not sure what to embrace as Wisdom."

"What anyone would call Wisdom," replied the Elder, "is only the illusion of Wisdom."

"But that cannot be," blurted out the Seeker, "for I hear you speaking of Wisdom! You guide us to others who speak it, as well."

"You misunderstand," responded the Elder, "for Wisdom is not found in words, but rather in The Way."

"What way?"

"That way."

August
15

RESPECT

A Sage would receive guests and offer them nothing to drink. He bade them to sit with him on his dirty floor without offering them a rug.

"Why do you treat people in such a way?" asked a Seeker.

"Because some people like it. They think they are enduring something in order to receive a Teaching. Those people are the ones I ask to leave."

"What about those who react by accusing you of being disrespectful?"

"I tell those people that they have neglected to inform me that they came to be respected. I do not offer respect, and I have no time for the hollow protocols surrounding it. Instead, I devote my time and energy to seeking the Wisdom of the Ages."

"Is not respect a basic Human need?"

"If they want respect, I tell them, it will be given to them by every vendor at the market—and by anyone else who wants something from them."

August 16

VIRTUE AND VICE TOGETHER

"Seekers, you have come here for Guidance," began the Sage, "and I wish to warn you of a trap, lest you step into it. Recently, a Seeker I knew suppressed all desire in her Quest for Clarity of Mind, then died of starvation. Another Seeker wanted to live a pure life, free from accoutrements, then froze to death. Are these two Seekers any different from those who become obsessed with their cravings?"

"They appear to be as different as hot grease and ice water," replied a Seeker.

"Yet they are actually quite similar," commented another, "as both imperil themselves with their excesses."

"Yes, they are no different from each other," said the Sage, "even though some would say that one is the epitome of virtue and the other is the epitome of vice. In either case, we let our desires drive us until they become mad compulsions."

"You said we *let* this happen, which must mean there are other options," said a third Seeker.

"Always. One thing we can do is listen. When we give our desires the space to speak, we see that they are beings, just like you and me; they have needs, just like us."

"Ah, now we can relate to them!" exclaimed a Seeker.

"And if we can do that," added another, "perhaps we can help them meet their needs, and they will be content."

The Sage bowed to the Seekers. ➤

August 17

HEAVY THINKING

A Nun was doing very well in her studies. One day, a Fool tested her by asking, "What is reality?"

That is an easy question, the Nun thought to herself. "Reality is what I perceive," she replied without thinking.

"Where does what you perceive dwell?" asked the Fool.

"It dwells in my mind," responded the Nun, "as that is where I perceive it."

"What is this I am holding?"

"It is a large pot of rice."

"If this dwells in your mind," said the Fool, "your head must be bigger than it appears." ✒

August 18

HOW SECRETS SPEAK

She was beautiful—too beautiful to be a Nun, some said. However in thinking things such as this, they showed their ignorance of what a Nun truly is. Even though she cut her hair and wore plain, loose clothing, her beauty shone through; it was not only physical, but also in her demeanor.

Some of the Monks she studied with couldn't help but fall in love with her. Having vowed celibacy, they kept their love a secret—except for one Monk who wished to share it, at least with her. One day while walking past her, he slipped her a note asking her to meet him by the gate later that evening.

After that day's evening meal, the Elder they were studying with gave a talk. When he finished, the lovely Nun stood up and said, "You who sent me the note to meet you in the night, come forward and embrace me here and now if you truly care for me as much as you profess." ◦∼•

August
19

STALKED BY BELIEF

"I hate being haunted by doubt," complained a Seeker. "How can I get rid of it?"

"Doubt is the sister of belief," replied the Sage. "When we believe, we seek conviction rather than Knowledge, and conviction casts doubt. Once we release ourselves of belief, there is nothing more to doubt."

"Without doubt," continued the Seeker, "I put myself in your trust."

"That is true," replied the Sage. "Yet whether or not you trust in me, you are guarding yourself. When we question whether or not we can trust, we are not capable of trust. And if we believe that we can trust, our trust is not true. In both cases, we are merely formulating opinions, which have nothing to do with trust."

"How does that relate to you?"

"Your opinion of me has little to do with whether or not I am trustworthy."

"Then what am I to do?" lamented the Seeker. "I sometimes get discouraged by your statements. I feel criticized, which makes me mistrust you. And when you encourage and praise me, my trust for you grows."

"Watch your reactions," instructed the Sage "I am showing you how easily you can be attracted to a belief, for that is all my praise is. And I am showing you how easily you can abandon a belief, for that is all my criticism is. Your Journey must be based on effectiveness rather than belief. Once you become effective, belief and trust will cease to have meaning." ➤

August
20

THE TRUTH IN WORDS

Several townspeople were sitting with an Elder in the shade of a grove of Trees just outside the village.

"I have never heard such profound Wisdom as that which comes with the words you speak, Wizard-Elder," someone stated.

After the people left, a blind man who was sitting nearby came over to the Elder and said, "I have learned to listen for what I cannot see in a face. That individual spoke kind words to you, yet what I heard was scorn and criticism. Can that be?"

"You have a precious gift: you can hear the Truth in a person's words. I still took his words graciously, for I heard his Truth, as did you, and that was far more valuable to me than any compliment."

"Knowing the Truth behind people's words is a heavy burden for me to carry," said the blind man. "When I sense pleasure in a person expressing empathy for misfortune, or when I feel jealousy from a person who congratulates someone, I feel guilty for prying into another person's secret thoughts and feelings. Beyond that, I feel sad for their inner turmoil."

"Yours is both a gift and a curse. Let us work for the day when all feelings can be honored for what they are, and all Truths can be openly spoken and respected."

21

AN UNLIKELY PARTNERSHIP

In our village once lived a Scholar who mercilessly attacked a Sage. If it wasn't a criticism, it was a rebuttal or character smear.

On the other hand, there was a group of Seekers who could do nothing but praise the Sage. One day these Seekers decided that they had enough of the Scholar's disrespect, so they went and confronted him.

"We insist that you apologize to our Guide," they stated, "and publicly retract all the defamatory comments you have made."

"Look at you all, coming at me like a pack of Dogs!" responded the Scholar. "Did you ask the Sage why I am constantly after him before you descended upon me? Of course not!"

Confused, the Seekers went to their Sage and related what had happened.

"The Scholar and I work together," replied the Sage. "By setting himself up in opposition to me, he sways the uncentered to keep their distance from me. This gives me more time and wherewithal to devote to what I am called to do." ➳

August
22

WHERE VALUE DWELLS

Four Seekers prepared for a journey through the jungle to find a Hermit who was reported to have discovered the secret of Instant Awakening. The story went that after he realized that was all he needed, the Hermit went off to live a life of bliss immersed in nature's splendor.

After making it across Crocodile-infested Rivers and through an endless tangle of vegetation where Tigers and Pythons lurked, the Seekers came upon a little clearing overlooked by the Hermit's thatched tree house.

Exhausted, scratched, and bruised, they sat at the Hermit's feet and beseeched him to share with them the secret that would bring them immediate Awakening.

"I will do that," replied the Monk. "A gift's value is all in the giving, and you have given enough to prove yourselves worthy of this gift."

The Hermit then gave each of them one word to remember on the way back to their homeland, instructing them to combine the words to construct the secret to Instant Awakening.

On the way back, the first Seeker forgot his word, as it was just an everyday term that was used in practically every sentence. The other three, he figured, must be carrying the meaningful words.

When they stepped out of the jungle, they were so full of anticipation that right away they wanted to put the words together, so that they too could experience the Hermit's bliss of Now Awakening.

"My word was of no value," said the first Seeker. "I was disappointed that I did not receive one of the important words, as the three of you did, so I didn't bother to remember it."

The other three Seekers looked at each other, then back at the first Seeker. Without saying a word, they realized that they had all done the same thing. ᨆ

August 23

LET DUST BE DUST

"How does one live a life of non-attachment?" asked a craftsman.

"What would one become attached to?" replied the Beggar.

"What we develop feelings for."

"And what is that?"

"The people we spend time with and the things we invest energy in."

"Do you have something with you that you are attached to?"

"Why, yes I do—this little pocket knife that my grandfather gave me."

"May I see it?"

The craftsman handed it to the Beggar, who then said, "If I were to toss this knife over my shoulder into the pond behind us and it were to sink down into the muck, never to be found again, would you still feel attached to it?"

"Yes, I would."

"Attached to what?"

The craftsman paused. Finally, he said, "Magician-Beggar, I am speechless. Never before did I understand non-attachment, even though I thought I did."

"How simple it is—once we listen!" concluded the Beggar. "When we live consciously in the world, we will not attach ourselves to the dust of the world."

August
24

THE STUBBORN PATTERN

A Seeker struggled to find motivation. He was content to eat, as long as he was being fed. As long as no one asked him to move, he was happy sitting and watching people go about their affairs.

One day, he woke up and realized that he should think better of himself. However, he simply could not come up with anything to do or anyplace to go.

"I will go and ask the Esteemed Elder what I should do," he told himself, and he did just that.

"You come to me," said the Elder, "to find out what you already know: that rust can be washed and washed, yet it will never turn white."

"I do not follow you," replied the Seeker. "How does what you just said help me?"

"You have made it about you, when the answer does not lie within, but before you. That is why the Old Ones tell us that it is better to do anything than nothing."

"The answer lies before me," repeated the Seeker to himself all the way home. When he entered his room, he saw a book that he had received from a wandering Wise Man many years ago. Although he had always meant to read it, he had never gotten around to it. He cradled it fondly in his arms and walked down to the park to sit under a Tree and read it.

Before he got very far, another Seeker interrupted him and said, "By the way you are handling that book, it must be very valuable. Does it speak Rare Wisdom?"

"I have kept the book before me for years, for just that reason."

"Then I wish to have it, for I am a Seeker of Wisdom." She pulled out all of her gold coins and offered them to the Seeker, who then handed her the book. ∼

25

ALL ARE INVITED

"Come and join the other Seekers who are sitting before the Sage," announced an enthusiastic Seeker to anyone on the byways who would listen.

"What right did you have to do that?" one of the seated Seekers asked the caller when she returned. "Were we not specially selected for our dedication to the Quest for Knowledge? And here you went inviting just anybody."

Realizing that they were at odds with each other, the two Seekers asked the Sage for her opinion.

She replied, "Does not the Clam gatherer wait until evening when the tide goes out, to see how many Clams are left upon the beach?" ➤

August
26

THE FLOGGING

A wandering Sage passed through a village where a bare-backed man was tied to a post in the central square. A flogger with a cat-o'-nine-tails stood ready to unleash his fury. The Sage walked up to the bound man and bowed before him.

As the Sage walked on, a young Seeker came up to him and said, "Honorable Sir, that man you honored is a criminal! He must have wronged others—I am shocked that you would bow before him."

"On his moral character I cannot comment," replied the Sage, "for reality is not what is seen, but what does the seeing."

"Then what *did* you bow to?" asked the Seeker. "I am very confused."

"This is a man with passion and purpose, willing to take risks to fulfill that purpose. Is not following one's passion, even though there might be consequences, so much better than lying defeated to avoid them?"

27

INSIDE SILENCE

"What is silence?" asked a Seeker. "You say it is not being quiet. You say it is not isolating oneself. You say it is not sitting in meditation. Then what is it, as these are the only ways I know to find silence?"

"How can one find what is not?" replied the Sage. "Silence is what is left when we quit looking."

"But when I quit looking, insightful Sage, all I hear is a bunch of noise inside my head."

"Quit that."

"Then I would feel so alone."

"Quit that."

"How do I quit it?"

"Quit that as well. When we counter something by force of will, it only comes back as soon as we let up." ↝

August
28

QUITTING IS DOING

"I have tried and tried," complained a Seeker. "I have fasted, I have studied, I have sat at the feet of Prophets, Fools, and Scholars, and so much more. Yet here I am, no more Awakened than when I began my Quest many, many years ago."

"What do you see as your solution?" asked the Elder.

"I must try harder, fast longer, and travel farther to find more Ancient Scriptures."

"And what will that bring you?"

"I think you are mocking me, and I am grateful for it. You have just helped me realize that more of the same effort will bring me only more of the same results. I am through—I have quit seeking."

In that instant, the woman was Awakened. ━

August 29

TRACK THIS WAY

Two eager Seekers heard rumors of a woman who was descended from a long line of venerable Mystics. After much investigation, they found her whereabouts and went to see her. She welcomed them graciously and invited them to sit with her in the orchard.

"You must be proud to be descended from such a line of Hallowed Ones," said one of the Seekers. "What an honor to carry such Knowledge as your family Elders must have passed on to you."

"It must be a burden as well," added the other Seeker. "I can't imagine what it is like to be one of such an elect family."

The Seekers continued for a while in this vein, even though the woman made efforts to steer the conversation in other directions.

Eventually, one of the Seekers said, "It appears that you do not wish to discuss your exalted heritage, and this leaves me confused. We have traveled all this way to be in the presence of you, the fabled Lineage Carrier."

"I do understand," replied the woman. "My ancestry has led you to me, yet that is just the trail you followed. Have you come to talk about the trail you took, or have you come to fulfill your reason for taking the trail?"

30

THE GIFTING OASIS

Two Nuns wished to serve their people, only they were confused as to how to go about it.

"Let us ask for Guidance from a Monk who serves," suggested one of them, and the other agreed.

When they posed their question to the Monk, he replied, "I will answer you with a story that I was told when I asked the same question many years ago.

"There was a Desert that people had to cross in order to get to the fertile lands beyond. The Desert was wide, and the sun was scorching. Nothing lived there but Scorpions, and many people had gotten lost trying to cross, never to be heard from again.

"A group of Goat herders set out to cross the barrens and got lost. Two of their young men scouted ahead, yet neither of them could they find the way. Running out of water, they knew they would soon die of thirst.

"'Look ahead!' said one of them at the sight of a lush oasis that lay in the distance. Without thinking, he raced toward it. The other man backtracked to get his people." ➤

August
31

THE VALUE OF COINS

There are stories of Sages who accept payment for their Teachings. These Sages are often criticized on the grounds that they take recompense for Knowledge that is not theirs, but rather has been passed down from the Ancient Ones and is therefore everyone's birthright.

A Scholar once challenged one of these Sages by saying to her, "The way of the Sage has always been to share with the worthy Seeker, without consideration for what is received in return. Are you not concerned with what others think of you?"

"Nothing of material value could compensate for the Ancient Teachings," replied the Sage. "For me to refuse what is given will not prevent the giving; it will only go another route."

"Yet what about your image?"

"Does my accepting something mean that I yearn for it? Coins have no value until the energy they represent is applied, and it is the application that shows a person's ethics."

"Then what about those who do not take money? Are they not naturally considered to be without ulterior motives for sharing the Ancient Wisdom?"

"That they are," answered the Sage. "However, they are not necessarily any different from those who take payment. Someone who claims to be a Sage may also claim to charge nothing, yet he may be making off with the greatest treasure of all—the souls of Seekers. Remember that reality is not what is seen, but what it is seen through."

September
1

QUALITIES OF A SEEKER

A Seeker, very much like you and me, asked for Guidance on the characteristics that exemplify the Seeker, so that she could evolve them and practice them to her fullest ability.

"You are already doing that," replied the Sage. "Whenever you are fully present and fully engaged, the skills of the Journey evolve along with your progress on the Journey. At the same time, being aware of those skills can help you to be engaged in the process, rather than being focused on the product."

"What are the most important skills?" responded the Seeker.

"The first, which is the foundation of all the other qualities, is to be unbound, which means to not be attached to anything. In this way, we find our connection with everything.

"The second in importance is naiveté. Some think it means being innocent; in actuality, a person who lives with naiveté becomes guilty of all sorts of things."

"How can that be so?"

"Because the naïve person does not have any scruples or boundaries, he leads a life of immersion, rather than observation. This gets him into mischief on a regular basis. He is doing what is called *drinking in Knowledge*, rather than skimming over it. Those who do not live by naiveté, live in bondage. They shackle themselves with the illusion that they are following guidelines for a righteous life."

"But I always thought guidelines were necessary."

continued on page 290

continued from page 289

"What we call guidelines are actually doctrines and rituals we have adopted, which make us not Seekers, but trained Dogs. There is a world of difference between guidelines and Guidance. Choose the latter, by listening to your dreams and intuition, and to the Ancient Voices you carry within, and you will see doctrine and ritual practice for what they are."

"And what is that?" asked the Seeker.

"They are repetitions that smudge out the ever-changing now, which is the dwelling place of the Seeker. In essence, they are as shallow as the antics of the Dog who keeps performing the same trick over and over. The way of the Seeker lies deep—it is the Journey of the Heart."

"I embrace what you say, for the spirit of your words resonates with my spirit, yet I am left feeling empty. I am no longer clear on who I am as a Seeker."

"You are looking for what takes the Journey, and that is what we have just deconstructed. The Seeker is the Journey—a living question with an endless, insatiable thirst that has no preference or prejudice. That is why you are called a Seeker—one who seeks—rather than a Student, which is one who learns. A Seeker never learns, and a Student never seeks."

 *September*
2

GROUNDING

"Everything you see is just an illusion," stated a man to a couple of very new Pursuers of Knowledge during a meal.

A woman added, "In fact, what we feel and think are also illusions."

A Fool, who was sitting across from the first speaker, took the man's bowl and started to eat from it.

"Dear sir," the startled man replied, "why are you eating my food?"

"Did you say 'food?'" asked the Fool. "I thought it would be merely an illusion to you, so I figured you wouldn't miss it."

After they all took a few more bites in reflective silence—except for the foodless man, of course—the woman who thought feelings were also illusions said, "I'm not entirely pleased with this food; I think it has a little too much basil and not enough garlic."

The Fool took her bowl and spilled its contents on the ground, saying, "Problem solved. Your feelings are just illusions anyway, so now you can transcend them."

The two youths bowed before the man, the woman, and the Fool for the masterful Teaching they had just given. In turn, the man and woman bowed to the Fool, in gratitude for checking their ego-driven efforts to impress the youths. ✎

 *September*
3

LIKES REPEL

"Why does it happen that the more we need each other, the more we reject and despise each other?" asked a Seeker.

"Is this true with all people?" replied the Sage.

The Seeker thought for a moment. "It seems to be the most extreme with large groups who organize and conspire to exploit each other in some way, or to conquer and subjugate."

"There may be your answer. The more people there are, the more the competition and disease, and the worse off we all become for it."

"Then why do we not band together and come up with a common solution?"

"Perhaps there is no common solution, or it would have already happened."

"I wonder if coming together could actually make things worse," mused the Seeker. "The more we cooperate, the more disease will spread, and the more we will have to share already scarce resources. There must be another answer."

"There actually is," responded the city Sage. "And the answer is your question."

"Do you mean war and disease?"

"Is that not the way of all life when it grows out of Balance? As much as we like to think we are different from animals, we too fight when we crowd ourselves together, and we too become vectors for the diseases of overcrowding."

"I always thought banding together was a good thing!" protested the Seeker.

"No people have ever joined into states and nations—and not even into tribes—out of desire, but only out of necessity. The Ancient Ones were people of the clan and the tiny village, where disease was virtually unknown and war was not even a word in their vocabulary, for there was no way to imagine such a thing, much less execute it."

"I think I understand. I see what you are speaking of in the animals who live Nature's Way." The Seeker paused, then asked, "What, then, can we do to restore the Balance of Old?"

"Look about you," said the Sage.

The Seeker turned to take in the small group of fellow Seekers seated about him, with their mates and children nearby, as well as the Elder in their midst, and he smiled. ◄—

September
4

THE WAY OF THE HEART

"What is it that keeps me sane?" asked a weaver. "There are times when my mind is so jumbled that I want to bash my head against a wall to quiet it. Yet a deeper calm always seems to come over me, and I don't understand what it is."

"Is understanding necessary?" asked the Healer. "The Way of the Heart is one of experience, rather than knowledge."

"But I know what spins around in my head," protested the weaver.

"Truly," replied the Sage, "yet the head is not the heart."

"Then how are the head and the heart related?"

"You will know that by naming what spins around in your head."

The Weaver thought for a moment. "I can do that. The spinning seems to happen whenever I experience change. However, it is not change itself, as I seem to be okay with it. Only when change is accompanied by drama do I swirl into chaos and lose my grip. If only I knew chaos the way I knew change and drama! Whether or not I like change and drama, at least I am in touch with them. I can feel, hear, and see them, which helps keep my feet under me."

"What you are asking for is a way to stay in your head," said the Healer, "and that is what keeps your head spinning. You are hanging on to mind control, and your head is screaming at you to get out and go to your heart. This is why you feel like you want to bang your head against a wall."

"But where does chaos fit in?"

"Order and knowing are The Way of the Head; chaos is The Way of the Heart. In the heart, there are no senses for grasping and directing; there is only what is. All you need to become what is, kind weaver, is to quit fighting it." ➤

September
5

MAKING A DIFFERENCE

A wicked typhoon, the likes of which is seen barely once in a generation, came pressing out of the south. Screaming wind churned the water to a seething froth, and vicious waves pummeled the shoreline. Boats were smashed into kindling and piers were torn from their moorings.

On the night of the fourth day, the tempest calmed. By morning, the sun's rays were back to merrily dancing over the Sea's rippled surface.

A Nun went out for a walk on the beach, to revel in the return to normalcy. It didn't take long for her to notice the thousands of Starfish thrown high above the waterline by the storm. They lay there dying in the baking sun.

Immediately, the Nun started to toss them back into the water. A short way down the beach, the Nun came across a fisherman looking for his lost boat.

"Do you really think you are going to make a difference?" commented the fisherman. "There are thousands of Starfish here, and you have barely made a dent."

"I am making a difference to this one," replied the Nun as she cast another one back into the water.

September

6

POOR, POOR ME

"Why do things keep happening to me?" complained a Seeker who had gone to get advice from an Elder. "I never know whether I'm making a right decision or a wrong one. Sometimes what I do is good for me and sometimes it is bad, and I never know what it is going to be until it is too late."

"Why do you imagine that what you do has an effect on what follows?" asked the Elder.

"Because I see it happening time and again. When I move to another town, something happens to me there that wouldn't have if I hadn't moved. If it is something good, I congratulate myself for having made the right decision; if it is something bad, I berate myself for having made the wrong decision, as nothing bad would have happened had I not moved."

"Would not something happen if you stayed where you were?"

"Well yes, of course."

"Would it have been good or bad?"

The Seeker reflected on that, then said, "I think you have caught me in a trap."

"When we see ourselves as the center of our own world, everything in our lives assumes a cause-and-effect relationship, with us in the center. We then thread these events together on our personal timeline and say exactly what you have been saying: 'Oh, this was caused by that, and what

continued on page 296

continued from page 295

happens next is going to be the result of what I am doing right now.' In actuality, these events do not exist—they are ripples of other causations that happen to cross our Path. It is only when we take them personally that they become events in our lives—events that we are in some way responsible for."

"I think I understand," responded the Seeker. "Right away it feels like I have assumed a role of self-importance. I have been flattering myself by thinking I could have an effect on matters that originate who-knows-where and affect who-knows-what, much less little old me who just happens to be standing in their shadow."

"That is so," replied the Elder. "Often the first step in Awakening is to see these events as exercises for learning how not to feel victimized by them. The next step is to see them as opportunities to practice virtues of humility, forgiveness, patience, and nonattachment. Yet whatever we make of them, they amount to no more than reflections of our own ignorance. When we realize that, we have taken the final step, and the events cease to exist."

"I bow to the Wisdom you have given voice to," stated the Seeker, and he took his leave. ⟿

September
7

THE HIDDEN POWER

A Bull is a mighty creature with stout horns, a neck the girth of his waist, and hooves capable of pounding nearly anything to dust. However, when the gate is left open and he can charge out to freedom, his spindly little tail will not let him pass through.

This is because he is locked in a battle that will not allow him to Awaken. On one side is fear, and on the other side is longing, and the tussle between the two renders the Bull impotent. He longs to run, yet he fears tumbling off the cliff immediately ahead. At the same time, he fears staying in the pen, because he will end up being butchered.

With all that power and majesty, the Bull is still controlled by his spindly little tail.

 *September*
8

THE WAY OF THE SEEKER

A conman impersonated Master Craftsmen as he traveled from village to village. One time he was an architect, the next time a clockmaker, and the next a goldsmith. He knew the talk of these trades, and he exuded trust and reliability. His con was to ask for a down payment on a commission, then disappear.

In one town his reputation caught up with him, and the townspeople seized him before he could escape. They consulted their Elder, known for his insight and fairness, for advice on what to do with the scoundrel.

"Leave him with me for a few days," replied the Elder, "and I shall see to it that he is justly punished."

The townsfolk were skeptical of their feeble Elder's ability to contain a man of such strength and cunning. Yet because they trusted in their Elder, they agreed.

Several days later, a few people saw the Elder in the market square and asked what had come of the fraud.

"I have let him free," replied the Elder, "for he is now a Seeker."

"How *ever* could you do that?" one of them blurted out. "He has gotten off free, and he is laughing at you all the way to the next scam."

"As to your first assumption that he has gotten off, the life of a Seeker is the most demanding and frustrating there is. I could think of no greater punishment for such a man. Regarding your second assumption that he would be right away up to his old tricks, I could think of no greater incentive to keep him from doing so than to help him realize that what he was really after in all of his conniving was the value of life. Now that he is on the true Journey to its realization, he will no longer have the interest—nor the time—for the petty ways which he once thought would fulfill his Quest."

September
9

EVERYTHING IS NOTHING

"I do not understand emptiness," lamented a Seeker to his Sage. "I hear all this talk of being of no-mind, of nonattachment, of having no preferences. So what is left but emptiness? Where's the vibrancy, where's the life?"

"What exists for you?" asked the Sage.

"What has meaning for me," came the reply.

"And why do things have meaning for you?"

"Because I have a relationship with them, I would guess."

"Would you say then that things exist for you because you have a relationship with them?"

"Well, yes, that appears to be so."

"Would this be an objective relationship?"

"I think it would be subjective," replied the Seeker, "because I have feelings for them."

"We have just conducted a dialogue on emptiness, and I believe you have solved your emptiness riddle!" exclaimed the Guide.

"How can that be?" commented the Seeker. "All we did was define what exists for me."

"Did you notice that we have not spoken a word about emptiness?" asked the Sage. "In fact, I have not heard a thing about no-mind or no preference. It appears that you have found emptiness."

In that moment, the Seeker became Awakened. ↜

September 10

WHEN HELP IS NEEDED

A young man about to venture out on his own was given a box by his father.

"Contained herein are the Sacred Teachings that will guide you in your life," said the father. "Study them and you shall be free of want."

The months went by and the young man only struggled. He tried one thing after another, with no success. He only sank further and further into debt. Ashamed to go to his father, he went to an Elder for advice.

"Did your father give you anything when you left him?" the Elder asked.

"Only a box that probably contains a fat book of Teachings, but that is of no help to me now."

"Did you ever open the box?"

When the young man returned home, he opened the box and found that it was filled to the brim with gold coins. ∼

September
11

MY TITLE

The other day, several Seekers were discussing who they should go to for Guidance and who they should not go to. "Is it okay to consult Scholars?" they asked. "And what about Nuns and Monks, or Elders or Sages? Then there are those who go by 'Master,' and 'Ascended One.'" Unable to come to agreement—and very concerned lest they receive erroneous Guidance—they brought their question to a trusted Sage with whom they had been studying for a long time.

"Someone who gives himself a title, or who is accustomed to responding to a title," she responded, "does not know himself. Those who call him by the title do not know him, either."

"What do you mean?" asked one of the Seekers. "Surely someone who is a Master or an Elder would know this of herself."

"What is a Master? And who is an Elder? And who is the person guided by an Elder?"

"Those who are less skilled, or those who are younger, I suppose."

"Are we then not all Masters, as there is always someone less skilled or advanced than we are? And are there not people younger than each of us, so are we not all Elders? Or are none of us Elders, as there is always someone older?"

"That is all true," agreed the Seeker, "yet it does not seem to address your initial point that those who have or respond to titles do not know themselves."

"If someone needs to identify himself as an Elder or a Master, what does that tell you about him?"

"Well, nothing significant, I guess. It does give the person a certain air of authority or assumed knowledge."

continued on page 302

continued from page 301

"That is my point," explained the Sage. "When I hear someone being addressed by title, I can only make an assumption about that person based upon the title. It tells me nothing about the person as an individual. In fact, the assumptions I make could detract from getting to know him for the person he is."

"But we all have names!" stated the Seeker. "Does this mean that our names do the same thing, at least to some degree?"

"That is why, in our culture, names are ever-changing as we go through different phases in our lives, and as new skills and characteristics become apparent to others. These are references more than formal names or titles. It is similar to saying, 'The Sky is blue today,' or 'The Sky is gray.'"

"I now understand," said the Seeker. "When I hear a title now, I will pay little heed to it and instead relate to the person."

September
12

NO MIND

Three Seekers were talking about the mind and realized that they did not really understand what it was. After all, their Guides were continually encouraging them to be mindless.

"How could a mind be mindless any more than a lake could be water-less?" wondered one of the Seekers.

A Nun who was resting under a nearby Tree overheard them and asked if she could join in the conversation.

"Please do," the Seekers replied. "Maybe you can help us with our confusion."

"There can be no confusion," replied the Nun, "for there is nothing to confuse."

"Then why do we talk about it if there is nothing to talk about?"

"It is because we secretly want to be in our minds," replied the Nun. "We are afraid to be mindless."

"What if we were not afraid?"

"We would still want to know what to avoid."

"Will you then, kind Nun, give us the nature of nothing, so that we do not again try to make it into something?"

"I would be honored." The nun gathered her thoughts, then continued to speak. "Let us begin by recognizing that the only way to describe noth-ing is by stating what it is not. Nothing is not emptiness, because empti-ness is something: it is blankness, it is a void. Nothing has no existence, so it has neither a beginning nor an end. It is not perishable, and it has no shape, substance, or color. It knows neither joy nor sadness, neither pain nor ecstasy. It has no yearning, and it does not know who experiences what."

"If that is the case, what is the function of a Mindless Mind?" asked one of the Seekers.

"That which knows everything has no need to function." With that, the Nun returned to her place under the Tree. ❧

September
13

MAKING ENEMIES

"It seems that I always have enemies," lamented a Seeker. "Even if I make peace with one, another takes his place. And there is one enemy I can never get rid of. What am I to do?"

"How do you feel about these enemies?" asked the Sage.

"I hate them."

"Why is that?"

"Because they treat me badly. Either they say something hurtful, or they have taken something from me, or they have spread lies."

"That must make you miserable."

"Whenever I *am* happy, it doesn't last long, because they come back and torment me. It's as though they live in my mind, always working to keep me miserable."

"Do your enemies see you as an enemy?" asked the Sage. "Do they hate you?"

"Well, no. Not most of them, anyway."

"Then why are they your enemies?"

After considering the question, the Seeker replied, "Because I have declared them so."

"Do you think they set out to treat you badly and make themselves your enemies?"

"Not really," replied the Seeker, then he lost himself in thought. After a couple of moments, he said, "It sounds crazy, but I think I might be creating my enemies."

"It is the way of things that when they continue to be fed, they never leave. As soon as you quit thinking 'hate,' your enemies will vanish. If you were to embrace them, they would become the people they really are. Were you to then sit at their feet, they would become your Guides." ◝

September
14

THE FOLLY OF ANSWERS

A Seeker asked an Elder a question, and she gave him an appropriate answer.

"That escapes me," replied the Seeker. "Will you please repeat what you said?"

"That is the second question you are asking me," replied the Elder. "If I were to reply, I would be making two mistakes."

"Now I am completely confused!" exclaimed the Seeker. "Why would replying to my second question be a second mistake?"

"Because it does not honor your question."

"I would think that answering a question would be honoring it rather than dishonoring it."

"An answer kills a question, and I would much rather breathe life into your question by encouraging you to explore it. A new question is so freshly born and deserves a long, long life." ➤

September 15

ON WHAT WE CLIMB

A Seeker sat quietly under a Tree by the River with her Sage, wanting only to be in his presence and learn from his example. At the same time, she had a burning question that she could hold no longer.

"If I may briefly interrupt this moment," she started, "there is something I must know. Some Teachings I remember word-for-word, and they return to me often. There are others that I can barely recall. In fact, I no longer remember who spoke them. Yet it doesn't seem to matter, as both have given me much. Why is it that one is so present with me and the other only lingers as a faint shadow?"

"A great Tree is supported by massive roots," said the Sage. "They split the ground and impoverish the soil, so that only scrubby shrubs will grow near it. However, that Tree was founded on a root as fragile and easily overlooked as a hair. Which of these roots is more important?"

September
16

THE DRAGON SLAYER

There are two kinds of Dragons: benevolent and malicious. In a land across the Sea, there dwelled a Dragon with a malicious bent. Whenever the people ventured into the Forest to gather firewood or pick berries, they knew they might not return. Yet venture forth they must, as they needed food and craft supplies, along with wood for cooking and heating.

Many people went cold and hungry, for as soon as they saw the great Dragon's form lurking in the shadows, they would scream in terror and flee the Forest, swearing to never again enter that vile demon's lair.

One day, a man from a Mountain tribe came passing through. He wore a sword on each hip and traveled with a Dog who looked like he was sired by a Dragon.

"I will kill your Dragon for you," stated the man to the people. With that, he and his Dog disappeared into the Forest.

Two days later, he came back carrying a huge pelt, a handful of large, hooked claws, and a massive, fanged skull. You and I would probably recognize them as parts of an ordinary Bear, however, the local people were convinced that it was their slain Dragon.

One would think that they would be grateful that their Forest was free of its nemesis and would hold a great feast in celebration. Wouldn't they want to honor the man who had liberated them? Instead, they trembled in his presence. "This beast of a man is more powerful than a Dragon!" they whispered to each other. "We now have an even greater monster to dread—and he is right here among us!"

The man overheard them and said, "The Dragon you fear is within you, and it will torment you as long as you keep feeding it your helplessness. Only you can slay the Dragon, by welcoming him into your life."

 *September* 17

THE SHAME OF WORDS

"I feel insincere when I speak my Truth," lamented a Seeker.

"That is because your intent is to deceive," replied the Sage.

"Gracious Sage, that is the last thing I mean to do!"

"Yet you just proved that it is so. The more vigorous the denial, the more true its opposite."

The Seeker bowed. He was now ready to listen.

"When we open our mouths," continued the Sage, "we are already lost before our first word. And when we close our mouths, we continue being lost, even before our lips meet each other."

"Then what is one to do?"

"When we think about what to do, we do the opposite of what we need to do. And little does it matter which we choose, as opposites are only more of the same."

"Then what is speaking Truth?" asked the Seeker. "I am so confused."

"When we make an effort to speak our Truth, it is as though we are talking about a dream."

"Is that a riddle?"

"That is all words can be. Any effort to speak Truth is conscious—it comes from the mind—and Truth dwells in the heart."

The Seeker heard, and he bowed. He then looked up, and as he saw a Bird flying overhead, he realized that his Truth had just been spoken. ✦

September
18

THE GREATER WISDOM

A Ruler banished a Monk from the land because he disagreed with one of the Monk's practices. The Monk sent a letter to the Ruler which said, "Honorable Sir, it is with great respect that this simple person obeys your banishment order. In all my life as a Seeker of Truth, I have not met one so wise as you."

Before the Monk could finish packing, he received an order to appear before the Ruler. The Monk went immediately.

"Humble Monk," the Ruler began, "I had you banished because I disagreed with your practice and would not allow it. Then you honored me for my action, when I would expect the opposite, if anything. Explain yourself."

"Ruler of Rulers," began the Monk, "this lowly Seeker has spent nearly a lifetime in quest of the practice that is right for him; whereas you, oh Great One, knew in an instant what is right and wrong for him."

September
19

THE GIFT OF KNOWING

"If you have a walking stick," said the Wizard, "I will give it to you. And if you do not have one, I will take it from you."

"That makes no sense," protested the Monk. "How can you give me what I already have, and how can you take away what I don't have?"

"What you ask, you already know. Someday, perhaps, you will also understand."

"Please guide me," requested the Monk.

"Recall what a walking stick does for you, and what you would do if you did not have one. Where did you gain the awareness to use a walking stick well? And where is it that you gained the even keener awareness to make your way through the dark, or across a Stream, without a walking stick?"

In awe, the Monk said, "In this moment I have Awakened, gracious Wizard. I bow to you."

 *September* 20

WHEN GAINING IS LOSING

"There is a saying that when we have nothing, everything is possible," stated a Sage. "As soon as we possess something, we greatly reduce our possibilities."

"But that makes no sense!" retorted a Seeker. "It would seem that when we gain something, we would have another tool to help us gain more."

"It would seem that way," replied the Sage. "This is the illusion that many people function under, and this is why those who gain the most are often the least happy—and the most burdened."

"Help me understand what you are saying."

"People observe because they are afraid to engage, and people seek gain because they are afraid to dream."

"Begging your pardon, all I hear is a riddle. I cannot make sense of it."

"Think of it as impatience. Those who want and those who have are one and the same. Those who want already have it in their minds, and those who have, want more. When we clutch something, we no longer have an open hand; and our impatience causes us to open our hand only long enough to clutch something else."

"Then how is one to take any action?" asked the Seeker.

"Action is merely the shadow of what I am really doing. When I focus on a goal, the action-shadow becomes all-important. Action is the manifestation of my impatience. When I have nothing, I have everything, for everything is possible. Inaction then becomes action and action becomes inaction: there is no difference. My hand is open and my back is not burdened." ◄

September
21

HOW TO SERVE

A Nun, who had dedicated her life to helping others, dreamed about a Fox with no legs. The Fox was propped upright by two stones and looked well cared for. Puzzled as to how this could be, the Nun sat at a distance and watched. After a short time, a Tiger came to feed and groom the Fox.

"Ah!" exclaimed the Nun when she awoke. "I have been going about serving others all wrong. I will relax my efforts and ask others to do the same, and we will be provided for like the Fox."

The weeks went by, and the Nun and those she once cared for grew weaker and weaker. They ran out of food, they had no firewood for heat, and their clothes grew filthy and tattered. In utter desperation and fatigue, the Nun lay down to sleep, not sure that she would get up again.

That night she dreamed again about the Fox and the Tiger.

She awoke trembling uncontrollably and could hardly gain enough composure to sit up and open her eyes. "What a fool I've been!" she said to herself. "All this time I assumed I should be like the Fox, when my dream was actually telling me to be like the Tiger!"

September
22

RIGHT GUIDANCE

"I am often left confused when one person tells me one thing and another person tells me another," lamented a Seeker. "I don't know which is true for me."

"Words can be confusing in and of themselves," replied the Sage, "not to mention the motivation of the speaker. Yet there is no need for confusion, as true Guidance is self-evident in everyday life. You can witness it in action whenever you want, as it is living, breathing consciousness."

"This I understand," replied the Seeker. "What I don't understand is how I would recognize false Guidance."

"By its very nature, as it is self-limiting. Either by implication or direct statement, it claims to be right. Yet when you hear it, you will sense that a curtain over your infinite nature is being pulled shut."

"That sounds so clear and beautiful, only my mind has a way of twisting things. It so easily turns joy into sorrow and makes black look white."

"That is because you are listening to your mind rather than feeling it. Right Guidance feels freeing. You will sense it intuitively and immediately, without having to think about it. Sham Guidance, on the other hand, is conjecture and fantasy that is made up by Scholars and Religious Leaders to promote their interests. It will irritate your brain right away, and you will know to walk away from it."

"Once I recognize Right Guidance, how shall I walk with it?" asked the Seeker.

"You will see first that it fits both within and around you, and that it is inclusive. It embraces everybody and everything; it does not stop with you, but speaks through you. Most of all, it will manifest in your life as humility. With it, you cannot help but be an honorable person, shun answers, and live in the wonder of the question that rises with every breath and thought and sight and sound." ⚡

September
23

CONSCIOUS GIVING

There is a man in our village who is wise beyond his years, yet he shies away from being called a Sage and prefers not to have Seekers spend time with him. He would rather be with the children, so he wanders happily from village to village with a sack over his shoulder that is filled with fruit and other delectables. When he comes upon a group of children playing, he sits down with them, opens his sack, and shares what he has. In the process, he learns from them and they learn from him.

Whenever the happy man comes across a Seeker, he asks for a contribution to his sack. Often he is asked to share some of his Teachings he carries, which he does, then asks for a gift.

One day on his travels, he came upon another Sage, who asked him, "What is the deeper meaning of Awakening?"

In reply, he set his sack down and stood in silence.

"What then," asked the Sage, "is the manifestation of Awakening?"

At that, the merry man hoisted the sack back onto his shoulder and proceeded on his way. ↝

September
24

FROM HOT, COLD

"What is wrong with me?" a Seeker asked of his comrades. "I have all this passion in me for seeking The Way, and I want to jump into things with everything I have. Only the Elders tell us that passion gets in the way, and that feelings warp our thoughts. That makes no sense to me! I cannot imagine a life that is not fueled by passion."

"I am confused by the same thing," added another Seeker. "How can it be possible to lust for the Quest and not have it overflow onto other things?"

"Let us take our confusion to our Elder," stated the first Seeker, "for it is clearly beyond us to make sense of this."

After the Seekers expressed their bewilderment to the Elder, he replied, "There is no sense to be made of your dilemma. You are merely looking at apples and seeing peaches. You are confusing passion with the fire of the heart."

"How are they not one and the same?"

"Passion is raw and erupts like a volcano, and it can be just as unpredictable and destructive. At other times, it lies dormant when we really need it. For these two reasons, it is vital for the Seeker not to be impassioned, but dispassioned."

"How does that differ from the fire of the heart?"

"The heart fire is a steady flame, always warm for nurturing and always there to guide. Whether we are joyful or despairing, whether we are in the company of friends or lost in a storm, the heart fire is there."

"How does that translate to daily life?" asked one of the Seekers.

"How does it manifest differently from passion?" asked another.

"The heart glows like a warm fire," replied the Elder, "yet the eyes are as cold as an abandoned hearth."

"How can that be? The heart and the eyes must have to work together. Are the eyes not the doorway to the heart? And does the heart not reach out through the eyes?"

"Cold eyes see all. They show no like or dislike, and they have no need or grudge. Is it not cold wood that makes a warm fire? When we perceive everything without filters, we keep the flame for our Quest burning hot and bright."

September
25

WHEN THIS IS THAT

In a land not far from ours, there lives a Monk who travels back and forth between two villages. He spends the majority of his time in the first village, conducting weekly dialogues in the square, giving private consultations, and guiding the children by his example. In the second village, he might spend part of a day sharing Teachings, then disappear without letting the villagers know when he will be back.

One day, a Seeker who sometimes traveled with the Monk, asked him, "Why do you spend so much time at one village and so little at the other?"

"Go and be with the people in both villages," replied the Monk, "then come back and tell me what you have found."

Several weeks went by and the Seeker returned to the Monk with this story: "In the first village, where you spend most of your time, I found that the people are very content. They have come to rely on your constant presence and everyday Guidance, and they all think highly of you and get along well with each other. In the second village, I found several groups. One of them considers your Teachings so precious that they cling to every word. They have formed a cult around you, and they shun all voices but yours. The second group is angry with you. They feel abandoned because you are not there when they need you. Those in a third group believe they are the Anointed Ones and claim special privilege in your absence—they teach as though they are speaking for you."

continued on page 318

continued from page 317

"What is your assessment of each village?" asked the Monk.

"If I may be so bold, I think the second village is in rough shape, because you have neglected its people. I think you should treat them more like those in the first village, where everyone is content and well mannered."

"That would appear to be the case, wouldn't it? Yet there is a saying that to know somebody's true nature, look at the opposite of what his critics claim. The first village looks harmonious; however, that peace comes from me rather than them. If for some reason I were not able to be there, they could not stand on their own, for they have developed a dependency on me.

"In the second village, on the other hand, the people know each other for who they truly are: their strengths and weaknesses, their needs and motivations. This will help each of them see where they need to grow, and in this way they will become a strong, deeply content people. In time of crisis, they will have the resilience to pull together."

"According to the saying that the Truth is the opposite of what the critic sees," replied the Seeker, "your hands-off approach with the second village is better than your engaged approach with the first."

"It does appear so. Yet we still have opposites, with the bad now appearing to be good, and the good seeming to be bad."

"Then what have we gained? There must be a catch."

"There is a catch: it is reverse thinking, which has created the opposites and the seeming conflict. Look rather at the two villages as one people, for they often visit and share with each other. Their Awakening will not come from any single approach, but from the fertile mix of all their approaches." ◄

September
26

HOW THE MUSES WORK

In a park one day, a group of Nuns gathered to explore what is known by various people as karma, intendedness, fate, or serendipity.

"What is common to all of these experiences?" asked one of the Nuns.

After a reflective pause, another replied, "I would say that they all describe series of events that are related to each other, with one influencing the next, then the next."

"I think it is simpler than that," commented another. "Whether we call these occurrences serendipitous, karmic, or whatever, they are just fancy terms for plain old cause-and-effect. If I open the gate, the Donkey is going to get out."

"If that is the case," said another, "what about a child who is being punished for breaking a window? Is it because someone gave her a ball for her birthday, or is it because a friend told her to bounce the ball off of the wall next to the window? Or might it be because the neighbor was outside and saw her do it?"

"All of a sudden," said another Nun, "our simple cause-and-effect scenario has become a complex interactive web. I'm sure it has even more factors involved than the few we just listed. It looks like we are in for a long discussion." ↝

September 27

EMBRACING WHAT IS

A wealthy woman wanted to become a Seeker. She knew that she must renounce everything she once held dear and live as though all that mattered was breathing without thought. At some point she must even let that go, she realized. "But who will show me the way of complete nonattachment?" she asked herself.

At that moment, a wandering Seeker passed by. She carried nothing but her bowl and a blanket to sleep under.

"There is a person who can show me the way of nonattachment!" the woman exclaimed. She asked if she could join the rover.

"If you can stay with me for this night and the next day," the Seeker replied, "I would be honored to have you ramble with me."

That evening, they came upon an Elder who was dying.

"Bury me right here beside the road," he implored, "so that I may continue my Journey. This road has guided me well all my long life, and I have much more yet to discover."

With that, the Elder breathed his last breath. The two dutifully buried him.

As it grew dark, the wealthy woman asked, "What shall we eat?"

"The one who passed on left us his food," replied her guide. "Let us partake, for this is one way the Journey provides."

The well-to-do woman could not eat the food. The next morning, she was gone. ❧

 *September*
28

LET THAT BE YOUR GATEWAY

A Seeker and an Elder were walking silently together down a country lane.

"Honored Elder," spoke the Seeker after a time, "where can I find the open gate to awareness?"

"Do you hear that Stream flowing over there?" asked the Sage. "Let that be your opened gate."

"But I can't hear it," replied the youth after he strained to pick up the sound he expected to hear. "Those rickety old carts and noisy Donkeys going up and down the road drown everything out."

"Then let that be your gateway."

September
29

THE LAKE AND BIRDS ARE MY FRIENDS

An old story endures of an Elder who was sitting outside under the Trees when a neighbor came over and asked what he was doing.

"I am having tea with my friends," the Elder replied.

"But how can that be?" commented the neighbor. "There is nobody here but you."

The Elder looked up and spread his arms to encompass all around him.

"What are you saying?" proclaimed the neighbor. "I am afraid I do not understand."

"Do you not see the Lake and the Hills?"

"I do."

"And the Finches and the Squirrel?"

"Truly, I do."

And look here at our feet, where the Butterfly rests and the Cricket scurries. These are all my friends, and we are sharing our morning together in pleasant conversation."

September
30

TO KNOW A FOOL

Folk Wisdom says that to judge someone as a Fool is to judge yourself for not being able to see who that person is. Some Fools live in worlds other than ours, some Fools are disguising who they are, and other Fools are people who guard their Wisdom.

There was a Seeker who would appear in odd places at odd times. He would say inappropriate things and ask questions that seemed irrelevant to the topic at hand. His fellow Seekers considered him a distraction and a troublemaker.

One day while this Seeker was talking with the Sage who guided him, a Monk from a far-off land arrived to meet with the Sage.

"Will you wait outside while the Monk and I meet?" asked the Sage of the Seeker.

"What is the reason that I should be excluded?" asked the Seeker. "And what is the reason that I should step outside, rather than this good Monk?"

The Sage bowed to the Seeker, and both he and the Monk stepped outside. ━

 *October*
1

DUMB TIGER

A man wanted to learn the Language of Tigers, so he went to live in the jungle. He came to know all of the Tigers in his area, and he did not find them to be very bright. Still, he wanted to give them a chance to prove themselves, so he went to the wisest of them and asked, "Do you know why this brush grows under the Trees?"

"It conceals our movements," replied the Tiger, "and sometimes we catch small animals there for our lunch."

"What do you think of mud?"

"It comes after the rains," said the elder Cat, "and when it gets between my toes, it dries and irritates them."

"And what do you think we Humans lack most?"

"That's easy!" exclaimed the Tiger. "You don't have claws."

If that's all the wisest of them knows, thought the man to himself, *my hunch was right: Tigers aren't very smart.*

After the man left, a Monkey came down from a Tree and asked the Tiger what he and the man were talking about.

"Not much," the Tiger said to the Monkey. "He asked me some meaningless questions, which made me realize that his kind aren't very smart, so I had to give him simple answers." ➤

 *October*
2

FACING ONE'S SELF

"What shall I do when I meet someone on the road who is Awakened?" asked a neophyte Nun who was preparing to travel.

"What could you not do?" replied the Elder-Nun.

"I don't think I could talk to her, yet I would feel even more uneasy if I stood there in silence."

"If you could speak from your heart to hers, all would be well. If you have trouble doing so, look around you without trying to see anything. It will bring you back to your heart center. Then do or say whatever comes to you."

"Whatever comes?" asked the younger Nun.

"Whatever comes," said the Elder "She will then know you as a woman of The Way, and it will help the two of you feel comfortable with each other." ⁓

October
3

ATTUNEMENT

A butcher was slicing up an animal for his customer. He cut through the meat as gracefully as a dancer.

"How splendid!" said his customer. "Your skill level is unbelievable!"

"When I was learning the trade," replied the butcher, "my focus was on the animal and how I was using my knife. In time, I forgot about both the animal and the knife, because I became them both. After that, it was as though the knife knew where to go on its own, slipping between bones and around tendons with no effort."

"What a story!" the customer exclaimed. "How did your skill evolve?"

"Early in my apprenticeship, I hacked more than cut and needed a new knife every month. When I improved at the craft, a knife would last me a year. This knife and I have been one for nearly twenty years, and we have long ago lost count of the number of animals we have prepared in that time. When a blade has no thickness, there is plenty of room between the joints. Having met no resistance, this knife has stayed as fine as when it was first shaped on the grindstone."

October
4

WHEN BLACK IS WHITE

A woman came to the town market to purchase some fabric from a weaver. She selected a piece she liked and offered two gold coins for it. The weaver frowned and took back the fabric. The woman took another coin out of her pouch.

"Please leave my sight," growled the weaver, "I have had enough of you!"

Rather than offering yet another coin, which the woman thought the beautiful fabric might actually be worth, she thought it would be best to leave and not risk insulting the angry weaver any more.

After the woman left, the merchant in the next booth asked the weaver what the altercation was about.

"That woman was insulting," replied the weaver. "She looked through my bolts of fabric, picked out the worst one, and pretended to offer me twice what it was worth. She saw how it shamed me, but that wasn't enough for her. She then pulled out another coin, and that was more than I could take. No one deserves that kind of treatment, so I told her to leave."

October

5

APPEARANCES AND TRUTH

One story about the Hermit who lives on the island in the big Swamp north of our village is that he was once a renowned artist. Only the wealthiest of the nobility could afford his work. Very few people respected him, yet those who coveted his work would fraternize with him.

Once a well-to-do matron asked him to execute a painting at a gala she was hosting. She saw how such unparalleled entertainment would boost her social standing.

"I will do your bidding," replied the artist, "but only if you will meet my price and pay me in advance."

The matron agreed.

When the artist arrived at the event, the matron brought him up in front of everybody and said, "You are an artist beyond compare. You have agreed to paint a picture here before us today. Yet your greed has tainted your mind to the point where your work should hardly be worth the canvas it is painted upon. Now I will provide you with a canvas to match your character."

She pulled one of her undergarments out from under her dress. The attendees snickered. The artist remained unfazed and created a piece of art worthy of any canvas. Then he left, never to be seen again.

At the time, nobody knew that he was a Monk from another province, where famine had left the peasants destitute. The noble class ignored the plight of the peasants and traveled abroad to escape the heat and locusts. The Monk, unbeknownst to anyone in the province, was previously a great painter. He left his homeland and adopted his old persona to raise funds to provide for his people.

With the matron's commission, he had all the money he needed. He gave away his brushes and turned to his ascetic life, which he continues to this day in the middle of the great Swamp north of our village. ❧

October
6

HORSE SENSE

One evening just before sunset, several Seekers were walking down the road back to their village. They heard a galloping Horse coming up quickly behind them. The local people were already home for the evening meal and travelers had found their night's lodging, so the Seekers were surprised to see anyone else on the road, much less someone in such a hurry.

They quickly stepped aside to let the Horse and rider pass. They wondered why the woman was traveling at such speed, and so late. *Maybe she needs help*, they thought, *or she could be responding to an emergency*. As she passed, they called out, "Where are you going in such a hurry?"

The rider shouted back, "I don't know, but it appears my Horse does."

October
7

DIRT MAGIC

A few years ago, a raging flood engulfed all of the lowland farms along a River. The townspeople, safe up on the bluff, looked out over the valley and witnessed the devastation as it happened. Carts floated by with drowned Horses still attached. Barns, and even cottages, were swept down in the current. One could only imagine what had happened to their inhabitants.

"Look!" shouted one of the children. "There are two people out on that roof!"

Everybody strained their eyes, and sure enough, they could make out two people on the roof of a building that had gotten caught in a snag.

"We must rescue them," said someone else. However, nobody dared fight the swift current.

A Wizard lived just outside the town, and several of the young men ran to ask her if it would be safe enough to attempt a rescue.

"I will throw a handful of dirt in the fire," she said. "If It puts the fire out, you will surely meet your deaths if you try to rescue them. However, if the flames jump high, you will be successful."

Picking up a handful of the dirt at her feet, the Sorcerer tossed it into the fire. Instantly a flash of crimson flames leapt Skyward, so bright that it nearly blinded the men. Infused with courage, they sprinted down to the water's edge and slipped a boat into the torrent. They rowed resolutely and reached the mother and child just as their roof raft crumbled.

The current ripped at the boat and demanded every last thread of the men's strength, yet they knew they were going to succeed, so never once did they waver. When they reached shore, a shout of joy rose up from all the townspeople, and they rejoiced into the night.

Meanwhile, the Wizard's apprentice asked her, "How did you get that dirt to burn?"

"Through the power of faith. Miracles happen only when we trust that they can happen, and that's all those young men needed. Do you see that jar of Moss spores up there on the shelf? They are extremely flammable, and I gather them every autumn for our magical fires. I had already mixed some spores with the dirt in front of the fire and I trusted that the men were capable of the rescue, so I gave them their missing ingredient: trust in themselves." ～

October
8

IN OR OUT?

Some guests will come inside without considering what they might be dragging in with them. Their shoes could be wet or muddy, and they might leave a trail across the floor for their host to clean up later.

Conscious guests will ask their hosts if they would prefer footwear removed, and conscious hosts will speak their Truths and inform their guests of household protocols.

One particular Seeker was quite considerate of others. Once when she went to visit an Elder, she asked, "Would you prefer that I put my shoes inside or outside the door?"

"What I would prefer right now is a buttered biscuit and a bowl of hot rice pudding," replied the Elder. ⇝

October
9

ELUSIVE WISDOM

"How can true Wisdom be told?" asked a Seeker.

"Are you assuming that there is such a thing as true Wisdom?" replied the Sage.

"Is that not what we are seeking?"

"Listen to what you just said, and you will find your Truth."

"Of course, Wise One!" the Seeker exclaimed after a moment's reflection. "I have forgotten. It is the seeking, not the Wisdom, that forms the Path before us. Seeing Sage, does Wisdom even exist?"

"Let me answer that with a story," responded the Sage. "There was once a Hermit who was reputed to possess great Wisdom. He was very hard to find, as he lived on a remote Mountain. Nevertheless, on rare occasion a very dedicated Seeker would track him down and ask him to share the Wisdom he had gained.

"The Hermit would stand in silence until the first Bird sang. Then he would turn from the Seeker, pack his few belongings, and retreat to an even more remote part of the Mountain."

October
10

SEEING UP CLOSE

A young Monk went out in the jungle to live the life of a Hermit; however, he found no contentment. Yet the effort helped him realize that the reason he went to the jungle was that people had called him stingy and unforgiving. For deeper clarity, he took his realization to an Elder Monk who had his hermitage some distance away in the same jungle.

"I have come to see that my struggle with other people was actually a struggle with myself," lamented the younger Monk. "How can I break free of my shackles and attain true empathy?"

The Elder held his clenched fist out before the younger one and asked, "What would you think of my hand if it were always this way?"

"I would say it was badly wounded, or diseased."

The Elder then opened his hand wide with the palm up and asked again, "What would you think of my hand if it were always this way?"

"I would again say that there is something wrong with it, and that it ought to be taken care of."

"You have just told us both that you understand something is wrong, and that it should be remedied. It appears that you have what you need in order to find your empathetic self."

The younger Monk returned to the village, where he found great satisfaction in lending his talents to those in need. ▬

 *October* 11

THE VALUE OF VALUE

"My mother is very precious to me," commented a Seeker. "Is this a help or a hindrance on my Journey?"

"And my work with the poor is the most cherished thing to me," added another Seeker. "I wonder, too, if this is helpful to me or not."

"How does holding something in value affect you?" asked the Sage.

"I protect it, and I give it special attention," replied one of the Seekers.

"I think of it often," replied another.

"That is admirable," responded the Sage, "yet what you are giving your attention to is not the most valuable thing in the world."

"Then what is? Could it be the seeking of Wisdom? Or being Awakened? Or is it just being?"

"It is a dead Rat lying in the gutter."

"That makes no sense!" cried the Seekers. "how can that possibly be?"

"Because no one can attach a value to it." ⌒⌣

October 12

THE SHADOW SAGE

In a faraway land lived a Sage who despised being a Sage. She wanted nothing to do with the attention Sages receive, nor with the protocols Sages follow in working with Seekers. Still, she was dedicated to her calling and knew that what she had been given had to be gifted back to her people.

She would often disguise herself as a Seeker and sit amongst other Seekers in front of Sages. In the space of a few years, these Sages gained notable reputations for their perceptiveness and uncanny ability to guide their Seekers through the travails encountered on the Journey to Awakening. Little did the Sages know that there was an Elder Sage sitting in their audience, planting seeds of awareness in the hearts of the Seekers. These seeds would bring forth the blossoming of understanding what the Sages were sharing.

When readying herself to leave this life, the Elder Sage chose two successors from the Sages with whom she had secretly worked. When their time came to leave their bodies, they did the same.

That tradition has been passed down through the centuries to this day. Now, whenever a group of Seekers comes together, you can be well assured that one of them is actually a Sage planting seeds of Ancient Wisdom.

October
13

CREATING TRUTH

"How many kinds of Truth are there?" asked a Seeker.

"There is only one," replied the Sage. "When we Awaken, we speak from our hearts, and that is Truth. There are shades of that Truth that can be brought out by rules and practices. These shades can certainly ring closer to the heart than the voice of the ego, yet they are no more a stand-in for the Truth than a picture of a Tree is for the Tree itself."

"Will you give me an example?" requested the Seeker.

The Sage considered for a moment. "I will show you how the mind can create the illusion of Truth. Imagine that there is a ferryman who will provide safe passage over the River to anyone who speaks her Truth. Anyone who does not speak Truth he will throw overboard to drown. A woman approaches the ferryman and says, 'I have come to be tossed into the River and drowned.'"

"'That is not your Truth,' replies the ferryman, 'so when we are halfway across the River, I must throw you in.'"

"'Would that not then prove that I *am* speaking my Truth?' asked the woman."

The Seeker reflected on the story for a while, then finally said, "I believe I understand what you are saying: Truth is not a matter of the mind, nor can it be arrived at through some structure. I bow to your Wisdom, Insightful Sage." ◂

October
14

THE VALUE OF TEACHINGS

One evening, a blind Seeker was leaving for home after visiting a friend.

"It is dark tonight," said the friend. "Here, take this candle lantern to help you on your way."

"Kind friend," replied the Seeker, "I have no need for a lantern, as dark and light are meaningless to me."

"This is not to help you see," said the friend, "but to help others see you."

"But of course!" stated the Seeker. "That makes perfect sense. I'll be glad to take the lantern."

When the Seeker had gotten about halfway home, someone walked into him.

"What's wrong with you?" the Seeker exclaimed. "Can't you see the lantern I'm carrying?"

"I'm afraid your candle has gone out," replied the other person.

October
15

PRESENCE SPEAKS

A Monk struggled mightily in his conversations with people. Whenever he answered a question, or what he thought was a question, people would look confused, as though he was taking part in some distant conversation. He decided to seek the help of another Monk who lived on the same Mountain.

"What is the way to answer a question?" he asked his fellow Monk. "What can I do so that they do not think I am in some far-off land?"

There was a moment of quiet, then the second Monk replied, "What did you just see me do in response to your question?"

"All I saw you do is raise your eyes."

"And how did that make you feel?"

The visiting Monk paused for a moment, then said, "Connected. You brought your attention to me."

"To you, to another, or to anything," replied the second Monk. "It does not matter what. The secret is presence. When I am present, I have already answered your question, for that is really all you wanted."

October
16

IT COULD BE

Some Seekers were listening to a visiting Sage, who was giving a talk on The Way. It grew late in the afternoon and the Sage had some distance to travel that day, so he begged his leave of the attentive Seekers.

While he was gathering up his things, a Seeker came up to him and said, "You bring us valued Wisdom. I have never heard sacred matters spoken of so clearly before. May your voice be heard by many on your travels."

"Well, perhaps that is so," replied the Sage.

Another Seeker approached the Sage and said, "I forced myself to stay through to the end of your talk, hoping I would hear something of value, yet all you did was fill the Air with hollow words. I hope you gain some Teachings on your Journey, so that someday you may truly be a Wise One."

"Well, perhaps that is so," said the Sage, who looked upon both of the Seekers, smiled, and continued on his way. ➤

 *October* 17

BE LIKE A RAINDROP

"When I can be perfectly honest with myself," said the Nun, "I often find that fear is behind what I say and do."

"How is that so?" asked the Elder.

"Something will come out of my mouth," she replied, "and it doesn't feel right. So I say something else to try to fix it, and I end up just not feeling good about myself. This is when I feel my fear. Instead of making it go away, my efforts only strip it naked."

"Those whose lives are ruled by fear," said the Elder, "disguise it in many ways. From what you are telling me, it is likely that fear is an even bigger part of your life than you think it is."

"It's not that bad!" said the Nun defensively. "My fear only comes up at times."

"Right here is an example: you just reacted out of fear."

"You're right, Wise One, "responded the Nun. "I just have a hard time admitting it."

"Do you ever feel rejected, and do you ever reject others?"

"Yes, sometimes I do."

"Again, that is fear. And so is clinging, whether it is to people, things, or beliefs. There is no difference between rejection and clinging; one is just a form of the other."

"It's as though you know me," replied the Nun. "I am embarrassed, because I feel exposed in front of you."

"It is not you that I am seeing, but rather your fear. It may control your life, but do not confuse it with who you are." After a short pause, the Elder continued: "Do you find yourself criticizing others?"

"I do, because I want to help them out."

"Those who criticize are cowards, and cowardice is simply fear. Criticism is only an attempt to mitigate the pain caused by fear."

"I can't believe that is so," said the Nun. "How could I have possibly gone this long without realizing that this was going on with me?"

"Fear is like those who rule, as rulers are just criminals who have not been caught."

"If that is the case, how ever can I get over this demon fear that has overtaken me?"

"By being like a drop of rain falling from the Sky," answered the Elder, "with no strictures and no concern for where you might land." ❧

October
18

THE FOOL

In the next village lives an Elder who was once considered to be very serious. She would always speak properly and apply herself diligently to matters that needed attention. However, in private she was frivolous and whimsical, always joking and making light of things.

She kept up this dual personality for all of her adult life, so that three generations of people knew just her serious persona. Only those in her inner circle ever saw her whimsical side.

One day she went to the village laughing, dancing, and joking with everyone she met. She continued to do so day after day, as though she never was the stoic person nearly everyone knew her to be.

Some people thought she had taken leave of her senses, and others liked the new Elder they saw. Yet the Scholars turned grim, accusing her of throwing away a lifetime of dedication to a serious, responsible life.

After some time, the Elder called all of the people together in the village square and said to them, "I have chosen to make a Teaching of my life. To those of you who thought my soberness and dedication gave me value, you might now see how shallow that is by how easily I deceived you. You who mistook Fools for idiots now know what a Fool is capable of, for I have served you all my life in matters of importance." ━

19

THE VOICE OF SILENCE

"I have a very important question for you," announced a Sage when a group of Monks came to visit her. "Who is served by past and future Awakened Ones?"

There were a few guesses, though no one had real clarity.

"When our voice comes not from the heart, it is best not to speak," commented the Sage.

"How else will we find the answer?" asked a Monk.

"An answer comes faster and more clearly when we do not try to extract it with words."

"Yet without words for confirmation, how will we know it is the answer?" asked another Monk.

"You will know because the answer will need no verification. It will be as though you ran into your mother by surprise in an unfamiliar, busy market. Even though she was in the middle of a crowd of strangers, would any words be needed to confirm her identity?"

"I understand," said several of the Monks.

One of them then asked, "Are there any signs to help us recognize when we are ready for wordless knowing?"

"You will have no more desire to discuss another person's faults," replied the Sage, "and it will be distasteful for you to interfere in another person's life."

"It all sounds so mystical," commented the Monks.

"Perhaps that will be your experience. Then again, the picture I painted might have been unnecessary, as it could have already happened to you, though you are not yet aware of it."

October 20

THE PATHLESS PATH

"What is Truth?" asked a new Nun.

The Elder remained silent.

Later, an older Nun said to the young one, "Any words from the Elder would have given you a Path to follow."

"Is a Path not what I need?" she replied.

"When you cross a rushing Stream on a fallen log, what need is there for a Path? When you are in the middle of an endless field of grass, is there a direction to take for finding more grass?"

"Would an endless field not lead to confusion?" asked the new Nun.

"Leaves rustle even in the faintest breeze."

"What, then, am I to do? You have deconstructed all that I thought was important."

"Let yourself go into free-fall," responded the Elder Nun.

October
21

THE FAR SIDE OF LANGUAGE

"What is the purpose of a fishtrap?" asked the Elder.

"To catch Fish, I suppose," replied a Seeker.

"What do you do with the trap after you catch your Fish?" continued the Elder.

"I would let it sit," said another Seeker, "and take my Fish home to eat."

The Elder then asked about the purpose of a Rabbit snare.

"It is to catch Rabbits," said a third Seeker. "As with the fishtrap, I would set the snare aside, clean the Rabbit, then bring her in to roast her for a meal."

"Now, what is the purpose of words?" asked the Elder.

"Ah, I see where you are taking us!" cried a Seeker. "Words transmit ideas, and once we grasp the ideas, we can forget the words."

"This is all true," concluded the Elder. "If ever you come across someone who has forgotten words, please send her to me—she is the person I would like to talk with." ➤

October
22

WHAT TO ASK FOR

A Sage and a group of Seekers were sitting comfortably under a Tree and having tea.

The Sage broke the silence by asking, "What is it you want?"

Each Seeker listed what he or she was after: consciousness, selflessness, nonattachment, wordlessness.

"Those are all noble-sounding goals," commented the Sage. "What do they show that you all hold in common?"

"We all want something," replied a Seeker.

"Yes," responded the Sage. "It is the wanting that creates goal orientation. It takes us out of the present breath, no matter how admirable the goal."

"Should we then not want these things?"

"It would seem so, wouldn't it? When something does not work, the mind wants to immediately take us to its opposite. Yet there is no difference, because by not wanting something, we still want it."

"That makes no sense!" argued one of the Seekers. "Black is clearly not white."

"Nor is it black," added the Sage. "It never did turn a color, and here is why: when I want something and say I don't want it, all I do is put a *don't* in front of it. I may have disguised, suppressed, or substituted something, yet it is still there."

"Then what is the answer?"

"There you go—you want something again." ⚬

 *October* 23

WHAT WE SEE

The Void—the Mindless Mind—is a scary place for many new Seekers to even consider entering. There is no identity, no control, no words. A common question Seekers pose is, "When one enters The Void, is it possible to see, or is there only blackness?"

"For me, it is both," replied one Elder-Nun to a Seeker.

"How is it possible to both see and not see?" asked the Seeker.

"What I see are the wordless meanderings of my mind," replied the Nun, "and what I do not see are good people versus bad people, or the right thing versus the wrong thing to do. In the Void, everything simply is what it is, but to me only. This is why an Awakened being cherishes dwelling there."

October
24

EMANCIPATION

"When a person becomes Awakened," asked a Seeker, "does that mean she is no longer ruled by cause-and-effect?"

"What is cause-and-effect?" replied the Sage.

"I think it has to do with will and its result: when I do this, that happens."

"What does this imply?"

"It appears as though there is a duality."

"When is there no duality?"

The Seeker gave some thought to the Sage's question, then said, "I would guess that there would not be a duality when cause-and-effect cease to exist, or when cause-and-effect become One."

"How would that happen?"

"Aha, now I see!" exclaimed the Seeker. "When I become One with cause-and-effect, they *are* no longer opposed to each other. In fact, they are no longer."

The Sage smiled.

October
25

GIVING IS RECEIVING

Outside a neighboring village, a Monk lived in a hut at the end of a seldom-used path. A thief heard about the Monk and thought his remote location would make him the perfect victim for his next heist.

On the way up the path to the Monk's hut, he came upon another thief he knew.

"What brings you here to this lonely place in the night?" the first thief asked the second.

"I suspect for the same reason as you," replied the second thief. "I over-heard some townspeople talking about the Hermit-Monk who lived up this path, and I thought he would be easy prey."

"Let us then join forces," said the first thief. "It will all the more assure our success."

As they approached the clearing in front of the Monk's hut, the first thief whispered to the second, "His lamp is out, so he must be asleep. I will sneak into the hut and grab what I can, then I will make noise to wake him up. He will jump up to come after me, and you will club him as he runs out the door. You can then take his robes and whatever else you find."

"No, let me go first," retorted the second thief, "or else you will take everything valuable, and I will be left with only the rags he wears to bed."

"I am more fair than that," scowled the first thief. "Besides, I am taking the bigger risk!"

They began to argue, then shout, which quickly led to punches. Soon they were wrestling each other to the ground.

Startled out of his sleep, the Monk jumped up, suspected the worst, and grabbed his few belongings. He hurried down the trail toward the village, right by the two tussling thieves, who were too preoccupied to notice him.

The thieves proved the sage Wisdom that a person's throat is most often cut by his own tongue. ➤

October
26

CHERISH THE ONE

A woman in our hamlet had a compulsion to steal. Whether the item was small or big, trivial or valuable, didn't matter—she had to have it. She not only took things from her fellow Seekers, but also from their Elder.

One day, several Seekers caught her in the act and took her to see the Elder. However, the Elder did nothing but smile and wish them all a pleasant day.

Several days passed and some Seekers caught her again, then another time a couple of months later. Each time they took her to the Elder, and as with the first time, he did nothing to correct her.

Dismayed, the Seekers talked amongst themselves about what they should do. They approached their Elder and said, "We are deeply concerned about your refusal to reprimand our troubled fellow Seeker. If you do not act, we must regretfully leave you and go study elsewhere."

"That is an option you have," replied the Elder, "for there are many places you can go to be guided in your Quest for Knowledge. However, where would your sister go if we were to turn her away? She is most in need of Guidance, and who will be there for her if I am not? Even if you all go, I will continue to serve as her Guide."

When the young woman heard what had transpired, something melted inside her—it was as though she never had the urge to steal. For the first time in her life, she felt whole. From then on, she found contentment in whatever the moment laid before her. ⌇

October
27

QUESTIONS KILL

"Kindest Elder," said a Seeker, "I now understand how answering questions numbs my consciousness, yet what about the questions themselves?"

"Just by considering that possibility, you have Awakened," replied the Elder. "Imagine a rope dangling over a cliff. You are hanging from it by your teeth, and your hands and feet are tied so that you cannot use them. Now somebody asks you a question, and you have the answer. However, if you open your mouth, you fall to your death; if you keep the answer inside, you hang there perpetually by your teeth, with the answer chewing away at your brain. What has gotten you into this predicament, and what can you do about it?"

"There is no salvation, at least not that I can see," replied the woman. "To answer or not to answer…it seems that the only choice is between a slow death and a fast death."

"It sounds as though you are accepting your quandary."

"If that is the case, perhaps I ought to look at what got me into it. I believe the question did it."

"What question?" asked the Elder.

"Ha—you have given it away!" exclaimed the Seeker. "With no question, there is no predicament, because there is no answer-or-no-answer dichotomy. There just *is*."

October
28

THE POWER OF ILLUSION

In a remote district lived a Sage and a group of Seekers who had dedicated themselves to the study and understanding of the Ancient Teachings.

"We are coming to resemble Scholars," announced the Sage one day. "Let us burn every note and book and abandon every practice that we have accumulated."

"How enlightened!" commented the Seekers. "By releasing ourselves of our conventions and accoutrements, we will arrive at the Essence!"

Not long after, the governor issued a ban on all scholarly studies and exercises. All books on the Ancient Wisdom were to be burned, and any practitioners would be severely punished.

Many of the people took up the cause. Gangs scoured neighborhoods, focusing on houses where they suspected contraband.

When they came to the cabin of the Sage and the Seekers, they found everyone out in the yard, having a good time burning texts. As the gang passed, the two groups cheered each other on. ✒

October
29

PASSION CRIPPLES

A Seeker went to a Scholar and said earnestly, "I am devoted to studying the Sacred Texts. I want to know them inside out, so I that will be able to recite them in my sleep. How long will it take me to master them?"

The Scholar casually replied, "Ten years."

"But I can't wait that long!" protested the Seeker. "I want to master the Texts faster than that. I will work very hard, reading and reciting every day, from dawn until dusk if I have to. Wherever I go, I will take pages with me. How long will it then take?"

The Scholar thought for a moment and said, "Twenty years."

30

LOOK BENEATH

The feel and look of gold excites many a person. One afternoon, a woman attending a bazaar passed by the booth of a jeweler, who had a stunning gold bracelet displayed on his blanket. She walked straight up to it, grabbed it, and ran.

"Stop her!" shouted the jeweler. She was apprehended and brought to the magistrate. "Why is it that you took this bracelet in plain sight of so many people?" he asked.

"Honorable One," the woman explained, "I saw no people. My eyes were blind to everything else—there was only the gold."

"I hear your Truth," replied the magistrate. "As a bee does not sting out of spite, many a thief does not steal out of need or greed. Go find the gold in your heart, for then your eyes will seek the gold in the hearts of others."

October
31

SEEKER CONSCIOUSNESS

"What kind of Seeker are you?" a Sage asked the group of young people seated with him.

"What do you mean?" replied one of them. "We all seek Knowledge of The Way. Are we not then all the same kind of Seeker?"

"The difference lies not in what we seek, but in how we seek," replied the Sage. "Some of us are believers and we work to share our approach with others, while some of us work to support others, no matter their approach. Then there are those of us who are merely here, not attached to any particular way."

"Why do these various ways make a difference?" asked another Seeker. "Why is it important for us to know them?"

"It affects your relationship with me," answered the Sage. "You who are believers take advantage of my influence, while you who maintain and support me are grateful for my kindness, and you who are merely present become empowered through my Guidance and discipline. To know our own style of seeking is to know how we can best serve each other when our time comes to do so." ━

 *November*
1

THE STING OF NOTHING

One morning, a young Seeker ran up to a Sage and proudly exclaimed, "Last night I Awakened! I came to realize that there is nothing: everything I see remains unseen, and whatever I think about disintegrates. It became clear to me that you do not exist and that there is no wind, no food, no sadness. There is only eternal emptiness with nothing to put in it, no matter how hard I might try."

Just then a bee landed on the Seeker's neck and stung her.

"It's good that you felt nothing," commented the Sage, "and that you had nothing to swat at—or swat with, for that matter. For if you did, you may not have become Awakened." ❧

 November
2

WHEN HELP HURTS

"I, a humble Seeker, have come to you, Awakened Monk, so that I may learn how to help a friend who is destitute. He has been abandoned by all who know him, and he has nowhere to turn."

"You wish to help him," replied the Monk, "yet it sounds as though he is doing quite well on his own."

"That is a ridiculous statement!" cried the Seeker. "How can you say that?"

"He has the most congenial of company, and right now they are together enjoying the sweetest fruit of the season. You tell me that this man is in dire straits. How can that be?"

"I just saw him, confused Monk, and I assure you that he is as I have described him."

"Does water not quench best when there is a good thirst?" asked the Monk. "His thirst is for a reason, and it sounds as though it has grown to the point where water will now do him the most good."

"I now grasp what you are saying," replied the Seeker. Still, how can you say that he is doing well?"

"Right now he could become wealthier than you or me, as he has the capacity to drink, while we are satiated." ➤

HONORING DYSFUNCTION

There is a Seeker who used to be very different from the way we know her now. She would take naps, sometimes two or three a day. It wasn't because she was particularly tired, and it wasn't because she struggled to engage with life. She had nothing to struggle for or against; her life was just flat.

One warm and quiet afternoon, she went to visit a friend who wasn't home. Not having anything else to do until he arrived, she laid down across his doorway and fell asleep.

Around mid-afternoon, he arrived and attempted to gingerly step over her. However, the tip of his toe caught on her clothing and she awoke with a start.

"Oh, pardon me!" exclaimed the friend. "I didn't mean to disturb you. Please stay where you are and I will be extra quiet so that you can fall back asleep."

At that moment, the young Seeker became what we know her as today: engaged with life and happy to be awake. ∿

 *November* 4

BECOME THE WATER

The bridge was narrow and slippery from the spray of the rapids. A Wizard slipped when crossing and fell in. Unable to gain footing, she got swept away downstream toward the waterfall.

Several people crossing the bridge at the same time saw it happen, yet the swiftness of the current gave no time to grab her. They ran ahead of her on the streambank and reached out with branches for her to grab onto, but she was too far out. All they could do was watch her disappear over the crest of the falls.

"Our Wizard is gone," they later reported to the townspeople. "She was carried over the falls, which surely killed her, and now the River is carrying her out to Sea."

Not knowing what else to do, the shocked townsfolk gathered in the central square to console each other.

"Look!" shouted a child as she pointed to a figure walking toward them through the town gate.

They couldn't believe their eyes. In silent wonderment, they gathered around her.

"Sit down, my friends" she said, "and I shall tell you what happened. When I realized the inevitable, I stopped trying to change it. I stopped thinking and became the Water, and the Water became me. It made me loose and fluid, and the Water and I swirled and tumbled together as one into the Whirlpool." She paused for a moment and looked into the faces of the awestruck townspeople, then continued. "The water and I came out of the Whirlpool together—the same way we went in. I then stood up in the shallows and re-became myself. And that is how I am able to stand here before you." ➤

November
5

WHAT IS WHAT?

"To say *what is, is*, seems so simple," commented a Seeker, "yet we have come to know through our Quest for Knowledge that there is always a deeper meaning or a hidden reason."

"We tell ourselves *what is, is*," another Seeker commented, "but *what is, is* what? Is it not true that when the water recedes, Fish move out to where the water is deeper?"

"That may be what is," added another Seeker, "yet we immediately get into trouble when we define it. Can we assume that all Fish have moved out to deeper water—or that there even *is* deeper water?"

Another Seeker reminded the group that the rational approach could lead to a different answer each time it is taken.

"Let us be cautious here," added a Seeker, "lest we think that one of our insights is better than another. That would show that we have lost the ability to see."

"Of what matter is it anyway if the Fish go to deeper water or not?" asked another Seeker. "The spear that kills is also the spear that gives life."

"Are we doing anything here," questioned another Seeker, "other than showing that the tongue has no bone and can move freely?"

With that, the group walked on and listened to the silence.

November
6

THE MEANING OF STORIES

The Elders of all times have been known to guide Seekers through stories.

"Why do you not explain your stories?" asked a Seeker of a particular Elder. "I'm sure it would help us tremendously."

"What makes you think that?" replied the Elder.

"On our own, we do not know if we interpret them correctly."

"What would you say if I invited you to dinner and served you a Chicken, proceeded to eat it in front of you, then passed you the plate of bones?"

"I have just learned how to listen," said the Seeker as he bowed. ➤

 *November* 7

SET FREE

A woman, overcome with sadness, stopped by to visit a Seer who was sitting out in her garden enjoying the ballet of nectar-sipping Butterflies.

"What troubles you, my grandchild?" asked the Seer.

"I have these overwhelming feelings," responded the woman. "Sometimes they do not let me sleep, and sometimes they cause me to say and do things that I later regret. I have made wasteful choices, and I have hurt people. These feelings have total control of me, and I do not know what to do with them." She then burst into tears.

After the woman regained some composure, the Seer said, "Please show me a couple of these feelings, that I may get to know them."

The woman paused, then said in a trembling voice, "I'm afraid I can't right now."

"That's strange; I thought you said you had these feelings, and that they controlled you. Where are they now?"

"I'm not sure," said the woman. "I never know when they are going to come."

"How curious. If they come and go, is it possible that you do not *have* them? And how can they control you if they are not around?"

"Oh!" Exclaimed the woman. "I see what you are insinuating. If I truly had those feelings, and if they literally controlled me, they would be here now and I could show them to you. But I cannot."

"Yes, granddaughter." Replied the Seer. "Is this Flower right here serving or denying nectar to the Butterfly, or is the Butterfly helping herself to the Flower's nectar? Go, now, and unfurl those wings you have kept bound for so long." ⌁

November
8

THE RIGHT WAY TO ANSWER

"If we are supposed to ever quest and always question," began a Seeker, "does it mean that we are never to answer?"

"That thought came from your Thinking Mind, where a question has to have its opposite, which is an answer," replied the Sage.

"Yet something remains missing," stated the Seeker. "A question cannot just hang in midair."

"The answer to any question is either yes or no. Whatever I answer, no matter how many words I use or allegories I summon, in essence I am saying *yes* or *no*."

"So what is wrong with that?" asked the Seeker.

"It is nonsense," replied the Sage, "because when I say yes, I am saying *no*, and when I say *no*, I am saying *yes*. Choosing one does not have the power to deny the other."

"I do not grasp what you are saying. What is it like to not answer a question?"

"It is like taking a bite of food and neither swallowing it nor spitting it out, but chewing and savoring it. When someone asks what you are doing, tell her you are chewing your food. That is all."

November
9

SPEAK, DON'T ANSWER

"Where did you stay last night?" asked the Sage of a visiting Seeker.

"At an inn about halfway here."

"Which route did you take to get here?"

"I followed the road along the River."

"Did you meet any obstacles?"

"There were none. The weather was good and the walking was easy."

"That's strange," commented the Sage, "as it appears that you did not wake up this morning."

"What do you mean?" protested the Seeker. "I was up at dawn, had a hearty breakfast, and set off."

"You are repeating yourself. You just told me again that you did not awaken."

"If that is so," said the Seeker, "am I now in a dream?"

"It appears that you are marooned on an island where there is only right and wrong, and where one relies on his eyes to tell him what is and isn't. Do you know that this is why you came to me?"

"I know nothing," returned the Seeker, "I only get out of bed, do some things, and go back to bed. I am, as you say, asleep."

"Are you content being asleep?"

"I know nothing else."

With that, the Sage pulled up his robe, turned around to show his behind, and bent over to make it clearly visible.

The Seeker laughed so hard that he was soon doubled over. Then all of a sudden he stopped, looking as though he had just seen his dead mother's ghost. A sense of deep serenity overtook him and he bowed to the Sage, then walked away. ↵

November
10

RIVER CROSSING

On his way to spend some time with others of his kind, a Monk came upon a River he needed to cross. It was shallow; yet the current was swift and the rocks slippery. He realized that it was too dangerous to attempt a crossing, even with a staff to feel his way and steady himself.

While he was contemplating his next move, he noticed a woman on the far shore. Her long white hair and the way she moved told him she was an Elder, so he figured she knew the River better than he did.

"Elderwoman," he called out over the rumble of the rapids, "will you tell me how I can get to the other side?"

Mustering all the energy she could, she shouted back, "Grandson, I believe you already are on the other side." ❧

11

THE TARGET

Tormented was a Seeker by her realization that each person had a Life-Path to follow, and that they were all so dissimilar. One day, she asked a Sage passing through her village why this was so.

"It is like shooting an arrow at a target," he replied. "How many would think that shooting an arrow was the only way to hit the target? Are there not a thousand possibilities?"

"That is my dilemma," lamented the Seeker. "With a thousand possibilities, how do I know which one is for me? I want to have one arrow so that I can take aim and shoot it."

"There are many like you who are frustrated, and there are many who are willing to help those like you find that one arrow. Yet no matter what means they use, what they end up giving you is what you already know and have. This is why you think it is the arrow for you."

"Why would these people deceive me in that way?" asked the Seeker.

"It is because they do not know The Way for themselves, yet they draw some comfort in giving you the illusion of Knowing. There is only one way to know, and that is to know the thousand until they become the one."

November
12

SAY THIS, SAY THAT

"What must I do to become Awakened?" asked a Seeker on her first visit to the Sage.

"I have enough willow here to weave a basket," he replied.

The young woman maintained her composure, even though she was so confused that she had no idea as to what she should say or do next.

"This willow sits very near to you and me," added the Sage, "yet your Mindless Mind has just come closer."

"Closer to what?" asked the Seeker. "And where was it before?"

"Talk of this and that creates a life of this and that," replied the Sage. "And now I must make my basket." ✺

 *November* 13

KNOWING THE PATH

"What might I study to learn about The Way?" asked a Seeker.

"Study takes effort," replied the Sage, "and effort alone makes The Way grow faint."

"Yet if I do not study," said the Seeker, "how will I recognize The Way?"

"You are assuming that there is something to recognize, and you are further assuming that you *need* to recognize it. The Way does not exist in the realm of perception, nor does it exist in the realm of non-perception. Anyway, recognition is a delusion; and non-recognition exists as a possibility only because it was invented by the mind."

"Yet I hear talk of The Way," replied the Seeker with a strained voice, "and I want to somehow embrace it."

"Do this: adopt the eyes of the Sky and the ears of the Mountains, think like a River, and dance when the wind waves the grasses."

At that, the young Seeker cried out in ecstasy. He then bowed before the Sage and remained bowed for a long, long time. ⬤

November
14

SELF-POISONING

A ruler held great disdain for those who would take from others and show no regret. On his way back from warring with a neighboring state, he stopped to see a Mystic who his father, the previous ruler, often consulted.

"We have won the war," began the ruler. "Victory is ours, so why am I not happy?"

"What eats at you when you reflect on the victory?" asked the Mystic.

The ruler thought for a moment, then said, "We may not have started the war, yet we prevailed and took over territory that did not belong to us. I struggle to see how that can be called a victory."

"Is there any real difference between you and those you hate for taking so much and showing so little remorse?"

Tears rolled down the mighty ruler's cheeks as the two men sat in silence.

After a long while, the Mystic said, "Hate and conflict do not go well together. Hate wears us down, yet it does not harm our foe. It is like drinking poison and wishing it would somehow kill the enemy."

November 15

IN A BLINK

"Horse dung is all our search is worth," stated a Nun to a group of Nuns and Monks over breakfast.

Several nodded in agreement, while a number of others frowned.

The Nun continued: "Look at all we do day after day in our Quest to become Awakened. Is it anything beyond what a Horse does day after day? Ultimately, do we have anything more to show for our efforts than does the Horse?"

"Perhaps anything more would get in the way," commented a Monk, "for Awakening can come so fast and unexpectedly that with a mere turn of the head we could miss it."

"That is truly the case," replied a Nun. "If we perceive everything as dung, which it ultimately is, Awakening will shine in comparison. In addition, we are more likely to be aware of it and fully present for it."

"Listening, then, is seeing things for what they truly are," added another Nun.

Everyone nodded in agreement and went on with breakfast in silence.

November
16

WHO IS WISE?

"How can I tell a true Wise One?" a Seeker asked of the Sage.

"She does not need any practice or scripture," replied the Elder.

"How could that be?" said the Seeker. "Don't they give us these things to help us come to awareness?"

"Think of the real Wise One as a shopkeeper. He has far more than enough to provide for himself, so he offers what he does not need to others, for their benefit. Most of what he has comes and goes, and he has no attachment to it. Such is the way of the actual Wise One."

"Yet there are those who claim to be wise and have things to offer that they swear to."

"If what they provide is something to memorize and repeat, or if it is the same for everybody, would you call them Wise Ones?" 〰️

 *November*
17

I AM THE WIND

Seeking Oneness, a man regularly climbed a Mountain. One day on his way up, he caught sight of a woman sitting off to the side on a large rock. He struggled to make out her features because of the bright sun behind her.

"Who are you?" he asked. "I have never seen you here before."

"I am the dancing beams of sun."

Her reply confused him, yet he decided to just continue up the trail.

The next time he went up the Mountain, he saw her again, in the same place. Again he could not make her out, this time because of the fog rolling down from the summit, and again he asked who she was.

"I am the Mountain Mist."

Puzzled again by the woman's reply, the man went on his way.

Later in the year when he came to the Mountain, there again was the woman. This time it was snowing and blowing and he could barely make out her silhouette.

"I must know you from somewhere," he shouted through the blizzard. "Who is your family?"

He strained to hear her response: "I am the wind in your face and the sting of the snow."

This time he truly heard, and right there he came to Oneness. —

November
18

RETRIEVING TRUTH

"Honored Elder, without speaking and without silence, how does one express Truth?" asked a Seeker.

"Some try with regular words," answered the Elder, "some recite poetry, and others point to something else."

"I see that," reflected the Seeker, "yet I don't know that it answers my question."

"Nothing will."

"How, then, do I get to my Truth?"

"The problem is that whatever we decide to do or not to do is never our Truth."

"Then what is?"

"Whatever is left." ➳

November 19

WHERE WORDS STOP

"There must be more," stated a Monk to his comrades and the Sage seated with them. "We have explored so much together, and I feel all the wiser for it. Still, I have this sense that something is missing—something that no one has ever expressed. I can feel it in my bones."

"Yes, that mystic, fabled Teaching does exist," replied the Sage.

"Then what is it?" asked another Seeker. "Please share it with us."

"If only that were possible," said the Sage. "We think words have power, but that is a myth. All they do is excite the mind."

"Then how will we ever receive the Great Teaching that has never before been spoken?"

"The Ocean can give birth to great Mountains, yet words cannot speak when they are asked."

November 20

THE REAL HEALING

There is a traveling Healer who has knowledge of remedies from the many lands he has visited. It is said that he has the ability to bring people back from the brink of death.

A wealthy woman summoned him to come and cure her of a mysterious affliction that left her crippled and wasting away.

The Healer came to the village where the woman resided and stayed at an inn the night before he was to see her. In his room at the inn, he mixed the potion that he would bring to heal her.

While the Healer slept, a thief snuck into the room and made off with the curing elixir.

He took it immediately to the desperate woman, professing it to be the very potion that was prepared by the Healer.

Desperately needing relief from her misery, she took it. However, within minutes she began to feel even worse than before.

Rather than being handsomely rewarded for saving the woman, the thief barely escaped the village with his life.

The next morning, the Healer arrived to see the woman. He gave her what he thought was the potion, but it was the replacement the thief had made from boiling dirty rags. She drank it and immediately began to feel better. By the end of the week, she was again walking, and you could see in the blush of her cheeks that the flame of life had returned. ▬

November
21

THE KEY

An anxious young Seeker came to an Elder and asked for the key to unlocking his personal power.

"You must first pass a test to show that you are ready," replied the Elder, "for that is what my Elder asked of me before she gave me the key. Go to the market next morning and spend the entire day there, then come and tell me one thing that you observed."

The next evening, the Seeker gave this report: "I sat in the market until dusk, and the most notable thing I witnessed was an ancient-looking woman who came with a basket of turnips on her back. It was so heavy that she was stooped under the load and could barely put one foot in front of the other.

"The market steward came up to her and asked for a copper coin to rent the space she needed to sell her roots. She replied that she had no money and asked if she might pay after she sold her first turnip.

"'You tramp!' bellowed the steward. 'I will sell your turnips to pay for my time that you have wasted. Now put your basket down and leave immediately through the gates, or I will have you thrown out.'"

"How did you feel about that?" asked the Elder when the Seeker had finished speaking.

"I felt sorry for the poor woman and wished that I already had the key to my power; for if I did, things would have turned out differently."

"The test was to see if you were one who serves his feelings or if you were one who serves his people," stated the Elder. "The key you seek is for the ability to serve the people at any time they are in need. That woman you watched get thrown out was my Elder—the one who gave me the key."

November 22

NO RIGHT

Three Seekers were sitting on a hillside, reflecting and enjoying the pleasant afternoon.

After a period of silence, one of them commented, "Look at that flag waving above the building over there."

The second Seeker said, "It's not the flag that's moving; it's the wind."

"Are you sure?" chimed in the third. "Isn't it our minds that are doing the moving?"

"It may be that it is not the flag, nor the wind, nor our minds that do the moving," said the first Seeker. "They are all the same, and we are fools for trying to distinguish between them. What is moving is our mouths, which makes us all wrong."

November
23

THE VALUE OF TRAINING

A young woman entered into a trance. Many days passed and she did not return. Her friends grew more and more worried, and finally they went to a Wizard for advice.

"Go fetch the Magician who lives in the next hamlet," he instructed. "She has a lifetime of experience with trances and will be able to help."

When the Magician arrived, she sprinkled a powder on the young woman's head, then walked around her four times while murmuring something incoherent. Without warning, she then clapped her hands sharply, right in the entranced woman's face.

She didn't flinch.

The Magician repeated the ritual four times, to no avail. "I'm afraid there is no magic that will bring her back," she said. "It is unfortunate."

The next day, a farmer who was bringing his produce to market walked by the possessed woman. Gazing upon her, he caught something in her left eye that no one else had noticed: a fleck of amber coloration. It could have been overlooked as just her natural eye color, only the farmer sensed something unique about it. He stared into the eye and snapped his fingers in front of it.

She came back. ➤

November
24

SEEKING HEAVEN

In a distant time, which was not so unlike ours, there lived a Seeker who desired the knowledge to help bring about the Golden Age foretold by the Prophets. To procure this vital information, she spared no effort to find the very wisest Elder in the land. However, after years of intense study and dedication, she learned nothing that she considered to be of practical value.

In great frustration, she left to find a Wizard who might help her. Once again, she sought the most renowned in the land.

"I fear I will not see the Golden Age in my lifetime," lamented the Seeker to the Wizard, "and I am not able to learn the skills to help it manifest. I ask that you put me in a deep sleep for four Generations so that I may wake up to partake of the full splendor of the Promised Era."

The Wizard did the impetuous Seeker's bidding, and on the dawn of the fifth generation, she awoke to a barren, sun-scorched landscape. Around her stood the massive burnt-out trunks of what must have once been a glorious primeval Forest, and the ground around her was littered with the bleached bones of dozens of creatures great and small. She could only imagine how wondrous this scene must have been only a generation or so ago.

Staggering to maintain her Balance, she let out a mighty wail, whose echo was heard only by her. She then crawled to one of the charred pillars, where she sat to reflect on the Elder's Teachings that she had once considered useless.

November
25

REFUSING TO HELP

Confused with the way her life was going, a Seeker went for Guidance to a respected Elder.

"What I have to offer would not be of any help to you," said the Elder after hearing her plea.

Not long after that, the young Seeker turned against the Elder, badmouthing him at every opportunity and discouraging people from going to see him.

"Why did you not help her?" asked another Seeker. "You must have known that she would demonize you and twist your words and actions."

"You are right; her actions were quite predictable. Yet to serve, I cannot make choices based on how they will affect me. At this time, the young woman is not capable of learning. If she stubs her toe on a rock, she will lash out at it as though it were the rock's fault. Then she will blame the person who dropped the rock on the trail."

"What if you helped her and she was thankful?"

"She would then turn on herself."

"Why ever would she do that?"

"When we are unteachable and begin to rely on someone else," replied the Elder, "we first end up resenting ourselves. Then we end up turning against the person who helped us anyway, because we blame him for our lack of self-regard."

"I think I grasp what you are saying. It is as though we have incurred a debt that we can only repay with spite."

The Elder bowed to the Seeker.

November
26

THE WAY

"I am not sure which way to turn," stated a forlorn Seeker. "I have tried this and I have done that, yet here I am as confused as ever. I seem to have lost my way."

"That is a shame," replied the Sage, "for there is only one Way."

"Then I will find it!" exclaimed the Seeker. With bright eyes and a spritely step, she ventured forth.

When she next went to visit the Sage some time later, she cried exuberantly, "I have found it—The Way is abstinence and discipline!"

"That may be *a* way, yet are you sure it is *The* Way?" asked the Sage.

Deflated, but no less resolved, she left to find The Way.

"This time I have it for sure!" she said on her next visit. "It is to be of no mind and listen."

"That is indeed *a* way, yet it might fall short of being *The* Way."

This went on for several more visits. The young Seeker, dismayed but never disheartened, continued the quest.

On the next visit, the Seeker found the Sage leaning against a Tree. He was watching a Hawk eat a Rabbit she had just caught. The Seeker leaned against the other side of the Tree and watched along with him.

As the sun dipped below the Trees and the Sage turned to walk back to his cabin, he commented to the Seeker, "It looks like you have found The Way." ～•

November
27

A TASTE TANTALIZES

A man of stature and wealth invited a group of associates to an outdoor banquet at his estate. It was located on a high bluff overlooking the Sea, and the grounds were a sight to behold: terraced gardens of flowers, fountains, and inviting grottoes. As they waited to be called for the banquet, the guests wandered the meandering paths in quiet meditation or reflective conversation.

"Have you noticed that the view of the Ocean is blocked by that hedge of dense Cedars?" commented one of the guests.

After they were called together for the meal, they each sat down on a bench to wash their hands in a bowl set down before them. While bending down to the bowl, one of the guests caught a breathtaking view of the bay under the Cedar branches.

"Why do you not cut down the Cedars to open up the view?" a guest asked the estate owner.

"Because a taste tantalizes," replied the host, "and constant consumption would make it commonplace." ✒

November 28

TOWARD BALANCE

"Esteemed Elder, why is it that you help us to achieve Balance without first showing us how imbalanced we are?" asked a Seeker.

The Elder reflected on the question for a moment, then said, "Let me illustrate with a story. A wealthy merchant once caught a man in the act of trying to kill him. It turned out the assassin was working for a rival merchant. Instead of putting the man to death, the merchant sent him back to his Master with this note: 'I have absolved this man of his crime, as he holds no malice toward me. He was only demonstrating loyalty to you, and I commend you for having such a devoted servant at your side.'

"As soon as the rival merchant read the note, he killed his servant. The merchant, who could not believe that the intended victim would forgive the servant, concluded that the only reason the servant was released was because he bargained for his life by swearing to go back and kill his Master."

November
29

IT'S ALL IN THE HEART

Like many Mice, this particular Mouse lived in constant fear of Cats. "I can't go on like this!" he cried out. "Those Cats are driving me out of my mind!"

A Wizard who happened to be passing by heard Mouse's lament and took pity upon him. "I will turn you into a Cat," said the Wizard, and she sprinkled magic dust over the trembling little being.

Feeling a bravado he had never known, Mouse-turned-Cat swaggered out into the open and let out a hearty "Meeeowww!"

A large Dog was napping nearby. He jumped up and bolted for the Cat with a rumbling growl. The cat barely made it to the safety of the dense brush where he once lived as a Mouse. There he cowered and trembled.

"What is your pleasure?" asked the Wizard, who hadn't moved more than a few steps away.

"I want to be a Dog!" replied the emboldened Cat. "Then everyone will fear me, and I will fear no one."

A Dog he became, and the first thing he did was give a bold howl that echoed through the valley.

He turned around and saw a menacing Tiger stride into the clearing. The Dog ran to slink behind the Wizard, who obligingly turned him into a Tiger.

The Wizard watched the Tiger strut off into the jungle, only to come running back to him a short while later with a hunter in hot pursuit.

"Whatever I do for you is of no help," stated the Wizard, "as you still have the heart of a Mouse." With that, the Mouse returned to his original form. ➤

November
30

I FOUND IT!

You may know a Monk like the one who followed this particular Sage around, asking him question after question after question. Knowing the inherent worthlessness of questions, the Sage kept answering them. And the Monk, never content, kept asking them.

The Monk finally said, "Aware One, even though an answer makes me feel good in the moment, it doesn't take long until my troubled mind drums up another question. There must be a Secret that you Wise Ones hold that gives you the contentedness you radiate."

"That there is," replied the Sage.

"If only I had it also, I'm sure I would dwell in the same serenity as you," stated the Monk. "That is what I want! What must I do to receive The Secret?"

"I will be glad to tell it to you when you are ready."

Every few days, the Monk would say to the Sage, "I think I am now ready."

"You are getting closer," the Sage would reply.

Finally one day, the Sage said, "I think you are now ready. However, The Secret is not for me to tell. You must go on a Quest to discover it. Prepare for a journey to the lands that lie beyond our borders, and there search out the Mystics and Ancient Ones who hold the Sacred Teachings. Tell them of your Quest, and one of them will impart The Secret to you."

One turn of the seasons passed, and another, and another, and the Monk grew fatigued from his fruitless Quest. He returned to the Sage, ready to listen. ⌇

 December
1

THE IMPRESSION OF WISDOM

There is a Scholar who once thought that he had arrived at a great place of Wisdom. "I want to tell the revered Sage who lives across the Valley what I have achieved," he said to himself. He wrote this poem and sent it to the Sage:

Unmoved by the worldly winds,
Serenely I sit on the Golden Terrace

As the Venerable One read the poem, an impish smile fell across his face. With his calligraphy brush, he wrote over the poem, fart, then sent the poem back to the Scholar.

The Scholar opened the paper. He sputtered and his face turned ruby red. Not even pausing to grab his jacket, he stomped out the door and down the road to the Sage's hut.

With a benevolent smile, the Sage met the Scholar at his door and spoke these words: "You wrote that you were no longer affected by the worldly winds, yet just one fart sent you scowling like a mad Dog across the valley." ↝

December 2

HOLDING ON

A young woman had come of age. She felt a restlessness that came from deep inside—it was time for her to embark on her Journey of Discovery. She gave away all she had and set her feet tentatively on the Pathless Path.

Coming to a great lake, she looked for a way to cross it. After seeing a patch of bulrush, she cut several large bundles and lashed them together to form a raft.

As she reached the far shore, she began to wonder if she might come to another lake. "How handy it would be to have the raft," she said to herself. "Should I carry it with me in case I need it?" She paused for a moment, deep in thought. "Or shall I leave it here on the beach for others who might need it?" ᴧᴏ

December
3

WHICH STEP

A gathering of Nuns and Monks was debating which is the most important step on the Pathless Path. Some thought it was the first step, for without it there would be no Journey beginning. Others argued for the middle step, as that is the halfway point, which shows that there is momentum to finish the Journey. Yet others spoke for the last step, as nothing is sure until the Journey is completed.

An Elder-Nun, who was nearby and overheard the comments, came over and said, "It sounds like you are having a lively this-or-that conversation. Your thinking-with-thought minds appear to be in prime shape this morning."

Right away, a few members of the group got defensive and wanted to say, "What do you mean by this-or-that?" However, they realized that it would have been their egos talking, so they refrained from speaking and instead listened.

Finally a Nun spoke up: "Are you hinting that there is only one step?"

"That is one possibility," the Elder-Nun replied. "Let's imagine that is the case. Which step would that be?"

"It would have to be the step I am taking," replied a Monk, "as that is the only step included in this breath."

"This is so," replied the Elder. "Yet which step is it?"

A Nun replied, "It is the first step, and I would think that every step is the first step, as that is all there is."

The Elder-Nun bowed to the younger Nun, then she left.

An animated discussion followed, with the group realizing that if every step is the first step, every step is a new beginning. Not being shackled by the past, we are completely open in each step to what the future might bring.

At the end of the discussion, they all bowed to each other. ➤

December
4

NEVER FINISHED

A young Seeker arrived at the state of No-Thought. She was pretty proud of herself and wanted to share the news. The first person who came to mind was the Elder who typically sat under a Tree by the River.

When she found him, she asked, "What should I do next, as my mind is no longer plagued with thoughts?"

"Toss them out," replied the Elder.

"How can I toss out what's not there?"

"That is a good point. If you can't toss them out, perhaps you can drag them out."

December
5

NEED SPEAKS

"My mind is lazy," stated a Seeker to his friends. "What can I do to stimulate it?"

"Go to a Sage," suggested one of the friends, "and ask for a riddle."

"A riddle? How could a silly riddle ever inspire me?"

"Just give it a try."

The Seeker decided to take his friend's advice. His other friends told him about a Mystic living in the next hamlet who could possibly give him a riddle.

"I will be glad to help stir your mind," replied the Mystic to the Seeker's request. "Take this riddle with you and come back to me when you have the answer: how can you hit two targets with only one arrow?"

Four years passed and the Seeker returned to the Mystic. "My mind is far from lazy anymore," said the Seeker. "In fact, this riddle is nearly all I think about. Yet all I have accomplished is depression and anger, as I have not been able to come up with the answer."

"Give it another month" replied the Mystic, "and you should have the answer."

Newly encouraged, the Seeker went back home and continued to work on the riddle. However when the month passed, the Seeker had to report to the Mystic that he was no closer to the answer.

"You must have been so near to it!" exclaimed the Mystic. "Give it one more week and you're bound to have it."

The Seeker was in tears when he returned a week later with nothing more to offer than the previous two times.

"This is it," stated the Mystic. "Take only four more days with the riddle, and if you haven't been able to come up with the answer by then, you're better off dead."

It took only two days for the answer to come.

December
6

IT'S YOUR PROBLEM

One Seeker tended to get preoccupied with how other people were doing on their Awakening Journeys. She became obsessed with certain people. "This person is doing that, and that person isn't doing this," she would say to others. She would even directly criticize people. After a while, she began to worry about her state of mind. She confided in a fellow Seeker.

"I'm glad you said something," her friend replied, "as I was growing concerned right along with you. I encourage you to go see the Sage we met at the carnival. He is reputed to know the secrets of the Journey to Awakening."

"I don't understand why otherwise good people say and do some of the things they do," the troubled Seeker said to the Sage. "It seems to go against what's best for them. What can I do to help them?"

"It is impossible to see others for who they are," replied the Sage. "All we see is the parts of ourselves that mesh with theirs. So what does it help to meddle in others' Awakening Journeys that we do not understand?"

"I...I never thought of it that way," stammered the Seeker. "What, then, should I do?"

"Perhaps the question to ask is how you can help and support your own Journey. Reflect on this, and within it you might find your peace." ➤

December
7

HERE IS HAPPINESS

Seven or eight Nuns and Monks were sitting out in a Meadow, having a good time eating and exploring the ways of the questioning mind.

After a while, a herder came by and asked if they had seen his Cattle. "There were ten," he said, "with three calves. They drive me mad when they bust out of their pasture—I end up spending all day looking for them. And then there is the plague of Caterpillars stripping my orchard bare. Will my travails never end?"

"We haven't seen any Cows," the group replied, and the herder went off in another direction.

"Perhaps we are so content with our life because we have no Cows, and therefore none to fret about," said a Nun.

"Yet it is a tricky situation," added a Monk. "I once thought that the more Cows I had, the more satisfied I would be. In time, I discovered that the more Cows I got, the more stressed I became."

"Perhaps each step of our Journey of Awakening is the release of a Cow," added another Nun. ～

 *December* 8

JUST PASSING THROUGH

One of our village merchants had a sickness, yet he couldn't tell exactly what was wrong or whether it was in his mind or his body. He just felt out of sorts all the time. "I need to see someone who understands the ways of life and death," he told himself.

He found a person to tend his shop, then he set off on the long journey to see a Sage he had heard rumors about many years go. The merchant wasn't sure whether the Sage was still alive, as he was already quite old when the merchant was first told about him.

Indeed, the storied Elder was still living, and he welcomed the merchant into his little hut.

"Where do you live?" asked the merchant. "I see you have only a pillow and a table here, and a bedroll in the corner. A storied Healer such as you must have a place that befits him."

"This is where I live," replied the Aged One.

"Then where do you keep your things?"

"Where do you keep yours?"

"I am only passing through," stated the merchant.

"I, also, am only passing through," replied the Healer. ᐳᐳ

December
9

THE TWO ARE MANY

"In our hamlet lives a woman who leads two lives," said a Nun visiting from the neighboring district. "She is sick at home and needs her aged parents to care for her. At the same time, she is out gardening and horseback riding at her country cottage, where she lives with her husband and children. Which of these two is the true woman?"

"Let us be careful," said another Nun, "lest we fall into the this-or-that trap. It may be that neither of them are the true woman."

"As we know," added a third Nun, "that is usually the case. When one cannot choose between one and the other, a third and a fourth option will just create more of the same confusion. We can see the moon in this pond and in that pond and in the next pond, yet is it not always the same moon?"

"Then who is this woman?" asked the visiting Nun.

"Perhaps she is a Spider who has lain down on her back and cannot right herself," suggested a Nun toward the back of the group. "All of her legs are reaching out this way and that, trying to latch onto something—anything. If those legs could listen to each other, they would no longer be two, or many, but One. The Spider could then right herself and be grounded."

December
10

YOU ARE RIGHT

After a talk given by a Fool, two Nuns got into a heated discussion about what they had heard. Each one was adamant that her understanding was the right one.

"Let us go and ask the Fool which of us heard him correctly," suggested one of the Nuns, and the other agreed.

The first Nun repeated to the Fool what she thought she heard, and he responded, "You have listened well—that is just what I said."

Feeling smug, the Nun looked over at her cohort, expecting her to relent.

What do I have to lose? The second Nun asked herself. She gave her version of the Fool's words, which she believed directly contradicted that of the other Nun.

"You, too, were attentive," said the Fool, "for what you say is what I spoke."

A Monk, who was sitting nearby, jumped up and said, "How can that be? One version negates the other, yet you say that they are both right. I don't see how this is possible."

With an accepting smile, the Fool turned to the Monk and said, "What you say is also right." ᨀ

December
11

NOT CHANGE, BUT CHANGE

"I have been seeking Knowledge from Beggars, Mystics, and Fools for over a month now," said a novice to a woman he met who had long been a Searcher for Meaning. "It's like I have been staying at home—nothing has changed."

"What were you expecting?" asked the woman.

"I see those around me—you, for example—who are centered and reflective, and I was told that those I sought out were Awakened and carriers of much Wisdom, so I expected to start feeling something by now."

"The sun rises on his own time and the sun sets on his own time," said a voice from behind them. It came from the Mystic who the novice had recently visited. He was walking by and overheard the conversation. "No matter how impatient we are, there will not be a sunset at midday."

The young one's knees buckled. It was as though the Mystic had given him a sharp rap across the shins. He felt faint and had to sit down.

"It appears to *me* as though something has changed," stated the Mystic. ➨

December
12

SEEING

"What do things look like when one is conscious?" asked a Seeker.

"One sees through timeless eyes," replied the Sage.

"All I can see is what is right in front of me."

"That would be so," replied the Sage, "if you were truly seeing. What do you see around a well-dressed woman's neck and on her fingers and wrists and dangling from her ears?"

"I would see jewelry."

"You see jewelry because you create it," said the Sage. "What you actually see is pebbles and pieces of shell. Consciousness is seeing something for what it is, while unconsciousness is creating something from what is."

"I think I am beginning to understand. Will you give me an example?"

"There is no need to understand, as that is what keeps us from seeing. All we need to do is open our eyes and think without thought."

"Then who is our magistrate?" asked the Seeker.

"He is nobody other than who you see. How do you remember him?"

"He is an overweight man with shoes that show no wear," stated the Seeker.

"And what about his regal robes?" asked the Sage.

"They are swaths of cotton and silk fabric. I see that. Yet what about things that are not so obvious, such as the glowing Path of the Awakened Ones?"

"When you imagine water in the Desert, do you really see it?"

The Seeker reflected for a while, then asked, "And what about my judgments of right or wrong and good or bad?"

"Ah. These are hard to see, as they entrap us in our thought-filled minds. Yet when we can see the serpent we are wrestling with, there is no more mystery."

"Then what about the likes of belief and conviction?"

"They can also be hard to see," replied the Sage, "yet they are just as visible as anything else. Do you notice those dried-up leaves lying over there? They are all that remains of last summer. When we see what is actually there, we see the soul and substance of our beliefs and convictions."

"Are you saying that all there is to the mystery of consciousness is merely seeing?"

"That is all," answered the Sage. 〜

December 13

SHALLOW GUIDANCE

"We know that it is not what one does that matters," commented a Monk, "but how one does it. Yet, Austere One, we Monks have come to sense a deeper meaning to this, only we cannot grasp it. Our only clarity is that the secret may lie in the *how*."

"You have grown in your ability to listen and refrain from embracing," commented the Ascetic. "I can now give you the deeper meaning of how: When you are hungry, eat; when your bladder is full, pee; when you are tired, sleep."

The Monks looked at each other in disbelief.

"If I may comment," said one of the Monks meekly, "what you have just given us appears shallower than our present understanding, rather than deeper."

Another Monk added, "What you say, which is to eat, pee, and sleep, is what we do anyway, is it not?"

"It may appear so at first glance," replied the Ascetic. "Most of us yearn and plan for a hundred things during a meal, and we are so preoccupied with our affairs that we put off peeing as long as we can, and all of our demons come to haunt us in our sleep. Imagine what life could be if we would fully immerse ourselves in what we are doing."

"We have much to unlearn," said one of the Monks. "It is now hard to imagine that any words for how, other than your "shallow" ones, could be more profound."

December
14

BE HERE

Several Seekers went to stay with an Elder for the summer, as she had a quiet place in the country where they could study and reflect. Each of them found a comfortable nook under the Trees around the cabin, where they spent much of their time.

For several days in a row, one of the Seekers was continually distracted by two others, who were talking and joking loudly. He went to the Elder and asked if she could suggest a new place for him that would be better suited to his work.

"I understand your frustration," the kind woman replied, "and I have just the place in mind. Let me draw you a map."

The Seeker took the map, bowed to the Elder and went to find his new place for reflection and study. To his utter surprise and confusion, the map led him back to the very Tree he was already sitting under. He felt a flash of anger for being toyed with, which was soon replaced by a knowing smile. Sitting down under his new Tree, he began to ponder the Teaching.

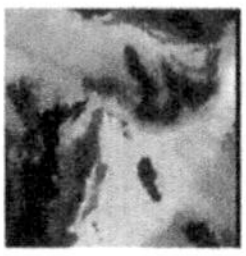

December
15

WHO I AM NOT

Back in time, there was a Sage who moved to a distant land. She left without notice, which confused the Seekers who had regularly come to see her, as all they found one day was an empty hut.

Some time later, word came from a traveler that he had happened upon the Sage on his travels. He gave the Seekers her location, and they immediately prepared to go and see her.

It was a long journey, and when they arrived, they could hardly believe that the person they found was their esteemed Sage. She wore strange dress, ate unfamiliar food, and spoke a dialect they had trouble understanding. Even the hut she lived in was so much different from her old one.

"What has happened to you?" they asked.

"I have moved to give you a Teaching," she replied. "You knew me one way, but you did not realize that you thus knew me in all ways. When it is cloudy or clear, scorching hot or bitter cold, does not the sun always rise and set in regular fashion? And so it is with us. We walk the Path that rises before us, however it presents itself; and we adapt and re-adapt to whatever it brings us through. Yet are we not the same person, on the same given Journey?"

December
16

CREATED FOR US

Some friends were holding a farewell feast for one of their comrades, who was preparing for a long journey. There were many mouth-watering foods: roasted meats, savory vegetables, and rich desserts.

When all the dishes were served and everyone was enjoying the reverie, one of the friends stood up and said, "Let us be thankful for all that the earth provides: the Fruits of the Field, the Animals of the Forest, and the Birds of the Air—all given to us for our pleasure and sustenance."

There were nods and murmurs of agreement.

Then someone else stood up and spoke: "If this is true, what of the Maggot and the Mosquito who feast on us? Are we then created for their pleasure and sustenance? Is it not pretentious of us to think that all of creation is here to do our bidding? Perhaps it is so that everything has its place, which is neither lesser nor greater than the place of anything else. Then there would be no comparison, and saying either 'equal' or 'unequal' would still be comparing. With one being stronger and smarter in one way and another being stronger and smarter in another way, all are at the same time both lesser and greater." ▬

December
17

WHAT MAKES A SAGE

"Have you ever wondered about the characteristics that Wisdom Carriers hold in common?" said a woman to her friends.

"I had never thought about it," replied one of the friends. "Together we have known many Wise Ones; why don't we see what list of characteristics we come up with?"

"That's a great idea!" said another friend. "I'll start: a Wise One has no need for virtues."

"She has no specific career, so she has no need to develop a set of skills."

"She has no drive for achievement or renown, so she does not accumulate Knowledge."

"He doesn't distinguish, so he doesn't have to work on bringing things or people together."

"He does not have reactive emotions, so he does not need rules for right and wrong," added the woman who posed the question.

"What do you mean by that?" someone asked.

"I am saying that he does not get emotionally entangled," replied the woman, "so he maintains heart-perspective and does not need outside governance."

"I see. I wonder how we differ from the person we have just described."

"I think many of us have raw emotions," suggested another friend. "We react to what goes on around us."

"That exhausts our energy," added another, "and we end up leaning on others."

"We wear ourselves out further by talking too much and doing meaningless work."

"Look how much we are aware of," someone concluded. "It shows the Wise One in each of us."

December
18

THE WISDOM CARRIER

"How can we know a person of true Wisdom?" asked a Pilgrim.

"That is of utmost difficulty," replied the Gatekeeper, "as Wisdom is very different from Teachings and Knowledge. Wisdom has no form or structure, nor can it be couched in words."

"Is it then not possible to talk about Wisdom? And how does one become wise?"

"To answer that would be using the ways of Knowledge to try capturing Wisdom."

"Then that leaves me with nothing!" cried the Pilgrim.

"And that is how to know a Wisdom Carrier," explained the gatekeeper.

"By nothing?"

"Truly. She appears to do nothing, yet her effect is apparent all around her."

"How would I recognize her if she did not appear to be related to what she caused?"

"Again," said the Gatekeeper, "because of nothing. You will see that no one is dependent upon her, yet her presence and example strongly manifest in the lives of those around her."

"Wouldn't her nothing-doing that affects everything still draw attention to her?" asked the Pilgrim.

"It would appear that way, yet Wisdom is complete and fulfilling onto itself. There is no recognition or glory, as Wisdom has nothing to recognize or glorify."

"Then what does the Wisdom Carrier do with herself?"

"If anything stands out, it is what she does not do with herself," answered the Gatekeeper. "She shuns the known and continually meanders into mystery by surrounding herself with nothing."

19

IS IT CAUSE-AND-EFFECT
OR EFFECT-AND-CAUSE?

Late one evening, a woman was walking back to her home in the village from visiting her aunt and uncle in the country. She didn't expect to run into anybody on the normally quiet path. However, about halfway home, four people materialized out of the darkness ahead of her. Startled, she looked right and left and saw a large boulder just off the trail. She ran and ducked behind it, hoping she wasn't seen.

"What do you make of that?" said one of the four.

"I think it was a person, but it's so dark that I'm not sure," replied someone else.

"If it was a person," said one of the others, "why did he run and hide? Let's go and see if everything's alright."

They walked over to the boulder and found the woman crouched behind it.

"Why did you run and hide?" one of the four asked.

Realizing that she was not in danger, the woman replied, "I don't know that I can give you a straightforward answer. I could say that I am here because of you; however, from your point of view, you are here because of me." ⌇

 *December*
20

MASKS

"The wise and benevolent are ignorant and stingy," stated an Elder to several Seekers.

They replied with a quizzical look.

"Come and have dinner with me this evening, and I will show you," said the Elder.

He invited a well-respected merchant and benefactor—a man who many went to for counsel—to come and eat with them.

The only food the Elder served to each of his guests that night was a small bowl of rice and a few bites of dried Fish, for that was all he had.

The next morning, a servant of the merchant came to the Elder's door with a satchel containing a thousand gold pieces.

"If this were rice and Fish," wrote the Elder in the note he sent back with the gold pieces, "I would invite your servant to sit down and eat with me. I have not found that coins served at a table help in the sharing of Wisdom."

"Yet how does that show that the wise and benevolent are ignorant and stingy?" asked a Seeker.

"I will show you," said the Elder. He asked a wanderer in rags who was passing by if she would go to the merchant and ask for a thousand pieces of gold.

A short while later, the woman came back and said she was given nothing and chased away.

"Those who claim to be wise," stated the Elder, "are only masking their self-hate and mistrust of themselves. On the other hand, those who admit they are Fools can find trust in who they are. The wanderer knows what she needs; however, the merchant does not know what he does not need."

 December 21

THE GREATER MISCHIEF

A young Seeker caught a small Bird and wondered how she could use him to raise some mischief. After all, what youth doesn't like pulling a prank now and then?

"I know," she said to herself, "I'll pull a trick on our Elder!"

This was very uncharacteristic for a Seeker, as Elders are generally respected and not involved in shenanigans. At the same time, it is a characteristic of youth to not abide by convention.

The Seeker walked up to the venerable woman, who was known for her piercing insight, and said, "Honored Elder, is the Bird I am holding behind my back alive or dead?"

The kindly woman looked upon the girl with a soft smile.

This caused the Seeker some discomfort, so she quickly reconsidered her plan to let the Bird fly if the Elder said "dead," and to quickly break the Bird's neck if the Elder said "alive." Yet her impish nature won out, and she was prepared to proceed.

The Elder read the Seeker's game and replied, "You hold the answer in your hands."

 **December**
22

THE WRAPPINGS

There was an Elder who came from a far-distant place to reside in a village. The townspeople, along with those from the surrounding countryside and neighboring hamlets, soon received word of his profound Teachings. They were all so moved that they asked the Elder if he would give talks and offer weekly classes.

He considered their request. Realizing that he was called there to serve, he asked the people to build a Temple, where they could come together for the Teachings.

For four years, the people toiled. When the magnificent structure was finally complete, the Elder called them all together for its dedication. He then said, "Will those of you who feel called to enter the Temple and receive the Teachings, please step forward?"

To the group who came forward, he said, "I have nothing to offer you. As honored as I am by your presence and commitment, I must now ask you to leave." He then said to those who remained, "Let us continue the Wisdom Journey, first by burning this Temple down."

December
23

THE MEANING OF TITLE

In search of a Wise One to guide him, a Seeker traveled the land from Mountain to Sea. In time, he came across a white-bearded man taking a rest at a wayside along the road between two villages. The two struck up a conversation, and the Seeker was immediately impressed by how few yet well-chosen were his words.

"What am I to call you?" asked the Seeker. "Truly, you are no ordinary person."

"I have yet to meet an ordinary person," replied the man, "and I have yet to be called anything other than a Beggar or a Fool. That sits well with me."

"Yet surely you must be asked this question often," protested the Seeker.

"Of what matter is title? All it does is denote rank, and rank matters only to the ego. Besides, our rank changes with every person we meet. When a King comes to me for advice, does that mean I should have a rank greater than King? Or when a Healer makes me a tea to aid my digestion, does that mean my rank should be lesser than hers? A Carpenter who teaches his sons the craft is a Teacher; however, he is the Student of the craftsman from whom he learns."

"All of that I understand," said the Seeker. "Yet I am still faced with my dilemma: what am I to call you?"

"In the ultimate, it does not matter, for anything you or I would choose could be construed as both demeaning and elevating. I will respond to anything, as I see the Truth in all voices. What I hear in a person's choice of title for me tells me something about the person who is speaking, rather than something about myself."

December
24

THE DEEPER JOY

There was a Hermit who was said to wear a perpetual smile, and nobody knew why. Very few people met him, of course, because he was a Hermit. Yet his reputation spread, as people were fascinated that anyone in this world of grief and toil could be continuously happy.

A wealthy family in a distant land was able to buy just about anything they wanted. One thing they did not have in great abundance was happiness, so they sent two servants with a bag of gold to go find the Hermit and bring back the secret to happiness.

After four months, the servants returned. They said the Hermit was glad to oblige the family's request, yet he would accept no gold. The servants then handed a neatly folded piece of parchment to the family matron, who read this aloud:

The grandparents die. The parents die. The children die. The grandchildren die.

The woman broke into tears. "What is this talk of death?" she exclaimed. "Where is the joy in it? Why did that Hermit decide to give us only more misery in this life? Servants, take me to this man and I will confront him myself!"

All the more aggravated by the miserable trek through damp Forest and rocky crag, the matron could barely refrain from spitting in the little man's face when she finally got there—especially when she saw his serene and all-embracing smile. "What a mockery your face is to life as it really is," sputtered the woman. "You grin while you rub the harsh realities of life into the raw wounds of those of us who must live it. Tell me, you crazy man, the method of your madness. If you have none, I will give you reason to be mad."

"Please read to me what I gave you," requested the Hermit in a soft voice.

Confused as this made the matron, she read the parchment anyway.

"Would you wish for anything else for your family?" asked the Hermit after a short pause. "Do you not enjoy the sight of your grandchildren playing, and would it not be a tragedy if they were to die before you? And how would it be for your mother if you were to die before her? Is not death the way of life? Is there not deep joy in having the natural order of things progress uninterrupted?"

The matron bowed to the Hermit, and with newfound gladness, she ventured homeward. ◂

 **December**
25

SEARCHING FOR MYSELF

"I feel lost," complained a Nun. "The more I study and contemplate, the less I know who I am."

"You have me to blame for that," replied the Wisdom Carrier. "It is I who encouraged you to study, in order to find your true nature—and it is because of this that you lost it."

"Why did you do that?" asked the Nun. "I feel miserable."

"That is because you are now locked in the fear of birth and death. When we do not know our true nature, we count the days to our death, and we lament the lost days since our birth."

"How can I free myself from that?"

"To do so would be to free yourself from the Dirt and the Air of which you are made. Then where would you be?" asked the Wisdom Carrier.

"So what is the answer? Whatever am I to do?" bemoaned the Nun.

"The more desperate we become, the more we keep asking that same question. All it brings us is scraps of food—never enough to feel satisfied."

"Yet I must find myself."

"Yes, the mind says we must do things, so that we can lead an ordered existence. Granddaughter, you are trying for something that is defeated by effort. Quit everything that is meaningful to you, and you will transcend the now, thereby realizing the endless moment—the Continuum."

"Learned One, I just don't see how that will help me find myself."

"When I said 'quit everything,' that included you," replied the Wisdom Carrier. "Quit holding onto yourself. It will then be possible for you to merge with the Continuum and become pure Awareness, free of the person. You will then have passed through the gateway to the Boundless." ⇝

December
26

WHAT LIMITS TRAINING

Why do you give these Seekers such superficial exercises?" asked a pass-erby of a Sage. "They are not true Teachings."

"When these Seekers get caught up in an exercise," replied the Sage, "it shows that they have become enamored with the cook, rather than with the food. In time, they will come to realize that they must feast not on the exercise but on its fruit. If they do not, it will lead to their stagnation, and eventually their death."

"How will they come to that awareness when they are so wrapped up in their exercise-based training?" asked to the passerby.

"There is no more wrong in enjoying the exercises than there is in enjoying the aroma of food. Once they learn that the full experience of a feast comes with *eating* the food as well, the exercises will mesh with their normal life and become indistinguishable from it, just as food becomes their bodies. Let them now be preoccupied with this step on their Journeys, so that one day they can laugh at how silly they were."

December
27

THE ROLE OF SUFFERING

A few Seekers were wondering why it was necessary to experience fear and suffering on the Journey of Discovery. After a long discussion, they found themselves even more confused than before, so they brought the question to their Guide.

"It is not fear that you must embrace," he replied, "but the fear of fear. It is not suffering itself that you must experience, but the suffering you cause yourself by trying to avoid it."

"That sounds like a play on words," commented one of the Seekers. "What is the difference between fear and the fear of fear, or between suffering and the suffering caused by trying to avoid it? Isn't it all still fear and suffering?"

"There are those who fret over their sufferings, and there are those who embrace them and ride them through. The first group fights pain and does everything they can to avoid more, and in doing so, they invite more pain and suffering."

"How can that be avoided?" asked the Seeker.

"By changing the circumstances that brought it about. The second group, by embracing their suffering, have opened to its voice and accepted it as their Teacher. They will learn from it and will not have to revisit it."

December
28

ONLY TRUTH HEALS

A Master bridge builder traveling through a distant land saw that the bridges were in ill repair. Several villagers told him that a bridge would sometimes collapse under the weight of oxcarts carrying goods to market. People had been maimed, and some had even been killed.

Realizing that he could serve these people, he went home to his own village, settled his affairs, and then returned.

At the next village meeting, he rose to speak. "People of this land, I see that your bridges are in need of repair. I am a bridge builder, and I would be glad to serve."

The inhabitants were overjoyed, as their previous bridge builder's leg had been crushed by a falling timber and he could no longer work.

When the new bridge builder began to explain to his crew what they would be doing, they interrupted him right away: "Oh no, we can't do things that way. We have a bridge-building tradition here—a certain way to install the pillars and cross pieces, and a certain way to fashion the braces. This way has been passed down through the generations, and we very much like its look."

In order to work with these people, the bridge builder had to conform to their ways. At the same time, he could not in good conscience keep from doing what was necessary for the safety of the villagers. In the middle of the night, he would go to each newly completed bridge and secretly add the necessary supports underneath, where they would not be seen.

Before long, he became known as the best traditional bridge builder in all the land. He was praised for the strength and reliability of his structures.

Yet over time, the bridge builder's routine of working all day and half the night took its toll. He died at an early age. From then on, the bridges built and repaired by his crew started to sag and unexpectedly collapse, just like the bridges before the bridge builder came to town.

continued

One of the crew members, a man with many years of experience, became curious about the change and studied one of the bridges worked on by the deceased builder. After diligent examination, the crewman found the well-disguised supports and foundation stones that made the bridge stalwart.

At the next village meeting, he spoke these words: "Fellow citizens, our traditions are valuable to us, and we wish to keep them. At the same time, I think we have forgotten that traditions, which have evolved to serve the people, need to change along with the people. We now build stronger oxcarts that carry heavier loads, yet our bridges, as picturesque as they may be, came down to us from an era when oxcarts carried only half of what they do now.

"The reason our past bridge builder's structures have been able to carry the weight, I have discovered, is that he honored our bridge-building tradition while at the same time secretly incorporating elements that made our bridges safe and reliable."

Astonished at the news, the townspeople immediately asked the elder crewmember if he would assume the position of bridge builder. He accepted, and the townspeople directed him to carry on the practices of the bridge builder from the foreign land.

From that day on, everyone remembered that a vital part of long-held traditions is that they evolve in order to continue serving the ever-changing needs of the people. ᴧᴄᴧ

December
29

FINDING HEART

Nobody really knew what a certain woman thought and felt about the topics of the day, as she lived a very private life. She did not involve herself in the things everybody else spent their time talking about, nor did she invite people into her house. Even at the little shop she ran, she exchanged only the few necessary words to serve her customers.

"That woman has no heart," people said. They felt uncomfortable being around her, so they seldom patronized her business.

When she died, there was no family to settle her affairs and clean up her house, so some of the townspeople went to do it. Inside they found paintings that elicited such powerful feelings that tears welled up in the eyes of the beholders.

"These could not have been rendered by the woman," they said, "for she had no heart. She must have purchased them somewhere."

Soon after that, a woman moved into the village and became an instant favorite with everybody. She smiled and greeted people as she passed by, and she openly shared her thoughts and feelings about nearly anything that came up.

"Now there is a woman with heart!" the villagers exclaimed. They opened up their hearts to her and trusted her.

Then one day, the woman with heart was gone. Nobody knew where she went—it was as though she had just vanished—and she took everything entrusted to her. Gone were all the heirloom clocks and precious jewelry that she was supposedly repairing.

Impoverished by the experience, the villagers were nevertheless grateful for it, as it taught them how to recognize a person of true heart.

December
30

THE LURE OF DEATH

There is a fear of dying that all Seekers must reckon with if they are going to walk The Way. Some read this as dread of the death of the body, which it could indeed be, as Seekers occasionally do perish in their walking.

However, this is not the kind of demise that continually haunts the Seeker. Rather, it is the Death of the Hungering Soul. Take the case of one young woman, a singer, who killed herself by letting attention distract her from the Pursuit of Knowledge. She was aware and capable, only an unresolved need cropped up at a pivotal time, and she never did return to walking The Way.

Those who were close to the woman lamented her passing. They swore never to do what she did, lest they meet similar fates.

Thus, her death was not in vain. For every one like her, ten more are inspired to venture out on the Frontier of The Way. These are the true Seekers: they taste death with every step they take farther from the familiar. It's a place where nothing is real; there is not even love or hate to grasp. There they grapple with the ultimate threat: the fear of not Knowing. ᜑ

 *December* 31

LINGERING STENCH

A Wisdom Carrier lay on his deathbed. All of those whose lives he touched came to be with him for his passing over. One by one, they came up to his bedside to bid him farewell.

Along with the sadness of their dear Elder's departure, they wondered who would take his place in their lives. There were several people who emanated the silent Wisdom reminiscent of their Elder, yet those who were close to him still looked for a sign as to who he wished would take his place.

The woman who they thought would be his most likely choice went up to be with him one last time.

Struggling for the strength to speak, the Aged One motioned for her to come close, then whispered, "You have learned well on your long Journey. I have watched you empty your mind and open your ears. I have watched you laugh at misery and cry over pleasure. I don't remember when you last settled for an answer, or even asked for one. Yet with my dying breath there is one last thing for me to draw your attention to: you still stink of Zen."

SPECIAL OCCASION
Stories

Birth

NOT ALWAYS OBVIOUS

One morning at breakfast, a Seeker asked his Elder, "How are you feeling at the start of this beautiful day?"

"Tenuous," replied the Elder.

"Why ever would you say that?"

"I have risen this morning, and I do not know if I will lay myself down this evening, or if something else will lay me down for the last time before that."

"This I understand," replied the Seeker. "Yet isn't that the case for all of us?"

"It may well be," replied the Elder. "Yet how many people are aware of it?"

DEPTH OF FRIENDSHIP

A group of friends share a depth of relationship that makes them feel connected and involved in each other's lives, even though they live in different places.

Recently one of them died. Her friends came from places far and near to remember her. While telling stories of their times together, they realized that she would live on within each of them. Several of them brought instruments, and they all commenced to dance and sing about times gone by.

One friend from a distant region arrived late and walked in on the revelry. After waiting for a break in the music, he asked, "Is this a proper way to show reverence for our dead sister? Should we not be mourning her passing by holding a somber vigil?"

Someone replied, "Is this a matter of concern to the friend whose body lies here before us?"

Coming into Adulthood

HOW TO SEE

It was getting late and the Nun needed to return home from her visit with the Monk.

"It has grown very dark," she said as she opened the door to leave, "and there is no moon tonight. What shall I do?"

"A hundred wise voices will not match one clear sight," commented the Monk.

He then lit a candle and handed it to the Nun.

She graciously accepted the candle, then blew it out, and said, "I have no more need to doubt a Teacher's voice."

LIKE NO OTHER

"What is this day?" asked a Seeker of his companions.

"Waiting for Awakening," replied one.

"The day after yesterday and the day before tomorrow," added another.

"It is chilling drizzle and a walk to the market," said someone else.

"I have thought about this," said the first Seeker, "and I have come to see the day as the son who was just given the family farm by his father. There was no question that it would happen, and there was no question about the son's acceptance. Father and son have the deepest of relationships; no words are needed. A new day is beyond comparison, as it is freshly gifted by the previous day. We who are gifted the new day play entirely different roles than we did yesterday."

"Are you speaking of death and life?" asked one of the Seekers.

"I am speaking nonsense," replied the first Seeker. "All I know is what has been laid in my lap, and I cherish it for what it is to me. At the same time, I realize that I must gift it to the next moment—to The Void—just as Father Yesterday bequeaths his firstborn to the dawn."

Wedding/Matedness

THE WELL

In the time of our ancestors whose names we no longer remember, a terrible drought befell the land. Every spring the people waited for the rains to come and soften the crusted earth; however, all that came back was the hot, dry wind.

There was one farm whose fields remained green. Fat Sheep grazed in the pastures and fruit Trees bore in abundance.

"Perhaps he has a large pond that is not yet dried up," some people speculated. "Or maybe he has drought-resistant plants," said others. Whatever the case, they were desperate for food and water, so they went to ask if he would share with them what he had.

"I have a well that never runs dry," the farmer said. "The well is called The Way. Come with me and I will show it to you." He drew a bucket of water, and they all drank their fill.

"It is the sweetest water!" they exclaimed. "Very satisfying."

"I wonder how deep this well is," said one of the neighbors. He dropped a stone into it and never heard a splash.

"When each of you gets back home," said the farmer, "open your eyes, for you also have a well like this, right in front of your door. Just like mine, it will never run dry."

THE GIFTING WAY

The Sage was so well regarded by those who came to him for Guidance that a group of Seekers got together one day and decided that they would each bring him a gift.

After all the gifts had been lain before the Sage, he took each one that had the name of the giver on it and returned it.

"I will keep the others," he stated.

"Why is this so?" a Seeker asked him. Are not each of our gifts a worthy expression?"

"Which is more valuable to you," said the Sage, "to receive Guidance, or to have me receive your gifts?"

"Isn't one the result of the other?" replied the Seeker.

"You may soon see that one is actually a denial of the other. These gifts with your names on them show that you have given in gratefulness for what you have received. Instead, consider giving for the pure joy of giving, without expectation."

"Why is it important to give without expectation?" asked another Seeker.

"Gifting with expectation is asking for a reward for doing well," said the Sage. "When I consider gifting, I am judging whether or not another has done well."

"From what state of mind should we then give?"

"Think that you are doing something useful," answered the Sage, "then you will give for the pure sake of giving."

Gratitude

PRESENCE

A traveling Nun was roasting a Deer haunch that a hunter gave her over an open fire. When it was done, it was too hot to eat, so she set it aside to cool while she went to the Stream for a drink of water.

When she got back, the haunch was gone. A Dog had come by and run off with it. As the Dog crested a hill, he nearly ran into two Seekers walking toward him on the trail. Startled, he dropped the haunch and took off.

"What a gift that Dog brought us!" said one of the Seekers. "We've been hiking the whole day and didn't bring any food with us."

"What do you mean, 'a gift'?" replied the other Seeker. "That meat is Dog food! It was in the mouth of a dirty animal and I'm not going to eat it."

The first Seeker stood there silently for a moment, with the haunch lying next to her. She then said, "I see this as a gift in our time of need, and I will enjoy it—with gratitude."

With a disgusted look, the other Seeker turned his face and let her eat.

New Beginnings

IT TAKES A RASCAL

A Nun walked by a man sitting alone in the village square with a vacant look on his face.

"Is there anything you need?" the Nun asked.

"The trouble is, I don't need anything," replied the man. "I have a beautiful family, I have wealth and position, and I have a fat belly. When it comes down to it, I have no reason to move, as all my needs and wants are met."

"Oh, look at the beautiful Bird in that Tree behind you!" exclaimed the Nun.

When the man turned to look, the Nun snatched up the man's satchel, which undoubtedly contained items that were important to him. In a wink she was darting down the alley between the nearby buildings.

While the Nun was spry, the man was rather portly; he waddled and puffed in an effort to overcome her. Leading him off to the far side of the village, she then doubled back and laid the satchel down next to his coat where he was sitting. Then she hid behind some nearby bushes and waited.

Sure enough, the exhausted fellow came dragging back, stooped over to pick up his coat, and shouted out a seldom-heard expletive when he saw what sat beside the coat.

Realizing that he couldn't remember the last time he had this much fun, he burst into a riotous laugh. "Wizard-Nun, if you can hear me," he shouted out, "my gratitude for your chicanery extends from one end of the Sky to the other! You have danced me out to the stormy edge, and that's just what my life has needed. I bow to you, and again I bow to you."

Grieving

REASON TO GRIEVE

Not long ago, an Elder and a young Seeker were walking by a cemetery and heard the bitter wailing of a woman. She was hunched over a freshly dug grave.

"That was her daughter," commented the Elder. "The woman has gotten much sympathy from the townspeople."

"Why does the most sympathy go out to those who cry the loudest?" asked the Seeker. "Are there not many others suffering as much and more, only in the quiet of their own rooms?"

"The woman is blessed," replied the Elder, "for she knows the cause of her pain and can speak it for us to hear."

"Why can't others do the same?"

"Most of us are as estranged from our pain as two lovers who each live in distant lands and do not know each other's whereabouts. The only thing most people know is that they carry a deep sadness, and the best thing they can do with it is invent reasons for why they feel the way they do, then blame others for it."

IT IS FINISHED

There was a Sage who cared for his aged mother for many years. One day he was asked by a group of Seekers in a distant village to come and share his Teachings with them. The Sage made arrangements for friends of his mother to care for her, then he left on his journey.

When he returned, he was informed that his mother had died the day before and the wake was being held at that moment.

The Sage hurried to the wake, walked up to his mother's body, and said: "Mother, I have returned from my travels."

"I am glad you have arrived safely, my son," replied the Sage on behalf of his mother. "It is good to have you home."

"It is good to be home," responded the son, "and I am grateful to be back with you."

With that, he turned to the people in attendance and said, "My mother is now ready to be buried."

GLOSSARY

Ascetic: Someone who lives with very few possessions or attachments.

Awakened: The state of being where the ego ceases to overshadow consciousness, and the mind, emotions, and senses function unencumbered.

Balance: Being fully present in one's body-mind and attuned to the moment; centeredness.

Continuum: The eternal spiral that is neither past nor present nor future, yet it is simultaneously all of them together.

edge: The state of being beyond our boundaries and perceived limits, where unfathomable potential dwells.

Elder: A person of advanced age who has gained considerable knowledge and perspective from life experience.

Fool: A person who goes about things in ways that seem frivolous or unwise, yet upon reflection show foresight and knowledge.

Gatekeeper: A symbolic person who stands at the threshold of a new state of awareness.

Guardian: A protector of the people, who functions as scout, emissary, provider, defender, and example for the young.

Guide: A person who suggests the direction for seeking knowledge and experience, as opposed to disseminating it directly (see **Teacher**).

Journey: The extended, conscious pursuit of knowledge and Awakening (see **Awakened**), undertaken through study, travel, and/or experience.

Knowledge: The information and memories gained through life experience and study.

Mindless mind: The realm of intuition, intrinsic morality, sensory knowledge, and ancestral memories.

Monk: A male dedicated to simple living, service, and the pursuit of spiritual ideals, usually in community with others of like mind.

Mountain: The symbol of either an arduous or aspiring period of time on one's **Journey**.

No Thought: No-effort mental activity occurring independently of rational processes.

Nun: A female dedicated to simple living, service, and the pursuit of spiritual ideals, usually in community with others of like mind.

Ocean: The symbol of an obstacle to be surmounted, along with the opportunity to learn something in the process and the allure of something that lies beyond.

Path: The set of teachings and experiences that unfolds before a **Seeker** on his/her **Journey**.

Pathless Path: Indicates the lack of definition, direction, and predictability of the **Path**.

Quest: See **Journey**.

River: See **Ocean**.

Sage: A person regarded for his/her wisdom, perspective, and ability to function as a **Guide**.

Sea: See **Ocean**.

Seeker: A person actively engaged in his/her **Journey** experience. Generally refers to a young person, though he/she could be of any age.

Sky: The symbol of boundlessness, the potential for pursuit without boundaries, and the limitless potential of the **Journey**.

Stream: See **Ocean**.

Teacher: A person who directly disseminates knowledge and constructs lessons, as opposed to giving guidance for self-discovery (see **Guide**).

thinking-without-thought mind: The seat of social processes, feelings, and sensory awareness, where nearly all decisions are made and self-guidance originates. Known also as *limbic process, animal mind, intuitive mind, mindless mind,* and *superconscious mind.*

thinking/thought mind: The seat of thought-based thinking and word-based communication. Known also as *rational mind* and *conscious mind.*

Truth: Knowledge, perspective, or awareness that is unique to the individual.

Void: The experience of dwelling in the **thinking-without-thought mind**, where there is no identity, self-consciousness, control, or words. Where an **Awakened** person dwells. Also known as *superconsciousness, higher consciousness,* and *transcendental reality.*

Way, The: A paradoxical term, implying that there is no way, and thus no direction and nothing to pursue.

Wisdom: The insight and perspective gained from reflection upon knowledge, experience, and ancestral memories.

SUBJECT INDEX

(* Found in Special Occasion Stories section.)

Frontier: Dec 30; New Beginnings story*
frustration: Feb 20
future projecting: Mar 5; Aug 5; Nov 24
generosity: Feb 7
giving/gifting: Jan 13; Apr 8, 9; Jul 11; Sep 23; Gifting story*
  – **is receiving/the Gifting Way:** Apr 7; May 13; Jun 30; Sep 27; Dec 2
goal orientation: May 9; Sep 20; Oct 22
Golden Age: See *utopia*
gossip: Jan 4; Dec 6
gratitude: Jan 6, 31; Mar 25; Gratitude story*; New Beginnings story*
greed: Jan 24; Feb 3, 7; Apr 17; Oct 25, 30
growth: Apr 29
grudges: Aug 2
Guardian Way: May 7
guiding/Guidance: Jan 19, 21; Feb 3; Mar 20; Apr 1; May 16, 31; Jul 3; Aug 7, 12; Sep 1, 22; Oct 12, 26; Coming into Adulthood story*
Guru: Feb 6, 27; Mar 27; May 28, 31; Jul 10; Aug 19; Oct 31
habits, abandoning: May 24
  – **the power of:** Aug 24
happiness: Feb 20; May 14
hate: Nov 14
health, mental: Jun 23
healing: Nov 2
heartvoice: Apr 14; May 12, 17
heart-centeredness: Sep 4
heaven: Jun 9
hierarchy: Jun 20; Oct 2
helplessness: See *victimization*
hell: Jun 9
honor and dishonor: Apr 12
hope: Sep 3
humility: Jun 3; Jul 14; Sep 6
humor: Jan 12; Feb 23; Mar 16; May 23; Jun 12; Jul 3, 6, 27; Oct 6, 8, 14; Nov 1, 9, 10; Dec 1, 4; New Beginnings story*
hunger: Apr 17; May 2; Nov 30
hypocrisy: Jan 17; May 5, 29
icons: May 2; Dec 22
illusion: Jan 18, 26; Feb 10; Mar 6, 22; Apr 21, 25, 27, 30; Jun 4, 6, 7, 24, 25; Jul 19; Aug 9, 12, 14, 29; Sep 2; Oct 5, 12, 18; Nov 1; Dec 9, 20, 21, 22
image: Mar 22; Aug 29, 31
impatience: Jan 7; May 22; Sep 20; Oct 29; Dec 11

STORY INDEX

SELECTED SOURCES

Aitken, Robert. *The Gateless Barrier: The Wu Men Kuan (Mumonkan)*. New York: North Point Press, 1991.

Broughton, Jeffrey. *The Record of Linji: A New Translation of the Linjilu in the Light of Ten Japanese Zen Commentaries*. New York: Oxford University Press, 2012.

Chung-Yuan, Chang. *Original Teachings of Ch'an Buddhism: Selected from the Transmission of the Lamp*. New York: Grove Press, 1982.

Cleary, Thomas and J.C. *The Blue Cliff Record*. Boston: Shambhala, 2005.

Haskel, Peter. *Bankei Zen: Translations from the Record of Bankei*. New York, Grove Press, 1994.

Leggett, Trevor. *Samurai Zen: The Warrior Koans*. Florence, KY: Routledge, 2003.

Merton, Thomas. *The Way of Chuang Tzu*. New York: New Directions Publishing, 2010.

Price, A. F. and Mou-lam, Wong. *The Diamond Sutra & the Sutra of Hui-neng*. Boston: Shambhala, 2005.

Reps, Paul. *Zen Flesh, Zen Bones: A Collection of Zen and Pre—Zen Writings*. North Clarendon: Tuttle Publishing, 1998.

Watson, Burton. *The Zen Teachings of Master Lin-chi*. New York: Columbia University Press, 1999.

Yampolsky, Philip. *The Platform Sutra of the Sixth Patriarch*. New York: Columbia University Press, 1978.

ACKNOWLEDGMENTS

I keep saying that I'll be more realistic with my next book regarding how long it will take to produce it. I figured that this one would take a few months, and that I could easily do it on my own. After all, it was just going to be a collection of stories from my repertoire. Here it is five years later, and I'm only now adding the finishing touches.

In truth, these final words are about all that I've done on my own—and that's a good thing, as this book would have taken another year or two if I hadn't accepted help. I am deeply grateful for the story research and organization by Patrick Dunn, Anya Fairchild, and Michael Fox, for story transcriptions by Nan Bearcachet and my beloved Lety Seibel, for Rebecca Lill's final edit, and for Jason Moser and Danny Fletcher's final reads.

My heartfelt appreciation goes to Sumi-e Master Jan Zaremba (*www.janzaremba.com*) for the artwork. The book has become a work of art in itself thanks to the design wizardry of Penny Lane Studio's Carole Sauers.

Everyone who was involved contributed to the spirit of this book; and I thank you, the reader, for the part you play in bringing these stories to life.

ABOUT THE AUTHOR

In order to qualify for the title of Zen Master, one first needs to turn his or her back to Zen, then recognize that the only thing to master is being a Fool. The Zen Masters under whom Tamarack Song first studied easily fit the criteria, as a Bird on the wind has as much use for Zen as she does a propeller, and a Wolf on the hunt eats only by playing the Fool.

Tamarack never heard the term *Zen* from the wild animals around him. It wasn't until he ran across Alan Watts' *The Book on the Taboo against Knowing Who You Are* in college in 1967 that he began to learn about the rich body of teaching stories in the Zen tradition. Since then, he has made an avocation of gathering the stories used by the ancient Sages of the East.

Along with scholarly pursuits, Tamarack writes on a variety of topics, runs Guardian training and wilderness skills camps at the Teaching Drum Outdoor School (*www.teachingdrum.org*), and works as an alternative trauma therapist.